Other books by the author

The Harper Study Bible
When You Pray
The World, the Flesh and the Devil
Handbook of Christian Truth
Missionary Principles and Practice

THE
BATTLE
FOR THE
BIBLE

Harold Lindsell

ZONDERVAN
PUBLISHING HOUSE

OF THE ZONDERVAN CORPORATION | GRAND RAPIDS, MICHIGAN 49506

THE BATTLE FOR THE BIBLE
© 1976 by The Zondervan Corporation
Grand Rapids, Michigan

Third printing June 1976

Library of Congress Cataloging in Publication Data

Lindsell, Harold, 1913 -
  The Battle for the Bible.

  Bibliography: p.
    1. Bible—Inspiration.   2. Bible—Evidences,
  authority, etc.   I. Title.
  BS480.L55   220.1'3   75-38794

Printed in the United States of America.

*This book is gratefully dedicated to four
of my teaching colleagues, all of whom stood or
stand steadfastly for biblical inerrancy —
Gleason L. Archer, Edward John Carnell,
Carl F. H. Henry, and Wilbur Moorehead Smith.*

Contents

Foreword

There is a pressing need for Dr. Lindsell's book *The Battle for the Bible* in the burgeoning evangelical branch of Protestantism. If evangelicalism bids to take over the historic mainline leadership of nineteenth-century Protestantism, as Dr. Martin Marty suggests, this question of biblical inerrancy must be settled. It is time for an evangelical historian to set forth the problem.

As evangelicalism grows, it becomes more and more threatened with incipient division. The perplexing question of the inspiration of Scripture is endangering the unity of the evangelical movement. Two prominent views are emerging. The adherents of both appeal to the Bible to support their position.

The first view considers all of Scripture to be inspired and true, including the historical, geographical, and scientific teaching. The second view holds that only the Bible teaching on salvation-history and doctrine is true. The Bible is authoritative for faith and practice only. Some who adopt the second view would say that the Bible is plenarily inspired, but that God intended the writers to use their limited knowledge — which is erroneous — in making nonrevelatory statements.

In evaluating this important theological difference Dr. Lindsell has written with accuracy, candor, an irenic spirit, and eminent fairness. Although he quotes individuals, he is not attacking personalities, but is attempting to set forth the different viewpoints. The time has come to warn evangelicals of the incipient danger to both faith and practice which comes from abandoning the essentially orthodox view of Scripture.

Dr. Lindsell and I have both been involved in many controversies over biblical inerrancy during the last several decades. In other situations, the issue has been raised in debate. All of these witness to the increasing importance of the topic and the need for a definitive word.

In the 1920s, while I was a writer for the magazine *Christian Faith and Life*, edited by Dr. Harold Paul Sloan, we were dealing with these problems in the Methodist Church. In the late twenties, the issue of inerrancy was seen in the Fundamentalist-Modernist controversy in the Presbyterian Church, U.S.A., over the Auburn affirmation and was expressed in the ultimate division of Princeton Theological Seminary in 1929. That year a group of us students at Princeton followed Dr. J. Gresham Machen, Dr. Robert Dick Wilson, Dr. Oswald T. Allis, Dr. Cornelius VanTil, and Dr. Ned Stonehouse to found Westminster Theological Seminary.

In 1942 the effects of the repudiation of the authority of Scripture in the Protestant denominations in the Federal Council of Churches caused us to establish the National Association of Evangelicals in St. Louis. The N.A.E. emphasized a return to biblical authority, authenticity, and truthfulness, and to a theological position derived from inerrant Scripture. In the early years of the N.A.E., many of us pastors in the old-line denominations repudiated our denominational membership in the Federal Council and aligned ourselves with the National Association of Evangelicals.

During the summers of 1944 and 1945 I convened a group of theologians at Manomet Point, Massachusetts, to discuss the need for the writing of a new evangelical literature, based upon evangelical principles and, in particular, upon an inerrant Scripture. Although the evangelical movement had begun to grow, it had to depend upon literature of a previous generation. Those two conferences brought evangelical scholars into contact with each other.

In 1947 Dr. Charles E. Fuller invited me to join him in founding a School of Missions and Evangelism, Fuller Theological Seminary. At that time Park Street Church had twelve members studying at Princeton Theological Seminary. They reported that authoritative Scripture was not taught at Princeton, and they felt the effect of it upon their own faith. We needed a highly academic theological institution founded upon an infallible Scripture. After discussion and seasons of prayer together, Dr. Fuller agreed to furnish the funds if I would direct the seminary. Dr. Lindsell, a founding faculty member, quotes the original creedal position of Fuller on Scripture, which unqualifiedly stated "biblical inerrancy."

In the conferences of the World Evangelical Fellowship, it became evident that there were two views of Scripture held by evangelicals. When this bifurcation began to manifest itself I called an international council of evangelical scholars to meet at Gordon College in Wenham, Massachusetts, from June 20 to 29, 1966, to discuss the issue of the inspiration and authority of Scripture. More than fifty men came from various parts of the world for this discussion. A clear position did not eventuate from the conference but rather the same lines of division were evident.

In 1955 at the suggestion of Billy Graham, a group of us met first at Bass Rocks, Massachusetts, and then in New York, to launch a magazine which would defend the evangelical faith on an intellectual level. The basic premise was our adoption of an inerrant Scripture. *Christianity Today* (of which Dr. Lindsell is editor) contributed to the evangelical theological revival through its faithfulness to this view of Scripture.

Neo-evangelicalism was born in 1948 in connection with a convocation address which I gave in the Civic Auditorium in Pasadena. While reaffirming the theological view of fundamentalism, this address repudiated its ecclesiology and its social theory. The ringing call for a repudiation of separatism and the summons to social involvement received a hearty response from many evangelicals. The name caught on and spokesmen such as Drs. Harold Lindsell, Carl F. H. Henry, Edward Carnell, and Gleason Archer supported this viewpoint. We had no intention of launching a movement, but found that the emphasis attracted widespread support and exercised great influence. Neo-evangelicalism differed from modernism in its acceptance of the supernatural and its emphasis on the fundamental doctrines of Scripture. It differed from neo-orthodoxy in its emphasis upon the written Word as inerrant, over against the Word of God which was above and different from the Scripture, but was manifested in Scripture. It differed from fundamentalism in its repudiation of separatism and its determination to engage itself in the theological dialogue of the day. It had a new emphasis upon the application of the gospel to the sociological, political, and economic areas of life.

Neo-evangelicals emphasized the restatement of Christian theology in accordance with the need of the times, the reengagement in the theological debate, the recapture of denominational leadership, and the reexamination of theological problems such as the antiquity of man, the universality of the Flood, God's method of creation, and others.

Because no individual carried the banner for the new evangelicalism and no one developed a theology or a definitive position, many younger evangelicals joined the movement and claimed the name, but did not confess the doctrinal position of orthodoxy. This brought neo-evangelicalism into criticism and often, both unwisely and unfairly, transferred these criticisms to the original leaders of the movement.

Dr. Lindsell mentions that acceptance of inerrancy is the watershed of modern theological controversy. He is right in declaring that the attitude we have toward the trustworthiness of Scripture determines our later position, not only on faith, but also on practice. The evidence that those who surrender the doctrine of inerrancy inevitably move away from orthodoxy is indisputable. It is apparent that those who give up an authoritative, dependable, authentic, trustworthy, and infallible Scripture must ultimately yield the right to the use of the name "evangelical."

Dr. Lindsell has done the church, and especially the evangelical cause, a great service in writing this book.

HAROLD J. OCKENGA
President, Gordon-Conwell
Theological Seminary

Preface

I regard the subject of this book, biblical inerrancy, to be the most important theological topic of this age. A great battle rages about it among people called evangelicals. I did not start the battle and wish it were not essential to discuss it. The only way to avoid it would be to remain silent. And silence on this matter would be a grave sin.

I have written this book largely for evangelical lay people in the pews who may not be aware of the central issue that faces them, their denominations, and their institutions. Because of this I have sought to write simply, avoiding technical language wherever possible. The book itself could be expanded almost indefinitely, for there is no end to the available material. The data I have used comprise only a small part of what I have personally collected for ten years.

This is a controversial book. It has to be. But I have tried to represent matters fairly and objectively. It should be understood and reacted to in the light of the facts. We all are responsible for what we say and write. I hope that I have not misquoted or misinterpreted anyone whose words appear in this book. There is sufficient material available that makes it unnecessary to do this. In my professional life I have been involved in a number of theological controversies regarding the question of miracles. I have repeatedly stated that the supernatural is taught in Scripture. When anti-supernaturalists try to persuade me that I am mistaken I reply that I did not write the Bible. I only try to reflect what the Bible says. No one can make a case against the supernatural from the data of Scripture. The same idea is true with regard to the people I quote in this volume. Anyone who doesn't like what he says should not blame me for surfacing his opinions. I didn't say those things. The people I quote said them. And anything people, including myself, write is subject to scrutiny by those who read what they write.

Christians everywhere should be concerned about biblical inerrancy. The least they should do is decide whether they believe it or not and then chart a course of action to follow up their choice. I hope that those who favor biblical inerrancy will make it known in every way possible and exert all the pressure they can bring to bear to see that the churches, institutions, and groups they have an interest in are committed to this viewpoint. And commitment must be accompanied by conduct in accord with the profession.

I have tried to tell it as it is. My responsibility ends at that point, except in those places where my own relationships give me the opportunity to carry through on my own commitment to inerrancy. Every reader of this book has a similar responsibility to do his thing in the place or places where he or she has the same opportunity.

THE
BATTLE
FOR THE
BIBLE

1

Inerrancy an Evangelical Problem

THE BASIC QUESTION

Of all the doctrines connected with the Christian faith, none is more important than the one that has to do with the basis of our religious knowledge. For anyone who professes the Christian faith the root question is: From where do I get my knowledge on which my faith is based? The answers to this question are varied, of course, but for the Christian at least it always comes full circle to the Bible. When all has been said and done, the only true and dependable source for Christianity lies in the book we call the Bible. This is the presupposition from which I start this discussion.

NATURAL AND SPECIAL REVELATION

Many Christians are aware of the distinction between natural revelation and special revelation. Natural revelation is God's witness to man through nature; consequently, theologians have written massive tomes through the ages on the ontological, the teleological, and the cosmological arguments for the existence of a supreme being. But natural revelation has inbuilt limitations. It is fair to say that in general no man can come to a saving knowledge of Jesus Christ through natural revelation alone, as much as it may bear an indirect witness to the existence of God. A sovereign God can apply salvation to whomever He wills, including infants, imbeciles, or to those who follow fully the light of conscience. Apart from a few exceptions, men need special revelation for salvation and this they have through the medium of the Bible.

I am making the claim that had there been no Bible, there would be no Christian faith today, nor, for that matter, would there be a faith called Judaism. I will not spend time to prove this, but only mention that other ethnic and cultic faiths would not exist either if there had been no Bible. Jehovah's Witnesses, Christian Science, Unity, and Mormonism are all cults that are rooted in the Bible, even though they are false religions. Islam and Zoroastrianism, two ethnic religions, owe a great debt to the Bible too.

THE RELIABLE GUIDE TO RELIGIOUS KNOWLEDGE

Since Christianity is indubitably related to and rooted in the Bible, another question follows inexorably. This is the one about which I have written this book. Simply stated it is this: "Is the Bible a reliable guide to religious knowledge?" Posing the question another way, people ask, "Is the Bible trustworthy?" There are only three possible answers to this question. The first is that the Bible is not at all trustworthy. If this answer is correct, then Christianity stands upon a false foundation. Anyone who professes a faith founded on a source that cannot be trusted is a fool, is naive, or is deluded. Certainly no thinking or honest person would embrace, recommend, or propagate a religion based on what he knows to be untrue.

The second possible view of the reliability of the Bible is that it can be trusted as truthful in all its parts. By this I mean that the Bible is infallible or inerrant. It communicates religious truth, not religious error. But there is more. Whatever it communicates is to be trusted and can be relied upon as being true. The Bible is not a textbook on chemistry, astronomy, philosophy, or medicine. But when it speaks on matters having to do with these or any other subjects, the Bible does not lie to us. It does not contain error of any kind. Thus, the Bible, if true in all its parts, cannot possibly teach that the earth is flat, that two and two make five, or that events happened at times other than we know they did. The Bible could not, if it is trustworthy, say that Julius Caesar was emperor when Jesus was crucified, or that Caesar Augustus perpetrated the sack of Jerusalem in A.D. 70. If it did these things, it then would be conveying information to us that is palpably false.

The third and last possibility is that the Bible contains some truth and some error. Part of what it says can be relied upon, and some of it must be regarded as false. In other words, the Bible is neither completely trustworthy, nor completely false. The proportion of the material that is truthful may be greater in volume than that which is untrue. But wholly apart from the proportion of that which is truthful and of that which is in error, the Bible is a mixture of both. It makes no difference whatever that the false information may have come about due to ignorance, carelessness, or any other reason. Indeed, no one need presume that any part containing error was introduced deliberately. For the purposes of this book it can be assumed that whatever errors there are (if there are any) came into the canon of the Bible incidentally and accidentally, not intentionally.

INERRANCY THE VIEW OF THE CHURCH

From the historical perspective it can be said that for two thousand years the Christian church has agreed that the Bible is completely trustworthy; it is infallible or inerrant.[1] The evidence for this statement will be presented later. But for the moment, a single quotation from a liberal New Testament scholar tells us what we need to know. We must remember that the author of this statement wrote at the height of the Liberal-Fundamentalist controversy earlier this century. While his statement makes specific reference to fundamentalism, it goes far beyond that particular school of thought and asserts that the view of the fundamentalist is indeed the historic view that has been the view of the Christian church through the ages. Kirsop Lake, an eminent New Testament scholar and a professor at the University of Chicago, said:

> It is a mistake often made by educated persons who happen to have but little knowledge of historical theology, to suppose that fundamentalism is a new and strange form of thought. It is nothing of the kind; it is the partial and uneducated survival of a theology which was once universally held by all Christians. How many were there, for instance, in Christian churches in the eighteenth century who doubted the infallible inspiration of all Scripture? A few, perhaps, but very few. No, the fundamentalist may be wrong; I think that he is. But it is we who have departed from the tradition, not he, and I am sorry for the fate of anyone who tries to argue with a fundamentalist on the basis of authority. The Bible and the *corpus theologicum* of the Church is on the fundamentalist side.[2]

THE SPECIAL NEED TODAY

In this book I propose to support the historic view of an infallible Bible. To do this one thing alone might be profitable, but the exposition of this viewpoint has been attempted a number of times successfully. No substantial new information has come to the fore that warrants another book on a subject well covered by eminent divines in the last hundred years. It is needed for another reason.

Fundamentalists and evangelicals (both of whom have been traditionally committed to an infallible or inerrant Scripture) have long been noted for their propagation and defense of an infallible Bible. But more recently, among those who call themselves evangelicals, there has been a marked departure from the viewpoint held by them for so long. More and more organizations and individuals historically committed to an infallible Scripture have been embracing and propagating the view that the Bible has errors in it. This movement away from the historic standpoint has been most noticeable among those often labeled neo-evangelicals. This change of position with respect to the infallibility of the Bible is widespread and has occurred in evangelical denominations, Christian colleges, theological seminaries, publishing houses, and learned societies. I will document this later and give specific examples.

While the departure of some evangelicals away from an infallible Scripture is significant, one thing needs to be said plainly: Just as it is possible for someone to affirm the full trustworthiness of the Bible and be unsaved (the devil knows that the Bible is true and the demons believe that Jesus Christ is God), so also it should not be inferred that because someone holds the opinion the Bible contains incidental errors he cannot therefore be a Christian. Belief in an infallible Scripture is not necessary to salvation. Indeed, one may never have heard of the virgin birth or know anything about millennialism and still be saved. This is not to say, for example, in the case of the virgin birth, that a truly redeemed person will deny it when he does learn about it. In any event it is important to note at the outset, particularly when persons and institutions are mentioned, that what I say should not be interpreted as a judgment that these people are outside the company of the redeemed or that the institutions are apostate.

GOING BEYOND INCIDENTAL ERROR

To acknowledge that a person who believes there are errors in the Bible can still be a Christian is not intended to undercut or underrate the importance of belief in an infallible Bible. The implications of the errancy view are tremendous and should be faced squarely by those who opt for it, even though they believe that by asserting this they are honest and nothing serious is lost. Indeed, many of them feel that something is gained by admitting that the jewels of the Christian faith are found in a setting that is marred and imperfect. It would be nonsensical, of course, to suppose that all who hold that truth and error are mixed together in Scripture stop at this point. There are those who go far beyond the notion that the Bible contains incidental errors and offer disclaimers about other matters. They deny things that the Bible itself clearly affirms. For example, the apostle John in the Fourth Gospel unequivocally states that the second half of the prophecy of Isaiah was written by the prophet himself. But there are some who believe there were two Isaiahs, one who wrote the first thirty-nine chapters and another or a school of prophets who wrote the rest of the book. Some do not regard the Book of Jonah as historical, although Jesus affirmed it to be. Still others hold that 2 Peter was written by someone other than Peter, and in the second century A.D. long after Peter was dead. Yet the Epistle itself claims to have been written by Peter and specific incidents support that notion. Among them is the assertion that the writer was present at the transfiguration of Christ, which could not be true if the letter was written in the second century. Moreover, some promote the documentary hypothesis of the Pentateuch which, in effect, denies the Mosaic authorship of the first five books of the Old Testament. They do this even though Jesus in the Gospels affirms the Mosaic authorship.

There is a wide diversity among those who believe in a fallible Bible and it is impossible to say that all who do so are of one mind. The best that can be said is that some who hold to errancy do not go beyond errors of science and history. This is as far as their pilgrimage has taken them to date. But there are others who have extended the principle and have rejected basic doctrines of the Christian faith deeply rooted in Scripture and in the heritage of the church. Some have reached the place where it is difficult to suppose they are still in the Christian tradition. But these are not the ones to whom I am addressing myself. I am speaking about evangelicals who, for the most part, have limited their changing viewpoint to embrace only a fallible Bible at this time frame of history, or about evangelicals who have moved only slightly beyond this and have capitulated in a few other areas. I am concerned that they, and evangelicals who still believe in an infallible Scripture, be made aware of what is happening, why it has happened, what the prospects are in the near future for further changes, and what history teaches us about the ultimate outcome when Christians cease to believe in an infallible Bible.

THE ETHICAL DILEMMA

One of the problems among evangelicals who have swung from an infallible to a fallible Scripture is ethical in nature. Most of them have operated within educational and ecclesiastical contexts that have been and are still governed by creeds or by confessions of faith that affirm an infallible Scripture. For them to function with integrity in this kind of situation is difficult. In effect, they deny what has been and still is being affirmed. In one way or another they face the ethical dilemma of subscribing to what they no longer believe, preach, or teach. At the same time, the institutions, publishing houses, and denominations where they labor generally tell the public that their theological stand remains the same as it always has been. But the facts tell us that if this is true, their stand for an infallible Bible is not being carried out in practice. The only way to clarify the issue would be for them to change their creeds and confessions to reflect the new reality. Two illustrations will help make this clear.

Fuller Theological Seminary was begun in 1947. The faculty drew up a doctrinal statement of faith that committed the institution to an infallible Scripture. But changes occurred and this view was no longer held by some members of the faculty and board of trustees. For a number of years the institution continued to affirm its loyalty to its confession publicly while divergencies from the confession were permitted privately. During this period of time the institution went to work on a new doctrinal statement in which a commitment to an infallible Bible was scrapped. When the new statement was adopted, the board of trustees announced it publicly around the country and published it in the catalog of the school.

For several years, before the new statement was forged and while some members of the Fuller Seminary family had ceased to believe in an infallible Bible, the institution was placed in the embarrassing situation of saying one thing to the public and another to itself. One can only feel the deepest sympathy for an institution when it gets caught up in this kind of predicament. But Fuller Seminary grappled with the problem and resolved it by changing its statement of faith to conform to the new reality. It used to profess belief in an inerrant Bible. It no longer does. It has so stated the change and delivered itself from the charge of ethical delinquency and misconduct.

Unlike Fuller Seminary, there are other colleges and seminaries as well as denominations that, though they have much the same problem, as we shall see, have not changed their creeds or confessions to reflect the new reality. By and large, they have continued to give the impression that they stand on the old truths even though change has come and the Bible no longer is regarded by some of their people as infallible. This poses a grave ethical problem that cannot be sidestepped. It puts those who no longer believe in an infallible Bible in the position of denying and actually undercutting what they claim to believe and propagate. Theoretically, when this occurs, integrity and honesty, which may well have occasioned the change of viewpoint in the first place, should cause the individual to demit the church, the institution, or even the denomination, and go to a new situation where his conscience is not compromised.

But we must not overlook an additional fact. Many who hold that the Bible is fallible are deeply convinced that those who think it infallible are wrong. Rightly or wrongly, they think they are doing the Christian faith a service by staying where they are and working to delete any commitment to an infallible Bible from the creeds and confessions. They are saying, to be sure, that the length of time infallibility has been believed and taught is no necessary reason to suppose that the viewpoint is true. Therefore they wish to deliver those who believe in it from their error. The decision to remain where they are and to work for this change is based on the conviction that to do so is more important than the ethical dilemma of signing statements of faith they do not actually believe.

INERRANCY A WATERSHED

The battle that rages over the Bible today centers around the question of infallibility — whether the Bible is fully or partially trustworthy. I am of the opinion that this is a watershed question and must be seen as such. Thus, little difference at a given point in history may seem to separate those who believe in an infallible Scripture from those who do not. This is especially true at the moment when the only discernible difference between them is over purely incidental matters. Otherwise they are fully agreed on all of the other great basic doctrines of the Christian faith. They believe in the Trinity, the deity of Christ, the vicarious atonement, the physical resurrection of Christ from the dead, and His second coming. Since they believe all of these things, and claim that the Scriptures that teach these key doctrines are trustworthy, what is the problem? What difference does this seemingly minor concession make? This question requires an answer, and it will be given. One part of the answer is the deep conviction based on past history that however small the differences may appear to be at this point, the gap will become enormous in due season, and the differences will increase as other doctrines, now believed, are tossed overboard, discarded with the doctrine of infallibility.

APPROACHING THE INERRANCY THISTLE

I intend to open up the discussion of infallibility from a historical vantage point to show how the contemporary situation has arisen among evangelicals. In the process I hope that light, not heat, will be generated. However sincerely and however deeply I believe in infallibility, I will not inscribe a diatribe against those who do not agree with my viewpoint. I will speak to the issue irenically, not polemically. I desire a return to the historic teaching and belief of the church by those with whom I am in disagreement. I would be less than candid if I did not also state my hope that this book will help those who believe in infallibility to maintain and to propagate that belief. I trust it will help those who read it to avoid capitulating to a view I consider dangerous to the church and impossible to defend from Scripture or from history.

To write about infallibility has risks attached to it. No matter how softly I speak, how irenic my presentation, and however much I have love in my heart, there are some reactions I can be sure will follow. There will be those who will get angry and react bitterly. This will be especially true of institutional administrators and denominational and publishing house executives who would prefer that public attention be diverted from inerrancy. For to talk about it is to create further problems automatically, even when the executives themselves may be in harmony with the viewpoint I take. It is risky to be honest, and to wash dirty linen in public before the eyes of those who are not, and probably never will be, the least bit sympathetic to evangelical theology. They may well delight in evangelicals being at odds with each other. Self-criticism among evangelicals, however, is healthy and exercises a cathartic influence, nonetheless. Evangelicalism needs more of this sort of thing. But bringing the inerrancy question out in the open may also open up the door for division and for possible schism. This is an important point to consider.

No one wants division or schism. But this possibility must be weighed against another possibility: that of the purity of the church. Peace at any price is always possible. There is no place in the world where peace may not be had with the Communists. All men need to do is to capitulate to their demands, and peace, their peace, will come. But peace at the price of theological purity for the church is too high a price to pay. We must by all means strive for both peace and purity. But when peace is threatened in the struggle for purity, it is a necessary risk that cannot be avoided.

The failure to open up the question of infallibility would lead inexorably to some undesirable results, in my opinion. I shall argue that once infallibility is abandoned, however good the intentions of those who do it and however good they feel their reasons for doing so, it always and ever opens the door to further departures from the faith. Once errancy enters an institution, it does not simply become one of several options. It quickly becomes the regnant view and infallibility loses its foothold and at last is silenced effectively. When one surveys the current scene in places where errancy has gotten a grip, it soon becomes obvious that there are few champions of inerrancy ready or willing to challenge the new reality.

No doubt a case for errancy can be made in such a way that the unlearned and unsophisticated will fall for it. This is true when its advocates are personable people, articulate and smooth, warm-hearted and committed to the saving gospel of Jesus Christ. Indeed, not only does it not appear to be dangerous, it can be made to look as though it actually bulwarks orthodoxy and removes unnecessary impediments that are stumbling blocks to some who would otherwise come to a saving knowledge of Jesus Christ.

ERRANCY PRODUCES EVIL CONSEQUENCES

I will contend that embracing a doctrine of an errant Scripture will lead to disaster down the road. It will result in the loss of missionary outreach; it will quench missionary passion; it will lull congregations to sleep and undermine their belief in the full-orbed truth of the Bible; it will produce spiritual sloth and decay; and it will finally lead to apostasy. No one should forget that the clearest example of this is the Unitarian Universalist denomination of which more will be said later. In turning away from Trinitarianism, this group of people turned away from the clear teaching of the Bible. Underlying their departure from orthodoxy was their disbelief in the infallibility of Scripture. In the early nineteenth century the differences between the Unitarians and the orthodox did not seem so great. But today the chasm is vast. Many Unitarians are atheists; many are humanists. In both the first and the second Humanist Manifestos the names of Unitarian clergymen are prominent. Among Unitarian Universalists the doctrine of sin has disappeared. The gospel is not preached. No missionaries go to the ends of the earth with the good news of Christ's salvation. Nor is the Bible preached in their churches. This group is utterly and completely apostate. No other conclusion is possible.

THE NEED TO SPEAK OUT

A great battle rages today around biblical infallibility among evangelicals. To ignore the battle is perilous. To come to grips with it is necessary. To fail to speak is more than cowardice; it is sinful. There comes a time when Christians must not keep silent, when to do so is far worse than to speak and risk being misunderstood or disagreed with. If we Christians do not learn from history, we are bound to repeat its mistakes.

In dealing with infallibility, there is one pitfall we must avoid by all means. We must not determine the rightness or wrongness of a man's position by his personal life. Surely there ought to be some correlation between what a man believes and how he lives. Yet Scripture itself teaches us that it does not always work out that way. David was a man after God's own heart, but at times he was quite defective in his life. He committed adultery with Bathsheba, and he plotted the death of Uriah the Hittite, her husband. His son Solomon was a man of great wisdom, but this did not keep Solomon from turning away from God in his latter years as a direct result of his intermarriage with heathen women.

A man's views should be examined for their intrinsic content or value, regardless of the kind of life he has lived. This is true for evangelicals as well as for those who no longer hold to an infallible Scripture. Evangelical theology should not be judged right or wrong on the basis of those who profess it. History affords examples of people who professed to be evangelicals but whose lives were no better and in some cases were even worse than those of some liberals.

I am not interested in trying to "prove" that belief in an errant Scripture leads to a dissolute life. The same kind of "proof" could be adduced from the life styles of some evangelicals. This would do no more than produce a standoff. I am interested in the theological viewpoint of those who hold to an errant Scripture, and wish to avoid dealing in personalities. If, at any point, I give the appearance of sniping at any person, or seem to be attacking anyone's person, it is not my announced intention. I will have to point out ethical inconsistencies on the part of those who live under creeds and confessions they cannot fully endorse. I am fully aware that circumstances vary widely in different cases and none of us is always consistent, despite the best intentions.

With the issue clearly stated: *Is the Bible infallible?* I go on to examine the evidences, put forth the arguments, illustrate the opinions by specific examples, and endeavor to make the case as impregnable as possible in a finite world in which the most passionate heart and the most enlightened intellect sees through the glass but darkly.

---

[1] A word needs to be said about the use of the words *infallible* and *inerrant*. There are some who try to distinguish between these words as though there is a difference. I do not know of any standard dictionary that does not use these two words interchangeably. All of them use them synonymously. Thus the synonym for *infallible* is *inerrant*, and vice versa. For some strange reason some people gag at the use of the word *inerrant* but do not seem concerned about the use of the word *infallible*. I shall use these words interchangeably and even speak about the Bible as trustworthy, authoritative, etc. Whatever particular word I use, it is to be understood that I have in mind the view that the Bible is free from error in the whole and in the part. Of this more shall be said later.

[2] Kirsop Lake, *The Religion of Yesterday and Tomorrow* (Boston: Houghton, 1926), p. 61.

2

Inerrancy a Doctrine of Scripture

In chapter 1 we discussed the purpose of this book. Now I must state more specifically what is meant by the subject under discussion: biblical inerrancy. It also will help to say what is *not* meant by the word *inerrant* as well as what *is* meant. But inerrancy does not stand in isolation from other important words. Key words intimately connected with biblical inerrancy include the terms *revelation, inspiration, illumination, authority,* and *interpretation.*

NATURAL AND SPECIAL REVELATION

The Christian faith originates in revelation. Had God chosen not to reveal Himself, man could never have known Him. And man can never know more about God than God chooses to disclose. God is incomprehensible so that if man were to know God in His totality, man himself would have to be greater than God. Whatever knowledge of God is available exists solely because God has chosen to make it known. This is His self-revelation.

Revelation comes to man in two forms: natural revelation and supernatural revelation, also called general revelation and special revelation. Natural or general revelation comes to man through nature, including man himself. The heavens declare the glory of God and the firmament shows his handiwork (Ps. 19:1). Paul says that "his invisible nature, namely, his eternal power and deity, has been clearly perceived in the things that have been made. So they are without excuse" (Rom. 1:20).

Natural or general revelation is rooted in creation and in the ordinary relationship of God to man. But natural or general revelation is deficient in itself. Nature has ceased to be an obvious or perspicuous (i.e., clear or plain) revelation of God, although it may have been so before sin entered the human race. Even if it were obvious now, man, because of sin, has been so blinded that he cannot read the divine script in nature. General revelation does not afford man the reliable knowledge of God and spiritual things that he needs for salvation. It is therefore inadequate as a foundation for the Christian faith. However, there is enough light in general revelation so that man is left without excuse if he does not live up to the light he has. The Christian, because he is a Christian and has a converted mind, not a reprobate mind, understands general revelation better through the Word of God, and thus he is able to see God's finger in nature and in history.

God also has disclosed Himself in special revelation. He has done so in at least three different ways: through theophanies, direct communications, and miracles. Theophanies are appearances of God Himself. He is spoken of as dwelling between the cherubim (Pss. 80:1; 99:1). He appeared in fire and clouds and smoke (see Gen. 15:17; Exod. 3:2; 19:9, 16f.; 33:9; Pss. 78:14; 99:7). He appeared in stormy winds (Job 38:1; 40:6; Ps. 18:10-16). He appeared as the angel of the Lord, not as a created angel. In some instances the angel of the Lord is distinguished from God (see Exod. 23:20-23; Isa. 63:8, 9) but he also is identified with God in such verses as Genesis 16:13; 31:11, 13; 32:28. Theophany reached its highest point in the Incarnation in which Jesus Christ became flesh and dwelt among us (see Col. 1:19 and 2:9).

God disclosed Himself a second way through direct communications. In doing so He made His thoughts and will known to men. Sometimes it was through an audible voice (Gen. 2:16; 3:8-19; 4:6-15; 9:1, 8, 12; 32:26; Exod. 19:9; Deut. 5:4, 5; 1 Sam. 3:4). He communicated through the lot and through Urim and Thummim (Num. 27:21; Deut. 33:8; 1 Chron. 24:5-32; Neh. 11:1). He worked through dreams (Num. 12:6; Deut. 13:1-6; 1 Sam. 28:6; Joel 2:28). He communicated through visions (Isa. 6; 21:6f.; Ezek. 1-3; 8-11; Dan. 1:17; 2:19; 7-10). And lastly, God has communicated His thoughts and will to men through the Holy Spirit, especially in the

New Testament (Mark 13:11; Luke 12:12; John 14:17; 15:26; 16:13; 20:22; Acts 6:10; 8:29).

God disclosed Himself a third way through miracles. These showed the special power of God and His presence. They often were used to symbolize spiritual truth. They confirm the words of prophecy and point to the new order God is establishing. The greatest of the miracles is the Incarnation (see here Acts 3:20, 21).

REVELATION: HISTORICAL AND INSCRIPTURATED

Revelation as I have thus far spoken of it is redemptive. It is a revelation of word and fact, and it is historical. It is intended to redeem lost men and to reveal the plan of salvation. It is the revelation of God in the Law, the Prophets, the Gospels, the Epistles, the history of Israel. All of this happened in history over many centuries. It was progressive and unfolding in character, dim at first, then gradually increasing in light until the fullness of the revelation had come.

This revelation of God of which I have been speaking has become inscripturated. It has come down to us in written form. Thus there are two Words: the Word of God incarnate, Jesus Christ, and the Word of God written, the Bible. It is the Word of God written that reveals the Word of God incarnate to men. The Bible, then, is *the* Word of God and it is of this Word we now speak. When we say the Bible is the Word of God, it makes no difference whether the writers of Scripture gained their information by direct revelation from God as in the case of the Book of the Revelation, or whether they researched matters as Luke did, or whether they got their knowledge from extant sources, court records, or even by word of mouth. The question we must ask is whether what they wrote, wherever they may have secured their knowledge, can be trusted. This brings us to the doctrine of inspiration, which is clearly taught in the Bible itself.

INSPIRATION DEFINED

Inspiration may be defined as the inward work of the Holy Spirit in the hearts and minds of chosen men who then wrote the Scriptures so that God got written what He wanted. The Bible in all of its parts constitutes the written Word of God to man. This Word is free from all error in its original autographs (of which more will be said in a moment). It is wholly trustworthy in matters of history and doctrine. However limited may have been their knowledge, and however much they may have erred when they were not writing sacred Scripture, the authors of Scripture, under the guidance of the Holy Spirit, were preserved from making factual, historical, scientific, or other errors. The Bible does not purport to be a textbook of history, science, or mathematics; yet when the writers of Scripture spoke of matters embraced in these disciplines, they did not indite error; they wrote what was true.

The very nature of inspiration renders the Bible infallible, which means that it cannot deceive us. It is inerrant in that it is not false, mistaken, or defective. Inspiration extends to all parts of the written Word of God and it includes the guiding hand of the Holy Spirit even in the selection of the words of Scripture. Moreover, the Bible was written by human and divine agencies; that is, it was the product of God and chosen men. The authors of Scripture retained their own styles of writing and the Holy Spirit, operating within this human context, so superintended the writing of the Word of God that the end product was God's. Just as Jesus had a human and a divine nature, one of which was truly human and the other truly divine, so the written Word of God is a product that bears the marks of what is truly human and truly divine.

Inspiration involved infallibility from start to finish. God the Holy Spirit by nature cannot lie or be the author of untruth. If the Scripture is inspired at all it must be infallible. If any part of it is not infallible, then that part cannot be inspired. If inspiration allows for the possibility of error then inspiration ceases to be inspiration.

Now no one will assert that the human authors of Scripture were infallible men. But believers in infallibility do say that fallible men were made infallible with respect to Scripture they indited. They were kept from error by the Holy Spirit. However, there are those who argue that this refers only to salvatory matters. The late John Murray has pinpointed the basic problem connected with this viewpoint. He argued the case this way:

> If human fallibility precludes an infallible Scripture, then by resistless logic it must be maintained that we cannot have any Scripture that is infallible and inerrant. All of Scripture comes to us through human instrumentality. If such instrumentality involves fallibility, then such fallibility must attach to the whole of Scripture. . . . If infallibility can attach to the "spiritual truth" enunciated by the Biblical writers, then it is obvious that some extraordinary divine influence must have intervened and become so operative so as to prevent human fallibility from leaving its mark upon the truth expressed. If divine influence

could thus intrude itself at certain points, why should not the same preserving power exercise itself at every point in the writing of Scripture?[1]

Need we add the obvious? If Scripture itself professes to be inerrant only with respect to revelational or salvatory truth, where is the evidence for this to be found? Not in Scripture. For when the Word of God speaks of its trustworthiness, at no point does it include any limitation. Nor does it indicate that some parts of Scripture are thus to be trusted and other parts are not. If there is any doctrine of infallibility based upon the biblical data, it must include all of Scripture or none of it.

Those who stumble over inerrancy do so because of the supposed errors they find in the phenomena of Scripture, by which they mean those parts that can be verified. Here the late Edward John Carnell makes an important point:

> B. B. Warfield clearly perceived that a Christian has no more right to construct a doctrine of biblical authority out of deference to the (presumed) inductive difficulties in the Bible, than he has to construct a doctrine of salvation out of deference to the (actual) difficulties which arise whenever one tries to discover the hidden logic in such events as (a) the Son of God's assumption of human nature or (b) the Son of God's offering up of his human nature as a vicarious atonement for sin. This means that whether we happen to like it or not, we are closed up to the teaching of the Bible for our information about *all* doctrines in the Christian faith, and this includes the doctrine of the Bible's view of itself. We are free to reject the doctrine of the Bible's view of itself, of course, but if we do so we are demolishing the procedure by which we determine the substance of *any* Christian doctrine. If we pick and choose what we prefer to believe, rather than what is biblically taught, we merely exhibit once again the logical (and existential) fallacy of trying to have our cake and our penny, too.[2]

WRONG NOTIONS OF INSPIRATION

There are some notions of what inspiration is that must be adjudged as constituting false or misleading opinions. Perhaps the most widely held view entertained by those who object to the definition just proposed regards the writers as mere secretaries, penmen of God who wrote down words that were *dictated* to them by the Holy Spirit. Not even the persistent and almost violent repudiation of the dictation theory by those of us who believe in inerrancy seems to make any difference. This libel surfaces over and over again. Let it be said succinctly that I do not know any scholar who believes in biblical inerrancy who holds that the Scriptures were received by dictation. Those who believe in inerrancy acknowledge that the whole Bible was written by men, and they make no effort whatever to obscure this fact, any more than they would deny the true humanity of Jesus. What believers in inerrancy are saying is that the Holy Spirit was also at work in the minds and hearts of the writers. These writers were guided in what they wrote so that they were preserved from error even as they communicated truth.

Inspiration is taken by some to mean that the thoughts of the writers but not the words were inspired. The idea that inspiration extends to the words (verbal inspiration) as well as to the thoughts appears obnoxious to their viewpoint. But thoughts, when committed to writing, must be put into words. And if the words are congruent with the ideas, the words no less than the thoughts take on great importance. Words have specific meanings. To suppose that thoughts are inspired but the words that express them are not, is to do violence even to the thoughts. This is apparent particularly in those areas of Scripture in which the writers profess to be speaking the very words of God. One cannot limit inspiration to thoughts, for if the words are not inspired, they will not properly convey the thoughts, and if they properly convey the thoughts, then they must be no less inspired than the thoughts.

Some use the term *inspiration* to mean genius of a high order. The writers of the Bible were no more inspired than Milton, Muhammad, Shakespeare, Confucius, and other great writers. Still others say that all Christians of every age are just as inspired as the apostle Paul so that there is no reason why another Bible could not be written today. Others hold to a view of partial inspiration, saying that the Bible contains the Word of God. This leaves man in the position of having to determine what is and what is not the Word of God. Emil Brunner says that what speaks to him is the Word of God and what does not speak to him is not the Word of God.

In addition to the erroneous views of inspiration, there are those who confuse inspiration and illumination. By illumination we mean the inworking power of the Holy Spirit in the life of an individual by which he is able to comprehend what the Scriptures say. Indeed, the Bible is objective truth whether a person believes it or not, or whether he understands, or fails to understand it. But the Scripture itself teaches that man, unaided by the Holy Spirit, will not understand it. It is spiritually discerned, and this ability to discern what Scripture means cannot be attained without the aid of the Holy Spirit.

INSPIRATION TAUGHT IN SCRIPTURE

I have stated what the doctrine of inspiration means. The question that now arises is: Whence does this idea of inspiration come? It is a doctrine taught in Scripture, just as the deity of Christ, the substitutionary atonement, the bodily resurrection of Christ from the dead, and the doctrine of the Holy Spirit are taught in Scripture. Certainly no one should be asked to believe anything that Scripture does not teach. Martin Luther appealed to this idea in his struggle against Rome. He offered to recant his opinions if his opponents could show him from Scripture that he was wrong.

The most conclusive claim for inspiration comes from the pen of the apostle Paul in 2 Timothy 3:16, 17: "All scripture is inspired by God and profitable for teaching, for reproof, for correction, and for training in righteousness, that the man of God may be complete, equipped for every good work." The Greek word for "inspired" is *theopneustos*. Literally, this word means "God-'spirated'" or "God-breathed-out." It means that God indeed is the author of Scripture, and Scripture is the product of His creative breath. The emphasis is not on inspired writers as much as it is on inspired Scripture. Scripture is "breathed out." This is not to suggest that the Holy Spirit did not move on the writers themselves, but that the writers produced a product, which, while it was their own, was also the Word of the living God.

Of course there is a mystery connected with a product that is the result of the confluence of the human and the divine. But it is a mystery only because it is exceptional, not normative, and does not happen frequently. The virgin birth of Christ has the same mysterious element in it. A baby was conceived in the womb of the Virgin Mary by the Holy Spirit. He was both human and divine. It also is true of the two natures of Christ in one person. He had a human nature and a divine nature. Thus there is nothing strange in the fact that the Scripture should bear the marks of both the human and the divine. And it is no more strange that the product, Scripture, should be free from error than that the human Jesus born of the Virgin Mary should be free from original sin.

A second biblical attestation for inspiration comes from 2 Peter

1:21: "No prophecy ever came by the impulse of man, but men moved by the Holy Spirit spoke from God." What is interesting here is that Peter claims that the prophetic word did not come from human impulse. It came from God Himself. And it was the Holy Spirit who moved on the hearts and minds of men to accomplish this purpose. Men were the divine instruments. Scripture did not come down from heaven. God used human instrumentalities to accomplish the divine purpose.

When Paul wrote to the Thessalonians, he made it clear that what they received and accepted was more than the mere words of men. It was the Word of God. "And we also thank God constantly for this, that when you received the word of God which you heard from us, you accepted it not as the word of men but as what it really is, the word of God, which is at work in you believers" (1 Thess. 2:13). In 1 Corinthians 14:37 Paul states, "If any one thinks he is a prophet, or spiritual, he should acknowledge that what I am writing to you is a command of the Lord." Paul claimed that what he said had come to him from God by revelation. He wanted the Corinthians to recognize that his words were not simply the words of a man, although they were communicated through human language and appeared in his style of speech; they were from God Himself. In Galatians 1:11, 12, Paul claims that the gospel he preached was not received from men. "It came through a revelation of Jesus Christ."

There are other reasons for believing in the infallibility of Scripture. The writers of the Old Testament professed more than 2,000 times that the words they wrote were given them directly from God. The phrase "Thus saith the Lord" or one comparable to it appears frequently. The pragmatic test by which we are challenged to prove the Scriptures in experience vindicates the claim of infallibility. Fulfilled prophecy adds to the case. Several scores of Old Testament prophecies relating to the life of Christ were fulfilled literally in the New Testament age. One of the greatest of the Old Testament prophecies foretold the Diaspora of the Jews because of their sins, with the promise of the regathering of Israel in the latter days. Who can doubt that the return of the Jew to Palestine, even though in unbelief, is anything other than a fulfillment of biblical prophecy? Archaeology also has verified the accuracy of the Bible. The spades of a thousand diggers over the centuries have not discredited the truth of Scripture nor has the turned-over earth proven the Bible to be untrue.

THE AUTOGRAPHS OF SCRIPTURE

Most evangelical writers and indeed many of the doctrinal statements that support inerrancy speak of it in connection with the autographs, that is, the original Scriptures. No one claims that the autographs exist, and certain questions must be addressed as a result of this. No doubt, God did not intend for the autographs to be preserved. They would have been accorded a treatment similar to that given to the *Granth*, the sacred scriptures of Sikhism. That writing is virtually worshiped and is kept encased in such a way as to place the emphasis on the book rather than on the god who lies behind it. Idolatry is hardly new, and we may be sure that the possession of the original books of Scripture would have been an incipient temptation to idolatrous worship.

God did not shield Scripture when it became a part of history. Moreover He did not shield Adam and Eve in the garden so as to make it impossible for them to disobey their Creator. Nor did He shield His son Jesus from the possibility of sin in His humanity. In the history of the Christian church it has been carefully stated that Jesus in His deity was not able to sin, and that Jesus in His humanity was able not to sin. He did not sin in His humanity, because He always chose to do the right. He did not sin in His deity, because deity cannot sin. Nor did God choose to preserve the mercy seat that was in the Holy of Holies in the tabernacle and the temple. It has disappeared. But in the providential care of God, He has preserved the Scriptures for us so that they have remained unadulterated, by which we mean free from error.

Any student of lower criticism admits that there have been copyists' mistakes made by those who diligently sought to reproduce the books of the Bible by hand. But a copyist's mistake is something entirely different from an error in Scripture. A misspelled or a misplaced word is a far cry from error, by which is meant a misstatement or something that is contrary to fact. Nor do evangelicals run away from the Old Testament problem due to the existence of the consonantal and the Masoretic texts. The consonantal text of the Old Testament used only consonants, no vowels. The Masoretic text supplied the vowel points. Anyone knows that it is possible to misread some words when the vowels are missing, and centuries have elapsed since the time the original material was written. But this sort of problem does not mean there are errors in Scripture.

Furthermore, it has always been acknowledged that Hebrew

numbers are a problem because the differences between the Hebrew words for a hundred and a thousand are so slight that a much-handled manuscript could be misread. It is hardly novel to say that lower criticism has worked through the thousands of manuscripts of the Bible that are available and in the reconstruction of the text scholars have produced a product that can be said to be the Word of God. Textual problems today in no way make the doctrine of biblical inerrancy impossible. It must be remembered, too, that those who scoff at the inerrancy of the autographs because they cannot be produced for examination have no better case arguing for the errancy of texts they cannot produce either. At the worst, it is a standoff.

I add one further word about the autographs of Scripture and the copies we now have. Anyone who has doubts about the accuracy of the Scriptures that have come down to us by transmission through copyists is misinformed. We can say honestly that the Bible we have today is the Word of God. This is not to deny the existence of textual problems, as we have already said. But the textual problems are minimal. Thus it is, that one of the world's foremost New Testament scholars, F. F. Bruce, has this to say in response to those who claim that infallibility is void because we do not have the original documents, and because of variant readings we cannot get back to them: "The variant readings about which any doubt remains . . . affect no material question of historic fact or of Christian faith and practice."[3] Therefore the variant readings offer no embarrassment to inerrancy advocates, for they do not impinge on the question at the point of the real tension. The places where the chief critics of inerrancy lay their emphases are, for the most part, places where there are no textual problems but where the claim in favor of errancy must be determined wholly apart from variant readings. Of this more shall be said later.

INTERPRETING SCRIPTURE

Those who advocate inerrancy take the Bible in its plain and obvious sense. The charge that they are "wooden-headed literalists" shows the bias of those who make the charge. All that is meant by saying one takes the Bible literally is that one believes what it purports to say. This means that figures of speech are regarded as figures of speech. No evangelical takes figures of speech literally. Nor does any evangelical suppose that when Jesus said, "I am the door," He meant He was a literal door. The Scriptures use phenomenological language, as we all do. To say that the sun rises and sets is illustrative of this device. To claim from its use in Scripture that the ancients who wrote this were saying the sun revolves around the earth is nonsense. We who are supposed to know so much more than the ancients still use the same kind of language, and no one in his right mind would conclude that we teach that the sun revolves around the earth.

Some people still believe the earth is flat. But to say that the Bible affirms this mistaken notion is hardly true. In Isaiah 40:22 the Scripture speaks of the God who "sits above the circle of the earth." That should be plain enough even for the skeptic. In Job 38:7 the morning stars are said to sing together. That sounds far-fetched and it has even been thought of as figurative language. But scientists now tell us that in the air there is music that comes from the stars.

Another gross distortion of the evangelical view of biblical inerrancy is one that supposes everything in the Bible is true. This is not the case. There are statements in the Bible that are false. All the Bible does, for example in the case of Satan, is to report what Satan actually said. Whether what he said was true or false is another matter. Christ stated that the devil is a liar. And we know from his words recorded in Scripture that he lied again and again. There are other incidents of a similar kind, as in Acts where Stephen is supposed to have made a misstatement about the number of Israelites who went down to Egypt. But this, too, like so many of the claims of error in the Bible, can be explained satisfactorily.

Furthermore, some men who ought to know better think that belief in an infallible Scripture carries with it the idea that all Scripture is of the same value. To say that all Scripture is inspired and that all is infallible does not mean that all Scripture has the same weight in teaching, or that no part is superior to any other part. All Scripture is profitable and all parts of it afford us knowledge and insight into God's self-revelation, but the didactic books such as Romans and Galatians, that open up to us the great teachings about justification by faith, are of more significance than some of the genealogical tables, or the details of the history of the kings, or some aspects of the journeys of the apostle Paul. The teaching books are more important to us than some of the material contained in the apocalyptic books. The latter are surely important, but less so than some of the other parts of the Word of God. The Proverbs of Solomon do not rise to the level of the gospel records. All of Scripture presents truth, but some truths are central, others peripheral; some parts are of the first magnitude in the scale of values and others of the second. Let no one imagine for a single moment that biblical infallibility connotes the idea that all Scripture is of the same level or degree of importance.

THE AUTHORITY OF SCRIPTURE

The Bible is authoritative. By this I mean that we are to believe what it teaches and to practice what it commands. It is the Christian's only rule of faith and life, and all the opinions of men and women are to be tested against it. What contradicts it we need not believe. For the problem areas for which we have no clear answer at the moment, we are to be content to wait until all the evidence is in. Apparent discrepancies are no more than that. Additional information in a thousand instances has proved that the Bible's critics were wrong. The authority of the Bible for man is viable only if the Bible itself is true. Destroy the trustworthiness of the Bible, and its authority goes with it. Accept its truthfulness and authority becomes normative. To accept the notion of the authority of the Bible and at the same time declare in favor of errancy is to rest on shifting sand. Infallibility and authority stand or fall together.

HERMENEUTICS AND SCRIPTURE

In our generation an old element that has assumed significant proportions has come to negate the doctrine of biblical infallibility. I refer to the field of biblical interpretation, more popularly thought of under the label "hermeneutics." This is defined as the science of interpretation. It is possible to destroy the idea of biblical infallibility neatly by providing interpretations of Scripture at variance with the plain reading of the texts. It can be accomplished also by consciously or unconsciously held *a priori* presuppositions that do the same thing. Several simple examples will make this clear. Take the virgin birth of Christ. The account of the virgin birth requires a belief in miracles, in the supernatural. No one can accept the virgin birth without also being a supernaturalist. But there are numbers of people who are convinced that the miraculous cannot occur. Their interpretation of Scripture rests on a presupposition that makes it impossible to believe in the virgin birth. For if the supernatural does not happen, the virgin birth could not have taken place. If one's basic presupposition is to accept the Scriptures, then the supernatural and the virgin birth are no stumbling block.

Perhaps the matter of hermeneutics can be summarized by a statement Harry Emerson Fosdick made some decades ago:

> This, then, is the conclusion of the matter. It is impossible that a Book written two or three thousand years ago should be used in the twentieth century A.D. without having some of its forms of thought and speech translated into modern categories. When, therefore a man says, I believe in the immortality of the soul but not in the resurrection of the flesh, I believe in the victory of God on earth but not in the physical return of Jesus, I believe in the reality of sin and evil but not in the visitation of demons, I believe in the nearness and friendship of the divine Spirit but I do not think of that experience in terms of individual angels, only superficial dogmatism can deny that the man believes in the Bible.[4]

This quotation perfectly illustrates the hermeneutical problem. Fosdick reinterprets what he admits the Scriptures clearly teach. But he does so because his hermeneutical presupposition is that the thought forms of yesteryear tell us something the writers did not know then but which we know now. He superimposes on Scripture his own thought forms, assuming that they are correct and the thought forms of Scripture incorrect. He ends up with interpretations that do violence to the Bible and in the process undermines its authority, not to say its infallibility. His views are not tested by Scripture. Rather they replace Scripture and, in making this choice, his notions reverse the process so that his norms become the test for Scripture. This is arrogant, to say the least.

Having laid a foundation by stating the doctrine of biblical inerrancy, we must take the next step. Does this view of Scripture, taken from Scripture, have support in the history of the Christian church? Or is it some esoteric opinion that finds no acceptance in the church's history? So we will seek to determine what the view of the Christian church has been through the ages with respect to biblical inerrancy.

[1] John Murray, "The Attestation of Scripture" in *The Infallible Word*, N. B. Stonehouse and P. Woolley, eds. (Nutley: Presbyterian and Reformed, 1946), pp. 4, 5.

[2] *Christianity Today*, October 14, 1966.

[3] F. F. Bruce, *The New Testament Documents* (London: IVF), quoted in *Inter-Varsity*, Spring Term 1965, p. 12.

[4] Harry Emerson Fosdick, *The Modern Use of the Bible* (New York: Macmillan, 1924), p. 129.

3

Infallibility in the Church

I have constructed a statement of what biblical infallibility means and have discussed the terms *revelation, inspiration, illumination, authority,* and *interpretation.* Now we must look at the church in history to see whether it has (a) accepted and propagated a view of infallibility as I have defined it, (b) entertained and promoted some other view, or (c) accepted and supported diverse views.

EARLY CHURCH CONTROVERSIES

When we look at infallibility in church history, one fact stands out in sharp focus. The dogma of biblical inerrancy never was an acute issue in the church until the nineteenth and twentieth centuries. The early church faced numerous controversies, none of which had to do with the question we are discussing here. Christology was an important issue in the early church. It had to do with the preincarnate and the incarnate Christ. The Arian controversy forced the church to decide whether Jesus was eternally subsistent and consubstantial with the Father and the Holy Spirit. The Arians believed that there was a time when Jesus Christ was not. This made Him a created being, however exalted above man He might be. The church agreed that Christ was eternal God and coequal with the Father and the Spirit.

The church had to grapple with the person and the nature or

41

natures of the incarnate Christ. Did He have a human and a divine nature? If so, did these two natures exist side by side? If He had two natures, was He two persons or one person? This Christological dilemma was settled by saying that Jesus had two natures, a human and a divine, that were not blended into one nor were they to be confused with each other, but they existed side by side in the *one* person.

The doctrine of man (anthropology), having to do with his nature, vexed the church also. It focused on the Pelagian-Augustinian duel that ended in favor of Augustine's view. Spiritually, man was dead. He was incapable of any act that would bring him into favor with God. He needed the grace of God through the new birth for spiritual life. The Pelagians taught that Adam's descendants did not inherit his guilt; Adam's sin injured only himself, not his posterity, and all men are born with the same freedom Adam had before the fall. Thus any man could fully keep the commandments of God if he willed to do so. Indeed, Coelestius declared that some men who lived before Christ were sinless. The semi-Pelagians adopted a middle view that man was neither dead nor unaffected by Adam's sin. Man's will had been impaired but not to the extent that he was incapable of achieving salvation through grace and the help of Christ.

All sorts of heretical groups and reactionary and reforming parties arose in the church and were dealt with. These included the Ebionites, the Gnostics, the Manichaeans, the Montanists, the Novatianists, the Donatists, and others. But in none of these controversies was the question of scriptural infallibility an issue. It formed no special part of the various movements and controversies. It is true that Celsus, in the third century, made light of Christians and Scripture, but he hardly represented a concentrated attack and he did not father a formidable movement.

At the time of the Reformation, as we shall see, biblical inerrancy was not a top-priority item. Whether anything could be added to Scripture or whether Scripture alone was the Christian's standard was an important subject, but at the heart of the reform movement were the doctrines of justification by faith alone and the priesthood of all believers.

Now if it is true that the question of biblical infallibility was not an important one until the nineteenth century, did the church believe and teach it through the ages? It is my contention that, apart from a few exceptions, the church through the ages has consistently believed that the entire Bible is the inerrant or infallible Word of God. Undoubtedly, some of the churchmen who believed in biblical infallibility differed about how the revelation of God was transmitted to men. Some apparently believed in what is termed "mechanical dictation," but they represented a minority. Moreover, whether one holds to this view or to the view that stresses the dynamic interaction between the human and the divine, acknowledging that Scripture is the product of both, one fact remains. In either event the outcome was the same: the people of God were given an inerrant Bible. Now, what are the evidences from the documents of church history that throw light on the view of the church about infallibility?

THE NEW TESTAMENT WITNESS TO INFALLIBILITY

When we speak of church history, it is obvious that we cannot overlook the New Testament itself and particularly the life of Jesus. I have already dealt with the issue of the claims of Scripture with respect to its infallibility. I now begin with Jesus Christ and His attitude toward the Word of God written. Kenneth Kantzer, dean of Trinity Evangelical Divinity School, has written about the testimony of liberal scholars who themselves denied biblical infallibility:

> H. J. Cadbury, Harvard professor and one of the more extreme New Testament critics of the last generation, once declared that he was far more sure as a mere historical fact that Jesus held to the common Jewish view of an infallible Bible than that Jesus believed in His own messiahship. Adolph Harnack, greatest church historian of modern times, insists that Christ was one with His apostles, the Jews, and the entire early Church, in complete commitment to the infallible authority of the Bible. John Knox, author of what is perhaps the most highly regarded recent life of Christ, states that there can be no question that this view of the Bible was taught by our Lord himself.[1]

Rudolph Bultmann, a radical antisupernaturalist, but acknowledged by many to be the greatest New Testament scholar of modern times, asserts that Jesus accepted the common notion of His day regarding the infallibility of Scripture. He wrote:

> Jesus agreed always with the scribes of his time in accepting without question the authority of the (Old Testament) Law. When he was asked by the rich man, "What must I do to inherit eternal life," he answered, "You know the commandments," and he repeated the well known Old Testament Decalogue. . . . Jesus did not attack the Law but assumed its authority and interpreted it . . . And from this time (After Jesus' day when Paul and others preached) came the well

known words, which Jesus surely cannot have said: "Do not suppose that I have come to destroy the Law and the Prophets. I have not come to destroy but to fulfill. I tell you truly, until heaven and earth vanish, no letter nor point can vanish from the Law until all is fulfilled. Whoever erases one of the smallest commandments and so teaches others shall be called least in the Kingdom of Heaven. But whoever keeps it and teaches it shall be called great in the Kingdom of Heaven (Matt. 5:17-19)."[2]

F. C. Grant, Union Seminary professor and a liberal biblical critic, agrees that the writers of Scripture, as well as Jesus, believed in biblical infallibility. He wrote:

The passage quoted from Second Timothy is the most explicit statement of the doctrine of biblical inspiration to be found in the New Testament. But its view of inspiration is not more advanced than that of any other part of the volume, as an examination of the passages cited in a concordance (s.v. "scripture" and "written") will show. Everywhere it is taken for granted that what is written in Scripture is the work of divine inspiration, and is therefore trustworthy, infallible, and inerrant. The Scripture must be "fulfilled" (Luke 22:37). What was written there was "written for our instruction" (Rom. 15:4; I Cor. 10:11). What is described or related in the Old Testament is unquestionably true. No New Testament writer would dream of questioning a statement contained in the Old Testament, though the exact manner or mode of its inspiration is nowhere explicitly stated.[3]

Grant's statement has interesting implications. He himself did not believe in biblical inerrancy. But he acknowledges that it was taught and believed by Jesus and the writers of the New Testament with respect to the Old Testament. In our day we have so-called evangelicals who, in one sense, hold a higher view of Scripture than Grant did, but who deny that biblical inerrancy is taught in Scripture. Grant was either a more perceptive scholar or a more honest one; he did not seek to hide his unbelief by claiming the Bible does not teach the view he refused to accept.

John Warwick Montgomery, a brilliant evangelical scholar, said this with regard to Jesus and Scripture:

Christ's attitude toward the Old Testament was one of *total trust:* nowhere, in no particular, and on no subject did he place Scripture under criticism. Never did he distinguish truth "in faith and practice" from veracity in historical and secular matters, and he told the Evil Foe in no uncertain terms that man lives "by *every word* that proceedeth out of the mouth of God" (Matt. 4:4, quoting Deut. 8:3). To his apostles, under whose scrutiny the New Testament would be written, he promised his Holy Spirit, who "shall bring *all* things to your remembrance, whatsoever I have said unto you" (John 14:26, cf. II Pet. 3:15, 16).

Inerrancy? Yes. Induction? Yes. The way out of the fly bottle? Approaching Scripture always and everywhere as did the Lord Christ.[4]

If Jesus taught biblical inerrancy, either He knew inerrancy to be true, or He knew it to be false but catered to the ignorance of His hearers. Or, He was limited and held to something that was not true but He did not know it. Whichever way anyone goes with regard to his Christology, certain conclusions follow inevitably. For example, if Jesus knew that the Scripture is not inerrant and yet taught that it is, He was guilty of deception. Thus He was a sinner rather than a sinless being. If He was a man of His times and in ignorance thought inerrancy to be true, then He was in no sense omniscient, and this leads to a strange Christology. The third alternative is the only one that holds water. Christ taught that Scripture is inerrant because He knew it to be so. This is the only view that fits the New Testament evidences about the person of Jesus.

GEORGE DUNCAN BARRY ON INERRANCY

I turn now from the person of Jesus to purely human witnesses. Fortunately, at least for the first five centuries, adequate research has been done on the subject, making it easier to grasp the opinions of the early writers without having to read through the voluminous tomes amassed in the Ante-Nicene, Nicene, and Post-Nicene Fathers.

George Duncan Barry's book, *The Inspiration and Authority of Holy Scripture, A Study in the Literature of the First Five Centuries,* is an excellent work that surveyed the early church fathers' views on Scripture. Barry observed:

> The fact that for fifteen centuries no attempt was made to formulate a definition of the doctrine of inspiration of the Bible, testifies to the universal belief of the Church that the Scriptures were the handiwork of the Holy Ghost. . . . It was, to our modern judgment, a mechanical and erroneous view of inspiration that was accepted and taught by the Church of the first centuries, seeing that it ruled out all possibility of error in matters either of history or of doctrine. Men expressed their belief in the inspiration and authority of the Bible in language which startles us by its strange want of reserve. The Scriptures were re-

garded as writings of the Holy Spirit, no room at all being left for the play of the human agent in the Divine Hands. The writers were used by Him as a workman uses his tools; in a word, the Books, the actual words, rather than the writers, were inspired.[5]

The words of Barry are important for three reasons. First, he makes it clear that the writers believed in an inerrant Scripture, and that since there was no question about that viewpoint, it required no special statements to offset any contravening opinions. Second, his witness is important because, while he himself does not believe in biblical inerrancy, he acknowledges that it was the predominant view. Third, he notes that these witnesses held such a high view of the divine activity in inscripturation that they talked as though the "words, rather than the writers, were inspired." He is saying that these witnesses believed in verbal inspiration, indeed perhaps in mechanical dictation. What is striking here is that whatever may have been the differences of opinions about *how* the Scriptures were indited — whether by mechanical or dynamic means or in some other way — the net result was the same: the Bible was looked upon as wholly without error in its entirety.

JOSEPHUS

With respect to Josephus, the ancient Jewish historian, Barry notes that he held a very high view of Scripture. He wrote, "In Josephus we are dealing . . . with an author who wrote more especially for Gentile readers. The high estimate which Josephus formed of the Sacred Books coincides closely with that of Philo: his reverence for them is based on his belief that their authors wrote under the influence of the Divine Spirit."[6] "In speaking of Moses, Josephus describes him as a prophet in so exalted a sense that his words are to be regarded as the words of God Himself. Of Isaiah he says that he was a prophet confessedly divine, and unhesitatingly avers that all the prophecies of Isaiah and of the twelve Minor Prophets have been literally fulfilled; and thereby the Divine authority of the writers has been vindicated beyond all suspicion."[7] "The fullest statement of the views held by Josephus of the authority and inspiration of the Bible is to be found in a celebrated passage of his treatise *Contra Apionem.* . . . 'There is no discrepancy in the facts recorded.' . . . 'The prophets learnt their message "by reason of the inspiration which they received from God" ': they compiled accurately the history of their own time."[8] "It is impossible to conceive language which could assign a higher authority to the Bible than that which he used."[9]

It was this same Barry, however, who balked at believing what he himself says the early writers taught. "Providentially, as we believe, no authoritative definition of inspiration was ever made, to which the Church stands committed: nowhere are we required to believe in the inerrancy of the inspired writings. The inspiration of the Bible and the Presence of our Lord in the Holy Communion, are alike the unshaken faith of the church; but, in either case the Church has been divinely guided, as one must certainly believe, not to define the mode of the Divine working."[10]

CLEMENT AND POLYCARP

In the writings of Clement appear such expressions as these: "You have carefully studied the Sacred Scriptures, which are the true utterances of the Holy Spirit. You know that in them there hath not been written anything that is unrighteous or counterfeit."[11] Polycarp held the Word of God in exalted reverence, calling it "The Oracles of the Lord" and saying dogmatically that whoever perverts it is the "first-born of Satan."[12]

THE LETTER OF BARNABAS

From the *Letter of Barnabas* Barry concludes that "he possesses great reverence for the Books of the Bible, and introduces quotations from them with the formula such as these: 'The Lord saith in the prophet.' 'The Spirit of the Lord prophesieth.' 'Moses spake in the Spirit.' 'The Scripture saith.' 'The prophet saith' (speaking of a Psalmist). 'The Spirit speaks to the heart of Moses.' . . . No theory of inspiration is attempted, but there is no doubt that the Books constituted for the author a final court of appeal; and that their teaching was uniquely authoritative."[13]

THE APOLOGISTS

Among the Apologists "we find that the belief in inspiration is carried a step further. These writers were feeling about for a working definition. . . . The first definite doctrinal exposition of inspiration is found in the *Appeal to the Greeks* which may have been written by Justin Martyr. We are told that the writers 'received from God' the knowledge which they taught. This knowledge was too great to have been acquired otherwise than by the Divine Gift which descended on men, whose sole function was 'to present themselves pure to the energy of the Divine Spirit, in order that the Divine plectrum itself, descending from Heaven and using righteous men as an instrument like a harp or lyre, might reveal the knowledge of things Divine.' "14 Moreover, "Moses, says the writer of the *Cohortatio*, wrote by the Divine Inspiration. . . . The writer sums up the whole argument with the statement that it is only from the prophets who teach us by Divine Inspiration that we can really learn about God and the true religion. Clearly, he believes in the verbal inspiration of the Books, and he makes it quite plain that the writers are inspired only for the purpose of imparting religious truths — such as are necessary for the salvation of men."15 Barry's interpretation here is open to question. The writer Barry quotes says:

> To him first did God communicate that divine and prophetic gift which in those days descended upon the holy men, and him also did He first furnish that he might be our teacher in religion, and then after him the rest of the prophets, who obtained the same gift as he, and taught us the same doctrines concerning the same subjects. These we assert to have been our teachers, who taught us nothing from their own human conception, but from the gift vouchsafed to them by God from above.

This can hardly be construed as saying that the writers "are inspired only for the purpose of imparting religious truth."

Justin Martyr "rests his whole case as an Apologist on the teaching of Holy Scripture. The authority of the Sacred Books is beyond question. His opponent Trypho describes him as 'holding fast by the Scriptures,' a phrase that is abundantly illustrated from his writings. . . . The Scriptures do not contradict each other, and are of undisputed authority, being the teaching of God through inspired men. He makes it clear beyond doubt that the words of the prophet were not his own, but were uttered by the Divine Logos, Who moved him. 'When you hear the words of the prophets spoken as though in their own persons, you are not to think that they are uttered by the inspired men themselves, but by the Divine Word who moves them.' . . . Beyond all doubt Justin held the plenary inspiration of the Old Testament and accepted its teaching as guaranteed by Divine authority."16

"Athenagoras" [second century], says Barry, "was committed to the view that the human instrument is practically passive in the hands of the Player to Whom all the praise is due. In the same language Athenagoras speaks of the Word as an instrument in tune, and he adores the Being Who harmonizes the strain and leads the melody — and not the instrument."[17] Ambrose says much the same thing, "speaking of the utterances of Balaam whom he describes as a 'lifeless instrument' in the hands of God. 'Thou shalt say, not what thou wouldst, but what thou art made to say.' " "Tatian had a clear grasp of the fact that the Books of the Bible attain a supreme standard of authority, because the writers are men whom the Spirit of God found responsive to His teaching; they are inspired."[18]

Theophilus of Antioch [second century] said that "the men of God, enlightened by the Holy Spirit, inspired and endowed with wisdom by God Himself were divinely taught and made holy and righteous." "Theophilus," says Barry, "insists in several other passages that the writers never contradict one another. . . . They were preserved from error in their description of events which precede their own time, by reason of the 'Wisdom of God' and 'His Divine Logos,' through Whom Solomon and Moses spoke."[19]

IRENAEUS

Irenaeus [second century] stated that the writers of Scripture "were filled with perfect knowledge on every subject." On the inspiration of the Bible, Barry says "he insists most strongly. The Spirit of God spoke through the writers. The Scriptures are the words of the Spirit; they are perfect, 'for they were spoken by the Word of God and His Spirit.' The prophets 'as recipients of the prophetic gift,' foretold the coming of the Lord in the flesh. . . . Irenaeus goes so far as to say that the very phrases of the Gospels were due to the prevision of the Holy Spirit. . . . Irenaeus shows that inspiration does not at all do away with individuality, or the literary style, of the writers of the Bible."[20]

TERTULLIAN

Tertullian [second and third centuries], according to Barry, had a high view of Scripture. "It would be difficult to overstate the reverence paid by Tertullian to the Scriptures of both the Old and New Testaments, or to imagine any language to describe the authority of the Books, stronger or more definite than that which he actually employs. . . . Tertullian teaches that all believers have the guidance of the Holy Spirit, but the inspired writers, the Apostles, knew everything. 'What man of balanced mind can believe that those whom the Lord gave to the Church as its Masters were left in ignorance on any matter whatsoever?" "Tertullian did not hesitate to say that the very phrases of Holy Scripture are the result of Inspiration; and that the foresight of the Holy Spirit cut away the ground from heretics. This is verbal inspiration in its most naked form. He admits that there are degrees of Inspiration in the Sacred Authors: and discusses the question in its bearing on St. Paul's teaching in I Cor. vii. 4 'This say I, not the Lord.' "[21]

CYPRIAN

Cyprian, third-century Christian martyr, and Bishop of Carthage, paid high tribute to Scripture. "The names which he gives to the Scriptures testify to his reverence for them. They are 'Divine Scripture,' 'precepts of the Gospel,' 'Divine commands,' 'Sacred Scriptures,' 'Scriptures from heaven,' 'precepts of the Divine Law,' 'wells of divine fulness,' 'voices of the Lord'. . . . The formulae of quotations are varied, and the several phrases are used apparently with entire impartiality. 'The Lord Himself saith in the twelve Prophets.' 'The Holy Spirit declares and saith through Isaiah.' 'The Divine Scripture saith.' 'The Holy Spirit declares in the Psalms.' 'Solomon, inspired by the Holy Spirit, testifies.' 'Paul, filled with the grace of the Master's inspiration.' 'The words which God speaks.' . . . In the summary of the Council of Carthage 'Concerning the Baptism of Heretics,' one of the Bishops gives his decision 'based on the authority of the Holy Scriptures,' and another complains of the blasphemous treatment by heretics of 'the Sacred and ever-to-be-revered words of the Scriptures.' To both men, as to Cyprian, the Scriptures are the final court of appeal."[22]

CLEMENT OF ALEXANDRIA

In the case of Clement of Alexandria [second and third centuries], "from his infancy he had been taught to reverence every letter of the Greek Bible, and he felt no difficulty in believing that He who inspired the prophecy had inspired the translation also. . . . Clement's view of the plenary authority of the Old and New Testaments is unequivocal: he admits the doctrine of verbal inspiration, but finds himself sorely tried by the difficulty of reconciling his reason with his faith, the philosophy of Greece with the teaching of the Law and the Prophets. . . . he advocates no bald mechanical theory which leaves no room for the exercise of men's faculties, but that the human side of inspiration must be allowed due recognition. . . . And once more,

Clement teaches us that the man who believes the Divine Scriptures with sure judgment receives in the Voice of God, Who bestowed the Scripture, a demonstration which cannot be impugned."[23]

ORIGEN

Barry writes, "To Origen, the Holy Scriptures and the teaching of the Spirit were the final and absolute spring of Divine truth. . . . Origen states categorically his reason for accepting the plenary inspiration of the Bible. 'The sacred volumes are fully inspired by the Holy Spirit, and there is no passage either in the Law or the Gospel, or the writings of an Apostle, which does not proceed from the inspired source of Divine Truth.' Indeed, so strongly does he acknowledge the Divine afflatus as operating on the writers of the Bible that he states his belief that in the words of his Master Christ, whether they are found in the Law or the Prophets, not one iota lacks a spiritual meaning, nor shall one of them pass away until all things are accomplished. . . . So complete is Origen's acceptance of each and every statement in the Bible that he does not hesitate to say that 'every letter, how strange so ever, which stands written in the Oracles of God does its work'. . . . The Books are writings of the Holy Spirit. They vibrate, for those who have ears to hear, with the harmony of God; indeed, the whole Scripture is His one perfect harmonious instrument. . . . We are justified in inferring that Origen believed the Bible to be the joint product of the Holy Spirit and human authors."[24]

ATHANASIUS

Athanasius, a fourth-century father, said, "The Holy Scripture is mightier than all synods. . . . The whole of our Scriptures, the Old Testament and the New Testament, are profitable for instruction as it is written." To him the Bible is "a Book wholly inspired by God from beginning to end." He even said that "each Psalm has been spoken and composed by the Holy Spirit."[25]

GREGORY OF NAZIANZUS (c. 329-388) AND BASIL THE GREAT (330-379)

Gregory of Nazianzus, one of the four great doctors of the East (Basil the Great his brother, John Chrysostom, and Athanasius being the other three), had this to say: "Nothing, he tells us, is without design in Scripture: Every stroke and every letter has its special significance. 'We trace the accuracy of the Spirit in detail to each separate stroke and letter; for it is blasphemous to suppose that exact pains were bestowed by the compilers of the Books, or even the smallest letters, without design.' " His brother Basil said that "the words of Scripture were dictated by the Holy Spirit. . . . No single syllable of the sacred writings is to be neglected.' 'Every word or action must be accepted on the testimony of inspired Scripture.' "[26]

CHRYSOSTOM

Chrysostom [fourth century] said, "There is divergence in the historical narratives of the Gospels. . . . but there is no contradiction." Barry says, "He clearly recognizes that while the writers of the Books are inspired, their message is given in their own words, and their individuality is always preserved. . . . He warns that we must not disregard even those passages which we might imagine to be of least importance. . . . The Bible presents us true history. . . and unless this principle be honestly recognized, it is useless to teach doctrinal and spiritual lessons as contained in the words, for that is to build a superstructure on a precarious and crazy foundation."[27]

THEODORET

Theodoret, fifth-century bishop of Cyrrhus who was thoroughly versed in dogmatic theology as well a defender of biblical orthodoxy, said that the peculiar function of a prophet is to "employ his tongue as a willing servant of the grace of the Spirit." "Discussing the authorship of the various Psalms, Theodoret dismisses the question as of no real importance. 'What advantage do I derive from knowing whether all were composed by one particular poet, or some of them were the work of other writers? It is enough for me to know that one and all are the handiwork of the Holy Spirit'."[28] It is only fair to add that Theodoret had questions about the canonicity of some of the New Testament books, but those he regarded as canonical he accepted as wholly free from error.

JEROME

Jerome, who produced the Latin *Vulgate*, and who probably was the most learned of the church fathers in the Hebrew language, had a high view of the Bible. "He states his conviction that in the Holy Scripture even the order of the words has a secret meaning. No single syllable lacks its own special force: 'every phrase or syllable or point in Holy Scripture is full of meaning.'. . . 'The heretics produce their witness from the most pure fount of the Scriptures, but they do not interpret them in the sense in which they were written. They are set upon reading their own meaning into the simple word of the Church's Books.' . . . The quotations are of interest, not only because they show that for heretics and for orthodox alike Holy Scripture was the final court of appeal, but also from the singularly clear testimony which they contain to the authority and inspiration of the Books, as taught by Jerome. The Scriptures are the 'most sure fount' from which knowledge is derived: they are 'written and edited by the Holy Spirit,' . . . .'Whatever we read in the Old Testament we find also in the Gospel: and what we read in the Gospel is deduced from the Old Testament. There is no discord between them, no disagreement: in both Testaments the Trinity is preached.' . . . Jerome recognized the existence of human faults (e.g. grammatical errors) in the writers of the Bible; yet he is careful to guard himself against any dangerous inferences that might be drawn from this admission. 'For myself, whenever I note a solecism or any such irregularity, I do not find fault with the Apostle, but constitute myself his champion.' His theory was that the Divine power of the Word destroyed these apparent blemishes, or caused believing Christians to overlook them. In a word, he taught 'that the external phenomena do not preclude the reality of the highest influences of Divine Grace.' "[29]

AUGUSTINE

Of all the church fathers none, perhaps, attained the stature that Augustine reached in his age and in the long history of the Christian church since then. Surely no other early church father had more influence on the life of Calvin and through him on the Reformed churches of the Reformation. His attitude toward the Scriptures should bear weight, especially among those in the Reformed tradition. He said, "The Faith will totter if the authority of the Holy Scriptures loses its hold on men. We must surrender ourselves to the authority of Holy Scripture, for it can neither mislead nor be misled." "The question," says Barry, " 'Why Christ Himself did not write any Book' is answered by Augustine in these remarkable words. 'His members gave out the knowledge which they had received *through the dictation of the Head*; whatever He willed us to read concerning His own words and acts, He bade them write, as *though they were His own very words*.' More unguardedly still, Augustine teaches that we see in the Gospels the very Hand of the Lord which

He wore in His own Body. . . . There are no contradictions of each other's writings in the Books of the Four Evangelists. 'We must demonstrate that the Four Sacred writers are not at variance with each other. For our opponents . . . frequently maintain that discrepancies are found in the Evangelists.' . . . Freely do I admit to you, my friend, that I have learnt to ascribe to those Books which are of Canonical rank, and only to them, such reverence and honour, that I firmly believe that no single error due to the author is found in any one of them. And when I am confronted in these Books with anything that seems to be at variance with truth, I do not hesitate to put it down either to the use of an incorrect text, or to the failure of a commentator rightly to explain the words, or to my own mistaken understanding of the passage."[30]

THE ROMAN CATHOLIC CHURCH

The view expressed by Augustine was the view the Roman Catholic Church believed, taught, and propagated through the centuries. The early church fathers came from both the eastern church and the western church. When the papacy evolved and later the church was split into the Greek and Latin churches, it was not caused by a difference of opinion relative to biblical infallibility. The Latin church, or the Roman Catholic Church, was the one out of which the Reformers came. It can be said that the Roman church for more than a thousand years accepted the doctrine of infallibility of all Scripture. There were two views the Roman church repudiated: one was the view that the Holy Spirit "secured the writers from error only in matters of faith and morals." This is one of the views that is being advanced in various forms today. But it is not a new view. It has simply surfaced again or has been advocated in slightly different forms. The *Catholic Dictionary* says that in 1685, Holden in his work *Analysis Fidei,* defended the limited inerrancy standpoint but got nowhere. The other view that the Roman church repudiated was mechanical dictation. For some reason they associated that view with the term *verbal inspiration* and in their differences with Protestants said that this view found wide acceptance among the older Protestant theologians. Suarez (*De Fide*, disp. 5, & 3. n. 3, 5) maintained it is "enough to believe that the Holy Spirit 'specially assisted him (the author of the inspired book, while writing) and kept him from all error and falsehood, and from all words which were not expedient.' " The same article says that Ballermin's *De Verbo Dei*, lib.

v. 15; Melchior Canus, *De. Loc. Theolog.* lib. ii. cc 17 et 18 say the same thing.[31]

The dictionary also says that "if Holden's theory sins against the received teaching and tradition [which it did], most certainly that of verbal inspiration as it has just been explained [the authors of the Biblical books were no more than scribes who wrote down the words which the Holy Spirit dictated] sins against the most patent facts. Evidently the style and method of the sacred writers is coloured throughout by their own individuality, and the differences in thought and language between Isaiah and Ezechiel [*sic*] are utterly inexplicable if we regard them as passive agents under a mechanical inspiration. St. Augustine in well known words formulises the prevailing belief of the Church without falling into the exaggerations of the theory that inspiration is mechanical"[32] (then follows the statement by Augustine quoted above).

What is important to note in this connection is that there are no evangelical scholars who hold to mechanical dictation, although it is true that those who hold to biblical inerrancy do believe in verbal inspiration in the sense that inspiration extends to the words, not just to the thoughts or ideas, and yet the writers kept their own styles and individuality. It is significant also that the Catholic church accepted Augustine's classic statement and used it in principle in the consecration of bishops. In the "Symbol of Faith," approved by Leo IX — and used in the consecration of bishops — God is affirmed to be the " 'one author' of the Old and the New Testaments."

In the latest *New Catholic Encyclopedia* there is a statement about inerrancy. "The inerrancy of Scripture has been the constant teaching of the Fathers, the theologians, and recent Popes in their encyclicals on Biblical studies (Leo XIII, Ench Bibl 124-131; Benedict XV, Ench Bibl 453-461; Pius XII, Ench Bibl 560). It is nonetheless obvious that many biblical statements are simply not true when judged according to modern knowledge of science and history. The earth is not stationary (cf. Eccl. 1:4); Darius the Mede did not succeed Belsassar (cf. Dan. 5:30-6:1)."[33] What the Encyclopedia is saying is patent to all. The church has *always* (via Fathers, theologians, and popes) taught biblical inerrancy. Some no longer believe it, despite the fact that it has been the church's viewpoint for centuries. The so-called errors pointed to are the same kinds of errors alluded to by modern evangelicals as the reason for supporting limited inerrancy, and in some cases not even that.

So we now come to the age of the Reformers to see what their witness to Scripture is and what they believed and taught. It would be a mistake to suppose that the Reformers formulated a viewpoint such as those expressed by the early ecumenical councils when they were dealing with Christology. It must be remembered that the Reformers spent their time talking about the issues that were important in the struggle against the Roman church. Since the Roman church held to a view of Scripture that was no different from that held by the Reformers, there was no real problem. The problem came from adding to Scripture, and was not concerned with whether Scripture could be trusted; it was about interpretation, not inerrancy. The role of the church as the unerring interpreter of Scripture over against the universal priesthood of all believers was important; and the Reformers believed that the church could err in interpretation.

MARTIN LUTHER

We come first to Martin Luther. And there is no better place to start than with his Ninety-five Theses. Their contents tell us what troubled him, and are a synopsis of the chief subjects Luther wanted to discuss:

Four of the theses dealt with the gospel doctrine of repentance.

Twenty-five covered the question of the pope's power over the souls in purgatory.

Eleven proclaimed that church penalties were cancelled at death and that indulgences could guarantee no one's salvation.

Twelve stressed that other Christian works were more important than buying indulgences.

Twenty-eight compared the value of indulgence preaching with the values of gospel preaching.

Ten dealt with related matters, such as the pope's wealth and prayers for the dead once an indulgence was obtained.

Five brought into sharp relief the difference between an indulgence religion and true faith in Christ.[34]

Luther did not spend any time arguing about biblical infallibility in the Ninety-five Theses, nor did he elsewhere. It was not a live question, for there was correspondence of belief between himself and the church on that score. Luther believed and taught that the Bible was infallibly true in all its parts. Of that there can be no doubt. But it is useless to look in his writings for a developed thesis to support biblical inerrancy. He believed it; it was not in dispute; he wrote all of his works based on his belief that the Bible was true. But he does leave us with much evidence as to his confidence in the truth of Scripture.

Luther quoted from Augustine's letter to Jerome in which he wrote, "This I have learned to do: to hold only those books which are called the Holy Scriptures in such honor that I finally believe that not one of the holy writers ever erred." Luther endorsed this view of Augustine and himself stated, "The Scriptures have never erred" (XV:1481). He also said, "The Scriptures *cannot* err" (XIX:1073). "It is certain that Scripture cannot disagree with itself" (XX:798). "It is impossible that Scripture should contradict itself, only that it so appears to the senseless and obstinate hypocrites" (IX:356). "One little point of doctrine means more than heaven and earth, and therefore we cannot suffer to have the least jot thereof violated" (IX:650). "For it is established by God's Word that God does not lie, nor does His Word lie" (XX:798).

When Luther found an apparent discrepancy with respect to chronology, he refused to side with "those rash men who in the case of a Bible difficulty are not afraid to say that Scripture is evidently wrong, I conclude the matter with a humble confession of my ignorance, for it is only the Holy Ghost who knows and understands everything" (I:721).[35]

J. Theodore Mueller in his book *Luther and the Bible* says that "Luther unfailingly asserts the inerrancy of Scripture over against the errancy of human historians and scientists. He writes: 'The Scriptures have never erred. . . .'" He also argues that the Lutheran "Dr. Reu champions the following theses, namely, that Scripture was the sole authority of Luther; that Luther's preface to the Epistle of James does not prove a different attitude; that Scripture remained Luther's sole authority of the Christian faith till the end of his life; that Luther never admitted any error in Scripture; that Luther considered even those parts of the Bible that do not concern our salvation as inerrant; that Luther ascribed absolute inerrancy to the original drafts of the Bible and that Luther did not teach a mechanical theory of inspiration. Luther indeed believed in verbal and plenary inspiration but not in a mechanical dictation theory." Mueller also quotes the Lutheran Dr. H. Echternach approvingly: "'The infallibility of Scripture was the consensus of the Church, irrespective of denominational lines, until long after 1700 A.D.'"[36]

Robert Preus wrote about the Lutheran Quenstadt who followed in Luther's footsteps. Of all the Lutherans of that era, perhaps none excelled Quenstadt, who has been charged with holding to a mechanical dictation view of inspiration. We must remember again that whether one holds to this or to some other view of *how* inerrancy came about, the fact remains that the end process, by whichever method one chooses, is an inerrant Scripture. But Quenstadt was hardly guilty of all the allegations leveled against him. Preus points out that Quenstadt believed Scripture was not brought into being monergistically (i.e., by God or by man alone). He quotes Quenstadt: " 'We must distinguish between those who have been snatched away and are in a trance and do not know what they are doing and saying and between the apostles whom the Holy Spirit activated in such a way that they understood those things which they were speaking and writing.' "[37] Preus claims that "the mechanical idea of inspiration was not only foreign to the dogmaticians, it was loudly and consciously condemned by them. They were opposed to every conception of inspiration which would degrade the writers to the status of inanimate objects which neither thought nor felt in the act of writing but to which God imparted revelation as one might pour water into a pail."[38]

Quenstadt, says Preus, "true to form, states the orthodox position in a manner which defies misunderstanding. He says: 'The holy canonical Scriptures in their original text are the infallible truth and free from every error, that is to say, in the sacred canonical Scriptures there is no lie, no deceit, no error, even the slightest, either in content or words, but every single word which is handed down in the Scriptures is most true, whether it pertains to doctrine, ethics, history, chronology, typography, or onomastic; and no ignorance, lack of understanding, forgetfulness or lapse of memory can be attributed to the amanuenses of the Holy Spirit in their writing of Holy Scriptures.' "[39]

One aspect of Luther's approach to the Word of God requires elaboration. Currently a number of Lutherans keep pointing out the fact that Luther, when using the term "the Word of God," did not have Scripture in mind, but Jesus Christ. Pelikan of Yale has stressed this as have those who are opposed to biblical inerrancy. Historically, it is true that Luther used the term "the Word of God" when he had Jesus Christ in mind and he did this frequently. But it would be incorrect to say that he did this all the time. Moreover, there are enough evidences available to prove conclusively that Luther also used the term "the Word of God" to mean Scripture. He also used the word *Scripture* and there are sufficient evidences to show that he regarded Scripture as inerrant. Clearly Luther knew there are two "Words of God," the Word of God incarnate and the Word of God written, and he held both of them to be completely trustworthy. So no one need get hung up on this issue nor spend time arguing whether on this occasion or that Luther meant Jesus Christ or the Scripture when he spoke of "the Word of God."

JOHN CALVIN

What can be said of Luther can be said also of John Calvin. He held the Scriptures in the highest esteem and believed them to be infallible in all their parts. Perhaps the best modern acknowledgment of Calvin's convictions about Scripture comes from the pen of Edward A. Dowey, Jr., who was the chief architect of the United Presbyterian's *New Confession*. His doctoral dissertation covered this question. He says of Calvin that we owe their (the apostles' and prophets') writings in Scripture "the same reverence which we owe to God, because it has proceeded from him alone and has nothing human mixed in. . . . We ought to embrace with mild docility, and without exception, whatever is delivered in the Holy Scriptures. For Scripture is the school of the Holy Spirit in which as nothing useful and necessary is omitted, so nothing is taught which is not profitable to know."[40]

Dowey says that when Calvin "does admit an undeniable error of grammar or of fact, without exception he attributes it to copyists, never to the inspired writer. There is no hint anywhere in Calvin's writings that the original text contained any flaws at all."[41] It is of more than passing interest to note here that critics like Charles Augustus Briggs, of whom more shall be said later, constantly criticized Benjamin Warfield as the inventor of the notion that inerrancy belongs to the autographs. He speaks of this as a late contribution brought about by an inability to demonstrate the infallibility of the copies. But Dowey here makes it plain that Calvin, where he does find a difficulty, lays it to a copyist's error, and this can mean only that Calvin regarded the autographs as infallible.

According to Dowey, "Neither in these places nor anywhere else does Calvin discuss in detail the method by which the Scripture was preserved. This leaves an interesting hiatus in his doctrine. It is interesting precisely because it is always to the text before him, never to the original text of Scripture, that Calvin attributes such errors as his exegesis discovers."[42] "To Calvin the theologian an error in Scripture is unthinkable. Hence the endless harmonizing, the explaining and interpreting of passages that seem to contradict or to be inaccurate."[43] "If he [Calvin] betrays his position at all, it is apparently in assuming *a priori* that no errors can be allowed to reflect upon the inerrancy of the original documents."[44] Here are Calvin's own words: "For if we consider how slippery is the human mind. . . how prone to all kinds of error . . . we can perceive how necessary is such a repository of heavenly doctrine, that it will neither perish by forgetfulness, nor vanish in error, nor be corrupted by the audacity of men."[45] "The question of authority supplies the dominant motif in Calvin's doctrine of Biblical authority, as well as his doctrine of faith in general. No hearsay about God can be the foundation of Christian assurance. . . . The divine origin of Scripture, the fact that it has come 'from heaven' is that to which the Spirit gives witness, and this transfers authority from men to God."[46]

Does Calvin's belief in biblical inerrancy mean he held that the mode of inspiration was by dictation? Dowey went into this question also, for there were evidences in Calvin's writings that might lead to such a conclusion. He says, "We must now consider whether Calvin's teaching about inspiration as so far presented requires the interpretation that Calvin held a mechanical or literal dictation theory of the writing of the Bible. He incontrovertibly did mean literal interpretation in his description of Jeremiah's inspiration, cited above (Supra., pp. 92f.). His emphasis as seen throughout our study of the miraculous accompaniments of inspiration upon the transmission of the message, in my opinion, add weight to the claim that he conceived the Scriptures as literally dictated by God. . . . Most of what today are recognized as idiosyncrasies in style and even mistakes in the text are attributed to the purposes of the Holy Spirit. To this end, the principle of accommodation is for Calvin a common exegetical device for explaining away irregularities that might otherwise, with a less rigorous view of the perfection of the text be simply attributed to inaccuracies. When he does admit an undeniable error of grammar or of fact, without exception he attributes it to copyists, never to the inspired writer. (Infra., pp. 104f.) There is no hint anywhere in Calvin's writings that the original text contained any flaws at all."[47]

Dowey then asserts that "R. Seeberg, O. Ritschl, and A. M. Hunter, . . . attribute unambiguously a dictation theory to Calvin. These are closer to the truth, but probably the solution of Warfield, curious as it appears at first glance, is the best formulation for doing justice to a certain lack of clarity or variation in Calvin himself. Concerning 'dictation,' Warfield comments, 'It is not unfair to urge, however, that this language is figurative and that what Calvin has in mind, is, not to insist that the mode of inspiration was dictation, but that the result of inspiration is as if it were by dictation, viz., the production of a pure word of God free from all human admixtures. . . .The important thing to realize is that according to Calvin the Scriptures were so given that — whether by "literal" or "figurative" dictation — the result was a series of documents errorless in their original form.' "[48]

One item in the testimony of John Calvin should be explained. A number of opponents of biblical inerrancy have attributed to Calvin the opinion that he rejected the Petrine authorship of 2 Peter. This is important because modern critics not only claim that this Epistle was not written by Peter; they also claim that it is a second-century, not a first-century, product. The problem of Petrine authorship, it should be stated, is not a modern one. It has existed in the church for centuries. Calvin was involved in this, too. Of 2 Peter he says in his commentary on that book:

> If it is received as canonical, we must admit that Peter is the author, not only because it bears his name, but also because he testifies that he lived with Christ. It would have been a fiction unworthy of a minister of Christ to pretend to be another personality. Therefore I conclude that if the epistle is trustworthy it has come from Peter; not that he wrote it himself, but that one of his disciples composed by his command what the necessity of the times demanded. It is probable that at the time he was very old; he says he is near to death, and it could be that at the request of the godly he allowed this testament of his mind to be signed and sealed just before his death, because it might have some force after he was dead to encourage the good and repress the wicked. Certainly since the majesty of the Spirit of Christ expresses itself in all parts of the epistle, I have a dread of repudiating it, even though I do not recognize in it the genuine language of Peter. Since there is no agreement as to the author, I shall allow myself to use the name of Peter or the apostle indiscriminately.[49]

From Calvin's own statement we should note several things. First, he acknowledges that if one accepts 2 Peter as canonical it must be admitted that Peter is the author simply because the Epistle so claims. Calvin would be at variance with modern critics who advocate the viewpoint that someone used Peter's name long after his death and that this device is acceptable. Calvin says no! Moreover, he makes it plain that 2 Peter was written during Peter's lifetime. He refuses to date it in another century even as he refuses to let it come from a forger who has used Peter's name. It is true, on the other hand, that Calvin had trouble with the language of 2 Peter and it was this that occasioned his suggestion that perhaps the Epistle was written by an amanuensis under the supervision of the aged apostle, in which case it was a genuine product of the apostle. Calvin does not hesitate to say that, allowing for the possibility that Peter had someone write it under his supervision and control, he uses the name of Peter or the apostle as the author indiscriminately. Thus the faith of Calvin in the inerrancy of Scripture overcame his scholar's questions and Peter remained for him the true author of the Epistle that bears his name.

Anyone who reads Calvin and Luther and compares them with modern writers who deny biblical infallibility cannot fail to note the difference between the attitude of the Reformers and that of the modern objectors to infallibility. The latter unfailingly seek to denigrate Scripture, to humanize it, to swallow a camel and strain out a gnat. The Reformers did not react in this way. Their attitude toward the Word of God was one of reverence, humility, and positive acceptance of it as both authoritative and infallible.

THE WESTMINSTER CONFESSION OF FAITH

Among the confessions of faith in the Reformed tradition, none ever written is superior to the Westminster Confession in scope, clarity, and precision. Chapter 1 sets forth the doctrine of Scripture. It is called "the only infallible rule of faith and practice." From this some have argued that the Westminster Confession in effect limited inerrancy to matters of faith and practice, excluding matters having to do with history, science, and cosmology. The error of this may be seen when two facts are taken into account. One is the entire statement on Scripture, which includes two phrases that destroy the limited inerrancy notion. The confession speaks of "the entire perfection" of Scripture and acknowledges the "consent of all of the parts." These portions of the definition rule out the notion of limited inerrancy. But more than that, the history of the times must be taken into account. We have noted that during the Reformation period biblical infallibility was a tenet accepted by both the Roman Catholic Church and the Reformers. It was not central to the dispute that occasioned the rupture. Had it been, the Reformers would have pinpointed the issue and the canons of the Council of Trent, in which the Roman Catholics answered the Reformers, would have included a counterblast. At the time the Westminster Confession was adopted, there was no serious challenge to the view of biblical infallibility, and the Confession did not speak to the issue the way it undoubtedly would have had there been such a difference of opinion.

No one can deny that in the United States, so far as the Reformed denominations are concerned, wherever the Westminster Confession was the controlling creed, it was understood to mean that the Scripture in all of its parts was without error. This was true of the northern and southern Presbyterian churches, as well as the United Presbyterian Church. During the Fundamentalist-Modernist controversy that swept through the Presbyterian Church in the U.S.A., the 1920s were the years of crucial decision. Clarence Edward McCartney was swept into the moderatorship of the church in connection with this issue. The General Assembly in 1924 voted to endorse biblical infallibility as the official view of the church. The Assembly did not vote this way as though this viewpoint represented a change of stance and constituted an addendum to the Westminster Confession, but only as a reaffirmation of what had been the standpoint of the denomination historically and of what had been established officially at an earlier date.

The evidences to support the contention that the Presbyterian Church in the U.S.A. (now the United Presbyterian Church) accepted the notion of biblical infallibility are so numerous that it hardly requires documentation. The former Dean of Princeton Theological Seminary, Dr. Elmer Homrighausen, says this: "Few intelligent Christians can still hold to the idea that the Bible is an infallible Book, that it contains no linguistic errors, no historical discrepancies, no antiquated scientific assumptions, not even bad ethical standards. Historical investigation and literary criticism have taken the magic out of the Bible and have made it a composite human book, written by many hands in different ages. The existence of thousands of variations of texts makes it impossible to hold the doctrine of a book verbally infallible. Some might claim for the original copies of the Bible an infallible character, but this view only begs the question and makes such Christian apologetics more ridiculous in the eyes of sincere men."[50]

This statement by Dr. Homrighausen clearly illustrates the truth that he was refuting a viewpoint that had once been held but was no longer acceptable. Unfortunately, his statement denigrates those who believe in biblical infallibility and casts them in the mold of stupid illiterates. Thus he says, "Few *intelligent* Christians can still hold to the idea . . ." (my italics). Anyone holding to biblical infallibility makes such Christian apologetics "more ridiculous in the eyes of *sincere* men" (my italics). Here Homrighausen speaks of disbelievers in biblical infallibility as sincere men and the implication is plain that those who accept biblical infallibility are less than sincere. Moreover, he inveighs against "the doctrine of a book [that is] verbally infallible." Now, if no one held such a view, he would not argue against it. It is plain that Homrighausen was talking against the common viewpoint of his own denomination that neither he nor a host of others in that denomination could accept any longer.

The founding of Westminster Theological Seminary was a protest against what was happening in the Presbyterian Church. That the struggle included the nature of biblical truth may be seen from what Edward J. Young, a long-time Old Testament teacher at Westminster, said in his volume *Thy Word is Truth*: "If the autographs of Scripture are marred by flecks of mistake, God has simply not told us the truth concerning His Word. To assume that He could breathe forth a word that could contain mistakes is to say, in effect, that God Himself can make mistakes. We must maintain that the original of Scripture is infallible for the simple reason that it came to us direct from God Himself."[51]

What is true for the Presbyterian Church in the north is true for the Presbyterian Church in the south as well. In 1962 *The Presbyterian Outlook* published a symposium entitled "Do We Need an Infallible Bible?"[52] On the face of it, such a symposium would have no meaning if no one was asking the question whether the Bible is infallible and if no one believed, or had ever believed, in an infallible Bible. The whole discussion was slanted to present one viewpoint, that of a fallible Bible. Every contributor to the discussion argued against biblical infallibility for the very reason that such a viewpoint was formerly believed. The arguments did not deny that the inerrancy position exists or that it had not been the view of the Presbyterian Church in the south. Rather, they were presented to destroy the belief in an infallible Scripture. What stronger evidence does one need to support the claim that biblical infallibility has been the historic viewpoint of the Reformed tradition?

AMERICAN AND BRITISH BAPTISTS

Among the Baptists, the same truth emerges. Until recently, Baptists of the north and the south have held to an infallible Bible. The New Hampshire Confession of Faith states that Scripture "has God for its author, salvation for its end, and truth, without any mixture of error, for its matter." The chapter on the Southern Baptist Convention will deal more specifically with the details of the struggle within that denomination relative to biblical infallibility. For the moment it remains only to make clear that the Northern Baptist Convention (now the American Baptist Convention) also held to inerrancy until the latter nineteenth century when German higher criticism invaded this and other denominations. During the Fundamentalist-Modernist controversy a continual battle raged between the differing viewpoints about Scripture and schism resulted with the formation of two new and distinct Baptist denominations. One was the General Association of Regular Baptists, which dates from 1932; the other, the Conservative Baptist Association of America, which began in 1947. The latter group comprised a number of fundamentalists who stayed within the Northern Baptist Convention after the GARB had come into being. They thought that the overwhelming majority of Northern Baptists believed in an infallible Scripture, and hoped to deliver the Convention from the control of the liberals. The Eastern and Northern Baptist Theological Seminaries were created as conservative institutions to combat the liberalism of the old-line denominational schools such as Crozer, Andover Newton, Chicago Divinity School, and Colgate-Rochester.

Alvah Hovey, president of Newton Theological Institute (which was later joined with Andover to become Andover Newton), defended biblical inerrancy. He argued against those who said that "infallibility in the original Scriptures requires for its complement infallibility in all copies, translations, and, some would say, interpretations of them. For otherwise, we are told, the benefit of infallibility is lost to all but the primitive readers. But this, again, is a mistake; for the errors from transcription, translations, etc., are such as can be detected, or at least estimated, and reduced to a minimum; while errors in the original revelation could not be measured."[53] Hovey was saying clearly that biblical inerrancy was the common viewpoint, but it was being challenged. And he responded to those who offered that challenge. He pursued this theme by alluding to questions of historical and scientific errors.

Hovey said: "On the supposed historical errors of the Bible we remark, (1) They relate, for the most part, to matters of chronology, generally numbers, etc. (2) Transcribers are specially liable to mistakes in copying numbers, names, etc. (3) Different names for the same person, and different termini for the same period, are quite frequent. (4) Round numbers are often employed for specific. Making proper allowance for these facts we deny that historical errors are found in the Bible." He also dealt with the so-called scientific errors, saying, "All references to matters of science in the Bible are (1) Merely incidental and auxiliary; (2) Clothed in popular language; and, (3) Confirmed by consciousness, so far as they relate to the mind. Remembering these facts, we say that the Bible has not been shown to contain scientific errors — astronomy, geology, ethnology. . . . Bearing in mind these facts, it will be impossible for us to find in the Bible any contradictions which mar its excellence."[54]

What has been said about the Baptists in the United States can also be said of the Baptists in Great Britain. They believed in biblical infallibility, although the same retreat from infallibility was to become serious in the nineteenth and twentieth centuries. The famed Charles Haddon Spurgeon was deeply involved in the changing fortunes of the Baptists as they moved away from a belief in inerrancy. Spurgeon, who was undoubtedly the best known and most popular preacher of his age, bore witness to the traditional view of the Bible. He delivered a sermon in 1855, a part of which was devoted to biblical infallibility. He said:

> Then, since God wrote it, mark its truthfulness. If I had written it, there would be worms of critics who would at once swarm on it, and would cover it with their evil spawn; had I written it, there would be men who would pull it to pieces at once, and perhaps quite right too. But this is the Word of God. Come, search, ye critics, and find a flaw; examine it from its Genesis to its Revelation and find an error. This is a vein of pure gold, unalloyed by quartz or any earthy substance. This is a star without a speck; a sun without a blot; a light without darkness; a moon without paleness; a glory without a dimness. O Bible! it cannot be said of any other book, that it is perfect and pure; but of thee we can declare all wisdom is gathered up in thee, without a particle of folly. This is the judge that ends the strife where wit and

reason fail. This is the book untainted by any error, but is pure, unalloyed, perfect truth. Why? Because God wrote it. Ah! charge God with error if you please; tell Him that His book is not what it ought to be . . . . Blessed Bible, thou art all truth.[55]

Perhaps the strongest evidence that Spurgeon was not parroting a new teaching when he proclaimed biblical inerrancy may be seen from what was happening in Britain after Darwin's *Origin of the Species* had been published and public fancy had responded to its ideas. The Baptist Union was "a very free and liberal organization which did not attempt to hold any person very strictly to doctrine or creed. Yet many of the strongest preachers in the Baptist denomination in and about London were members of that Association. In the membership there were also a number of pastors who taught in their pulpits some of the modern ideas of science — so called — and who advocated the theories of higher criticism and a more liberal and loose construction of the Old Testament records." Upon this subject Mr. Spurgeon wrote:

No lover of the Gospel can conceal from himself the fact that the days are evil. We are willing to make a large discount from our apprehensions on the score of natural timidity, the caution of age, and the weakness produced by pain; but yet our solemn conviction is that things are much worse in many churches than they seem to be, and are rapidly tending downward. Read those newspapers which represent the Broad School of Dissent, and ask yourself, How much further could they go? What doctrine remains to be abandoned? What other truth to be the object of contempt? A new religion has been initiated, which is no more Christianity than chalk is cheese, and this religion, being destitute of moral honesty, palms itself off as the old faith with slight improvements, and on this plea usurps pulpits which were erected for gospel preaching. The Atonement is scouted, the inspiration of Scripture is derided, the Holy Ghost is degraded into an influence, the punishment of sin is turned into fiction, and the Resurrection into a myth, and yet these enemies of our faith expect us to call them brethren, and maintain a confederacy with them![56]

Spurgeon's words portray what the situation was among Baptists in his day. They indeed were turning away from the old faith. But their turning is itself a witness that the old faith included full confidence in the totality of Scripture. And this was the witness of Spurgeon who continued to believe in biblical inerrancy. Moreover, he bore down on the consequences that always follow disbelief in the full reliability of the Bible. This disbelief leads inevitably to a denial of many of the basic doctrines of the Christian faith. Whatever these new-style Baptists believed and however much they departed from the old benchmarks, their departure witnessed to what had been the common viewpoints of the English Baptists.

THE ANGLICANS AND METHODISTS

What has been said of the Reformers and of the Baptists may also be said about the Anglicans and the Methodists. But they came out of a different tradition, and their views must be understood within that context. The Anglican Church came into being as a direct result of Henry the VIII's marriage dilemma with Catholic Catherine whom he wished to divorce. When the papacy refused to accede to his desires, Henry broke with the pope and established his own church. But that church stood then and remains in the tradition of Catholicism. It traces its apostolic succession back to the apostles and believes as Roman Catholics do in the historical episcopate. It accepts the real presence of Christ in the sacrament of the supper, and in a number of ways stands within the tradition of Roman Catholicism. Among the doctrines it inherited from the Roman Church was its view of the Bible as the infallible Word of God. It rejected some of Rome's teaching, such as those of the seven sacraments, the headship of the pope, and the like. But it did not declare itself against the Roman Catholic Church's teaching with respect to biblical infallibility. It followed this doctrinal teaching until it, like so many of the denominations that sprang out of the Reformation period, discarded it in the late nineteenth and twentieth centuries. (There are still some orthodox Anglicans who stand in the tradition of evangelical Christianity and still believe in an infallible Bible.)

The Methodist denomination came from the loins of Anglicanism and its founder, John Wesley, lived and died within the fold of the Anglican faith. It too holds to the historic episcopate and traces its own holy orders through the Anglican Church back to the apostles. Like the Anglican Church, Methodism believed in an infallible Scripture. Neither the Anglicans nor the Methodists enshrined their belief in an infallible Scripture in creeds and confessions with the precision and accuracy that marked those of the Reformed tradition, the Baptists, and the Lutherans. This may also explain why it was that the Anglicans and the Methodists were the most easily led astray from a commitment to biblical infallibility, and why these two groups in our generation include among their numbers large bodies of theological liberals whose theological beliefs are quite extreme.

George A. Turner of the evangelical Asbury Theological Seminary wrote this about John Wesley:

> Wesley believed in the full inspiration and inerrancy of the Bible. His view would now be described as pre-critical, as would the view of most eighteenth-century writers. The problem of authority which Luther faced was less acute in Wesley's day than the problem of indifference in the Church. Thus Wesley was less bold than Luther in determining the relative value of different books of the Bible; to him they were all equally inspired and hence authoritative. . . he did not feel the need of establishing the authority of the Bible or defending it from destructive critics. Jean Astruc, "the father of Pentateuchal criticism," published his views on the authorship of Genesis in 1753, but there is no evidence that it was noticed by Wesley and his colleagues.[57]

Wesley's own view of the Bible was a high one indeed. He never believed for a moment that because the writers of Scripture were human they therefore erred in what they wrote. In his *Journal* he wrote, "Nay, if there be any mistakes in the Bible there may as well be a thousand. If there be one falsehood in that book it did not come from the God of truth."[58] It would be inaccurate to suggest that Wesley spent much time on the question of biblical infallibility. He believed it and so did those who became Methodists. He preached, taught, and labored on the basis of his underlying conviction that the Bible is the inerrant Word of God.

Among the Anglicans and the Methodists today there are strong defenders of biblical inerrancy just as there are strong opponents of that viewpoint. And no one can suppose for a moment that either of these denominations now or in the discernible future will become strong advocates of inerrancy.

THE CONCLUSION OF THE MATTER

This survey of biblical inerrancy in the history of the church could be extended indefinitely. There are all kinds of material available to show that the church through the ages has held to an infallible Bible. This truth can be stated negatively as well. There is no evidence to show that errancy was ever a live option in the history of Christendom for eighteen hundred years in every branch of the Christian church that had not gone off into aberrations. It can also be said that what was true for eighteen hundred years is no longer true today. In the last two centuries inerrancy has become a live issue and increasingly there has been a turning away from this belief until the point has been reached where it is safe to say that a great proportion of scholars and ministers in the Christian church in all of its branches no longer hold to biblical inerrancy. However, there has been a strong evangelical strand in the church that has held to inerrancy in the last two centuries. Among these people were men like Spurgeon, B. B. Warfield, Charles Hodge, J. Gresham Machen, Edward John Carnell, as well as a host of scholars who are members of the Evangelical Theological Society today.

In recent years evangelical Christianity has been infiltrated by people who do not believe in inerrancy. This penetration into the evangelical spectrum is my deep concern. Having laid a foundation to demonstrate that the church historically has been committed to biblical inerrancy, I must now show that among evangelicals who have carried on this long tradition there are evidences of concessions and departures that require attention. So I now will paint the picture of what has happened among denominations and parachurch groups that long have been committed to evangelical truth and biblical infallibility but who now have begun to stray from that viewpoint.

[1] Harold Lindsell, ed., *The Church's Worldwide Mission* (Waco: Word, 1966), p. 31.

[2] Rudolph Bultmann, *Jesus and the Word* (New York: Scribner's, 1934), p. 61.

[3] Frederick C. Grant, *An Introduction to New Testament Thought* (New York: Abingdon Cokesbury, 1950), p. 75.

[4] *Christianity Today*, March 3, 1967, p. 48.

[5] George Duncan Barry, *The Inspiration and Authority of Holy Scripture, A Study in the Literature of the First Five Centuries* (New York: Macmillan, 1919), p. 10.

[6] Ibid., p. 19.

[7] Ibid., p. 20.

[8] Ibid. pp. 20ff.

[9] Ibid., p. 28.

[10] Ibid., pp. 30f.

[11] Ibid., p. 37; *The Ante-Nicene Fathers* (hereafter cited as A.N.F.) (New York: Scribner's, 1899) *The First Epistle of Clement to the Corinthians*, Vol. I, p. 19 (LIII), p. 17 (XLV).

[12] Ibid., p. 40; A.N.F., *The Epistle of Polycarp to the Philippians*, Vol. I, p. 34 (VII).

[13] Ibid., pp. 41-43; A.N.F., *The Epistle of Barnabas*, Vol. I, pp. 142 (IX), 147 (ILV), p. 143 (X), p. 140 (VI), p. 144 (XII), p. 146 (XV), p. 147 (XVI).

[14] Ibid., p. 43; A.N.F., *Justin's Hortatory Address to the Greeks*, Vol. I, p. 276 (VII).

[15] Ibid., p. 44; A.N.F., Vol. I, p. 277.

[16] Ibid., pp. 45-47; A.N.F., Vol. I, Trypho, p. 230 (LXV); p. 256 (CXV), p. 175 (XXXVI).

[17] Ibid., p. 49; A.N.F., Vol. II, p. 133 (IX).

[18] Ibid., pp. 50, 51; A.N.F., Vol. II, pp. 65-82.

[19] Ibid., p. 52; A.N.F., Vol. II, p. 97 (IX).

[20] Ibid., pp. 54, 56, 57; A.N.F., Vol. I, pp. 414, 420, 440.

[21] Ibid., pp. 60-64; A.N.F., Vol. III, p. 442.

[22] Ibid., pp. 67, 68.

[23] Ibid., pp. 71ff.; A.N.F., Vol. II, pp. 222ff., 348, 349.

[24] Ibid., pp. 79, 80. (Homilies in Jeremiah, XXI; Philocalia, C. XII, X.)

[25] Ibid., pp. 93, 96.

[26] Ibid., pp. 105, 108.

[27] Ibid., pp. 121-124.

[28] Ibid., p. 129.

[29] Ibid., pp. 130ff.

[30] Ibid., pp. 140ff.

[31] *A Catholic Dictionary* (New York: Addis and Arnold, 1884), p. 450.

[32] Ibid.

[33] *The New Catholic Encyclopedia* (New York: Mc Graw, 1967), Vol. II, p. 384.

[34] *Christian Heritage*, June, 1975, p. 9.

[35] Theodore Engelder, *Scripture Cannot Be Broken* (St. Louis: Concordia, 1944). Engelder quotes from Luther's work as indicated in the text.

[36] J. Theodore Mueller, *Luther and the Bible*, pp. 99, 103.

[37] Robert Preus, *The Inspiration of Scripture, A Study of the Theology of the Seventeenth Century Lutheran Dogmaticians* (London, 1955), p. 58.

[38] Ibid., pp. 66, 67.

[39] Ibid., p. 77.

[40] Edward A. Dowey, Jr., *The Knowledge of God in Calvin's Theology* (New York: Columbia, 1952), p. 91.

[41] Ibid., p. 100.

[42] Ibid., p. 103.

[43] Ibid., p. 104.

[44] Ibid., p. 105.

[45] Ibid.

[46] Ibid., p. 109.

[47] Ibid., p. 99.

[48] Ibid., pp. 101, 102.

[49] John Calvin, *The Epistle of Paul the Apostle to the Hebrews and the First and Second Epistles of St. Peter* (Grand Rapids: Eerdmans, 1963), p. 325.

[50] Elmer Homrighausen, *Christianity in America* (Nashville: Abingdon, 1936), p. 121.

[51] Edward J. Young, *Thy Word Is Truth* (Grand Rapids: Eerdmans, 1957), p. 87.

[52] *The Presbyterian Outlook* (Dec. 24, 1962), pp. 1ff.

[53] Alvah Hovey, *Manual of Systematic Theology and Christian Ethics* (Philadelphia: A.B.P.S., 1880), p. 83.

[54] Ibid., p. 85.

[55] Russell H. Conwell, *The Life of Charles Haddon Spurgeon* (Edgewood Publishing Co., 1892), pp. 574-576.

[56] Ibid., pp. 468-470.

[57] George A. Turner, "John Wesley as an Interpreter of Scripture," in *Inspiration and Interpretation*, John W. Walvoord, ed. (Grand Rapids: Eerdmans, 1957), p. 161.

[58] John Wesley, *Journal*, VI, 117.

The Lutheran Church - Missouri Synod Battle

The three largest Lutheran bodies in the United States are the American Lutheran Church, the Lutheran Church of America, and the Lutheran Church - Missouri Synod. Of the three, the Missouri Synod (as I shall call it) has been the most orthodox. Across the years it has remained faithful to its tradition and part of that tradition has included a strong conviction that the Bible is the inerrant Word of God. But things have been changing in the Missouri Synod in recent years and the denomination is currently embroiled·in a controversy that many have labeled a battle for ecclesiastical power. In a sense that is true. It is a war for the soul of the denomination and the control of it by parties of varying persuasions. Charges and counter-charges have been hurled back and forth, involving the dissidents, the moderates, and the conservatives. What does all of this have to do with the present struggle over the inerrancy of the Scriptures?

MISSOURI'S BASIC QUESTION

It is true that the Missouri Synod has been shaken by an ecclesiastical battle. It is true that people on all sides of the controversy have said and done things that do not measure up fully to the ethical principles laid down in the Scriptures. It may be true that some of the people in the controversy have ulterior motives, whatever they may be. Perhaps there has never been a church controversy that has not brought forth the worst in many people, and no ecclesiastical battle has ever been waged in full accord with the teachings of Jesus. Defective human nature makes sure of that. But when due allowance has been made for all of this, no one can fail to see that a theological question is at stake in the struggle, and the key doctrine in the struggle is biblical inerrancy. The historical-critical method, form and redaction criticism, etc., all have a role in the battle, but they are subsidiary. They simply express methodologies that are secondary to the primary question: Is the Bible completely trustworthy in its entirety?

MARTIN E. MARTY ON LUTHERAN CREEDS

Martin E. Marty, professor of the history of modern Christianity at the University of Chicago, and also associate editor of the liberal *Christian Century,* wrote a pamphlet entitled "Lutheranism, a Restatement in Question and Answer Form." In his discussion he asks, "Don't the confessions or creeds define Lutheranism?" His answer to this question is "Indeed they do, but they define it in a special way. In effect they say, 'This we believe!' and not 'This you must believe!' It is true that some Lutherans use them to build fences, to rule heretics out and the orthodox in, to enforce loyalty."[1] In speaking about what Lutherans believe, Marty goes on to ask the truly important question: Whence do Lutherans get their religious data? He then says that it is the Bible, which Lutherans regard "awesomely," to use his own word. Lutherans "yield to no other Christians in their regard for its authority. . . . Lutherans believe that the Bible is divinely inspired, that in some special way God saw to it that the humans who wrote it, without stepping outside their own personality and style, imparted His own truth. They believe that it is 'infallible' and unerring in its setting forth of all that one needs to be made right with God; Scriptures will not mislead believers. Some Lutherans go a step further and speak of the Bible as being 'inerrant' in the sense that its details are unfailingly accurate even when they talk about matters of geography, of history, of 'science.' Most Lutherans do not begin with such statements, however; they adhere to the Bible because it brings them Jesus Christ and speaks with authority to them in matters of faith and hope."[2] The two ideas expressed so aptly by Marty lie at the heart of the problem of biblical inerrancy.

THE BIBLE AND THE CREEDS

In the first place, creeds and confessions always have been used as a touchstone to determine whether one belongs to the group that has constructed the confession or creed, despite the intimation by Marty that they should not. Those who cannot accept the creed or confession are not Lutherans (in this case), and there is no reason why they should remain within the fellowship of those who adhere to the confession or creed. The group that holds to the confession or creed has every right, even the obligation, to remove from their fellowship anyone who does not hold to the statement of faith. Any Lutheran body that does not use a creed to fence the faithful in and rule the heretics out will shortly lose its distinctive identity.

Also, Marty, while not saying so in these words, admits that the source of religious data for Lutherans is the Bible. When he does this, he opens up the question concerning whether the Bible can be trusted. For if all other sources of data disagree with Scripture, then one must make a choice between belief in Scripture and belief in the sources that contradict it. It is here that Marty makes his neat distinction, one that is at the center of the Missouri Synod troubles today. The Bible can be trusted. It "will not mislead believers." But he quickly qualifies this statement, which on its face assumes that *none* of it will mislead believers. He mentions some Lutherans who go a step farther and speak of the Bible as inerrant, especially in matters of geography, history, and "science." He says that many Lutherans do not hold to a fully inerrant Bible. He intimates here, and writes elsewhere, that he does not believe that the Bible is free from geographic, historical, or scientific errors. When all is said and done, the Missouri Synod's real problem is biblical inerrancy. The denomination is riddled by voices that deny this doctrine and seek to wrest control of the denomination from those who are determined to preserve this basic belief in the life and the confession of the Synod.

LUTHER AND THE AUGSBURG CONFESSION

Lutheran bodies confess and use the Augsburg Confession of faith. This confession does not have a specific section dealing with the doctrine of Scripture. Many sections of it have no particular relevance today, for the matters discussed are no longer controversial. The absence of a dogmatic statement on Scripture in the Augsburg Confession does not mean, however, that Luther and his followers were unconcerned about the truthfulness of the Word of God.

Neither Luther nor the Roman Catholic Church, which he fought, had any real dissent about the Bible. Both believed the Bible to be the true Word of God (see the earlier quotations about Luther in chapter 3). The Roman Catholic Church added to Scripture, and also did violence to Scripture by making the church the authoritative interpreter of it. Luther strongly supported *sola Scriptura*, by which he meant he would not believe anything that could not be proved from Scripture and he would believe anything taught in Scripture even though the Church denied it. It was this principle of biblical trustworthiness that led to the use of the second principle, *sola fide*. Man is saved by faith alone. The Roman Catholic Church taught faith plus works. The Scriptures taught faith plus nothing. Luther believed that salvation by faith plus works could not be proved from Scripture, and he was equally convinced that salvation by faith alone could be proved from the Word of God. On this he stood resolutely, but ever and always it was the Scripture that brought the gospel and Christ to him.

THE MISSOURI SYNOD'S BRIEF STATEMENT

The Missouri Synod, from its earliest beginnings, was not unaware of the implications of its Lutheran heritage. The people of this Synod knew that Martin Luther was a man of his times and they were discriminating in how they followed him. Neither Missouri nor other Lutheran groups have been happy about Luther's diatribe against the Jews or about the other crude things he said at times. But he was sound on the essentials and loved the Word of God.

The Missouri Synod learned one thing from Luther and from the history of the Christian church. At any given time in the history of a denomination one issue may surface that demands resolution. In Luther's day his Ninety-five Theses and the Augsburg Confession are a fair reflection of the crucial issues he and the early Lutherans had to deal with. But those issues are dead today and others have taken their place.

From its founding, the Missouri Synod held to an inerrant Scripture. It was not then an issue in the denomination, for there was no dissent. Then came the Fundamentalist-Modernist controversy. The Missouri Synod was largely untouched by this controversy, but it would be a mistake to say that the controversy had no influence on the Synod. The influence was there, but the timing of it was delayed. Thus, Missouri is experiencing now what other large denominations experienced decades ago. By 1932 there was enough of a cloud in the sky to show that the Synod might have the beginnings of an infection that centered around the inerrancy of the Bible.

In 1932 the Lutheran Church – Missouri Synod adopted a *Brief Statement* of its doctrinal position. In 1947, at the centennial celebration of the denomination, the *Brief Statement* was incorporated in the official proceedings of the convention. It was not made part of the Constitution along with the confessions contained therein. I have heard some argue in effect that the *Brief Statement* contravenes the Constitution; that the Lutheran Confessions do not teach or require an ordinand to believe in biblical inerrancy. Certainly, however, the *Brief Statement* did reflect the dominant views of the Synod which understood that the *Brief Statement* did say what the Confessions really say. The first article of the *Brief Statement* said thus:

> 1. We teach that the Holy Scriptures differ from all other books in the world in that they are the Word of God. They are the Word of God because the holy men of God who wrote the Scriptures wrote only that which the Holy Ghost communicated to them by inspiration, 2 Tim. 3:16; 2 Pet. 1:21. We teach also that the verbal inspiration of the Scriptures is not a so-called "theological deduction," but that it is taught by direct statements of the Scriptures, 2 Tim. 3:16; John 10:35; Rom. 3:2; 1 Cor. 2:13. Since the Holy Scriptures are the Word of God, it goes without saying that they contain no errors or contradictions, but that they are in all their parts and words the infallible truth, also in those parts which treat of historical, geographical, and other secular matters, John 10:35.[3]

BRETSCHER'S CASE AGAINST INERRANCY

For almost a century and a half the Missouri Synod has been identified with this view of the Bible as the infallible Word of God in its entirety. Today the doctrine of biblical infallibility is being challenged, and many voices claim that the Bible is more like that described by Martin E. Marty and less like that enunciated in the *Brief Statement* of 1932. One of the best formulations of the basic issue in the Missouri Synod was advanced by Paul G. Bretscher in his book *After the Purifying*. His argument is worth study.

Bretscher says the term "the Word of God" is being used in the Synod, but points out that two different meanings are attached to it. The one meaning is that spelled out in the 1932 *Brief Statement*, which says that all of the Bible is the Word of God and all of it is without error. Bretscher differentiates as follows: "For example, Article II of the Synod's Constitution declares that the Synod and every member 'accepts without reservation' the Scriptures 'as the written Word of God.' But what do the members of the Synod have in mind when they hear and use that phrase, 'the Word of God'? To many, perhaps most, it means the inspired and inerrant Scriptures, with God as the true Author of every word. To a minority, however, 'the Word of God' means the Spirit's proclamation of grace in Christ to sinners, and the Scriptures as the fountain and norm of that Word."[4]

Bretscher continues his argument, using the term *dross* from which the Synod needs to be purified, by giving to the phrase "the Word of God" a different meaning from that attached to it by the *Brief Statement*. He distinguishes between the gospel and the Scriptures. He says that for the believers in inerrancy

> the Scriptures are regarded as broader than the Gospel. Beyond their content of Law and Gospel there remains the "rest of Scripture." The Scriptures contain also "information about other matters." Christians must also accept matters taught in the Scriptures which are not "a part of the Gospel." Thus, in the mind of the dross [i.e., those who believe in inerrancy], the message which Christians must accept to be true Christians is *more* than Christ alone! It is *more* than "the Gospel of the gracious justification of the sinner through faith in Jesus Christ." "Anything and everything that the Scriptures teach" now belongs to our Synod's faith and confession.[5]

Bretscher, in his distinction between the Word of God as understood by the believer in inerrancy, as against the minority for whom he is speaking, says this: Not all of Scripture has to do with the gospel; Luther's definition of the Word of God had to do only with Christ and the gospel; those who apply the term "the Word of God" to all of Scripture are mistaken. His conclusion is obvious: Whatever is not of the gospel may have error in it, and to extend the meaning of the term "the Word of God" to all of Scripture is wrong and misleading. He wishes to limit the term to what is to be found in some of the Bible but not all of the Bible; only a part of it. So he writes that the school of thought he represents, which opposes inerrancy, understands "the inspiration, authority, and inerrancy of the Scriptures in terms of the Gospel. They found this understanding of the Word to be both Scriptural and Confessional. By it they affirmed their loyalty to Article II of the Synod's Constitution 'without reservation.' Scripture is indeed 'the written Word of God and the only rule and norm of faith and of practice.' "[6] The sum of it is this: Whatever has to do with the gospel in the Bible is inspired and can be trusted; whatever does not have to do with the gospel has error in it — it is not inerrant. This, of course, leaves it up to those who hold this view to decide what parts of the Bible have to do with gospel and what parts do not. And it ends up by assuming that whatever it is the individual wishes to disbelieve can be labeled as not part of the gospel.

The allegations of Paul Bretscher demand a response. He apparently is arguing that the Missouri Synod in 1932 and 1947 did something that is not in accord with the teaching and practice of Luther. It is, he says, un-Lutheran to relate Scripture and gospel in such a way that anyone must believe in biblical inerrancy. If, for the sake of argument, we concede that his point is valid, it still is possible to show that he has no leg to stand on. What is there to prevent the people of the Synod from improving on Luther himself if they so choose? Or from carrying out in this generation the implications of what Luther taught at a time when biblical inerrancy was not a pivotal issue? Or of standing firm with Luther on his basic presupposition that it is from Scripture alone we get our religious data? And in following through on this to show they are merely saying that the Bible itself, which is the source of their religious faith, teaches biblical inerrancy? Since Luther and the Synod both agree on the principle *sola Scriptura*, are not the opponents of biblical inerrancy wrong when they refuse to believe what Scripture teaches about itself?

What the Missouri Synod has done in its *Brief Statement* is not something new; it has been part and parcel of the Synod's views since it was founded in the United States. Bretscher was raised in this environment. If he personally believes that the Synod has erred in demanding adherence to an infallible Scripture, and he cannot convince the Synod that it is wrong, he is free to remove to another Lutheran group more to his liking. So long as he wishes to remain within the Synod, he is bound by his ordination oath to believe, teach, and propagate what the Synod is committed to. He has every right to change his views and to depart from synodical teachings. He has no right to remain within the church when he does this.

We need to explore what it means to be a Lutheran, keeping in mind what Martin E. Marty said about who Lutherans are. If a man denies what a Lutheran church teaches, is he truly a Lutheran? Let me illustrate this. Suppose Bretscher denies the deity of Christ, the vicarious atonement, the bodily resurrection of Jesus from the dead, and His second coming. Does he then have any claim to the title

"Lutheran"? Does he have any right to remain with a church that calls itself Lutheran? More than that, does a Lutheran church not have the right to exclude from its fellowship those who deny the truths that their confession says a Lutheran believes? Does a church have a right to permit those who disbelieve Lutheran teaching to remain in its fellowship? Does not the presence of those who disbelieve Lutheran teachings almost surely guarantee further infection in the church and at last the loss of the church to historic Lutheranism in all except name? Since any church has the right to determine what its own confessional standards shall be, men like Bretscher have no right to deny those teachings or to defy the authority of the church that has set up those standards. This is an ethical issue that cannot be avoided.

The great weakness of Bretscher's case is that he misunderstands Luther. And this misunderstanding stems from the need to believe that his ordination oath, properly understood, enables him to dissent from traditional Missouri Synod teaching. His situation might possibly be legitimate if his allegation about Luther's teaching happens to be accurate. It isn't.

In the chapter on the teaching of the church through the ages about infallibility, statements were quoted to show that Luther believed in an infallible Bible. It is hardly possible for any scholar to say that this is not true. There is too much evidence in its favor. Who can read what Luther said in a sermon of John 3:16 and refuse to agree that he believed in biblical infallibility? Here are his words:

> If a different way to heaven existed, no doubt God would have recorded it, but there is no other way. Therefore, let us cling to these words, firmly place and rest our hearts upon them, close our eyes and say: Although I had the merit of all the saints, the holiness and purity of all virgins, and the piety of St. Peter himself, I would still consider my attainment nothing. Rather I must have a different foundation to build on, namely, these words: God has given His Son so that whosoever believes in Him whom the Father's love has sent shall be saved. And you must confidently insist that you will be preserved; and you must boldly take your stand on His words, which no devil, hell or death can suppress. . . . Therefore no matter what happens, you should say: There is God's Word. This is my rock and anchor. On it I rely, and it remains. Where it remains, I, too, remain; Where it goes, I, too, go. The Word [and he is not talking about the gospel; he is talking about the written Word of God, not the incarnate Word] must stand, for God cannot lie; and heaven and earth must go to ruins

before the most insignificant letter or tittle of His Word [and to make this apply to Christ would make nonsense of what Luther is saying] remains unfulfilled.[7]

Bretscher's case, even if it were true, which it is not, that "the Word of God means the Spirit's proclamation of grace in Christ to sinners" and that to believe in biblical inerrancy is not part of the gospel, is poles apart from Martin Luther. For Luther affirmed his belief in the Bible as free from error in the whole and in the part. If Luther did so in his day, no one has any right to suppose that he would approve of someone like Bretscher coming along today claiming the opposite. Indeed, the Missouri Synod is most Lutheran in standing for a belief about the Scriptures that is no different from that which was entertained by Luther himself.

KELLER ON ADAM AND EVE

Relating Scripture to law and gospel as part of the Missouri struggle can be seen by listening to another writer who makes it plainer than Bretscher. Professor Walter E. Keller, chairman of the Department of Theology at Valparaiso, wrote in the *Cresset* of that institution, saying, "I cannot say that the distinction between Law and the Gospel will answer the question as to whether Adam and Eve were historical, but that distinction releases me from the burden of having to say that Adam and Eve must have been historical. They may have been; from the viewpoint of the distinction between the Law and the Gospel the question of their historicity is an indifferent matter."[8] In a nutshell, what the Missouri liberals are saying is that it does not matter if the Bible contains error, since error does not invalidate the message of law and gospel. God can also work through error. Whether what happened was historical makes no difference. Theirs is a theology that "sees all the intention of Scripture in a Gospel understanding only, thereby making unimportant the historicity of the narrative described."

TIETJEN AT CONCORDIA

When President Tietjen was defending Professor Arlis Ehlen of the Concordia Seminary faculty at St. Louis, he revealed clearly the real state of affairs at the seminary. Ehlen, when explaining his position on angels, wrote, "In this matter as in all others connected with Biblical exegesis, I am concerned to be totally faithful to the intention of the Divine Author . . . . I accept [in connection with the

Red Sea crossing of the Israelites] what the Sacred writers evidently intended by their elaboration of the miraculous details; namely, to magnify the glory of God's great act of Salvation and to heighten its impact on those who hear in faith. In this case, too, my ultimate concern therefore, is to be faithful to the intended meaning of the Biblical text." So Tietjen could write: "I have had a number of doctrinal discussions with Dr. Ehlen in recent months. In those discussions he has specifically affirmed the authority of Scripture in its entirety and in all its parts. He has stated that he affirms the *facticity of what the Scripture intends to present as facts*" (my italics).[9] In all of this, the use and meaning of the word *intended* is what makes the difference. Both Ehlen and Tietjen knew and understood that by the use of this device they were saying they do not think "that Scripture intends to present as a fact what the clear sense of Scripture presents as a fact." By this methodology, the historicity and facticity of anything in Scripture can be destroyed.

THE HISTORICAL - CRITICAL METHODOLOGY

In the Concordia Seminary dispute the use of the historical-critical method was high on the agenda. Some of the defenders of this methodology declared that it is neutral. Tietjen, the president at the time, stated flatly that "it would not be possible to operate a Department of Exegetical Theology at a graduate school without the use of the historical-critical methodology."[10] He said this despite the fact that there are graduate schools where it is not in use. Robert Preus of his faculty stated that most of the members of the Concordia faculty used the method but it leads to a rejection of many of the miracles, the temptation story, and the details of the story of Jesus' baptism (including the descent of the dove and the voice of God from heaven).

Professor Dean O. Wenthe of Concordia Seminary at Springfield wrote that "the historical-critical method is not a neutral tool, but rather a very special instrument that is inseparable from its own presuppositions, procedures, and results. As one surveys the anti-supernaturalistic presuppositions, the secular procedures and the far-reaching results, it becomes obvious that a wedding between the bride and 'Lutheran presuppositions,' is as impossible as the marriage of light and darkness."[11]

The situation at Concordia at St. Louis and the Missouri Synod has advanced beyond that of Fuller Seminary, which has only gone so far as to reject inerrancy in principle. This can be illustrated by the support and use of the historical-critical methodology, which men at Fuller repudiate. Professor George E. Ladd of Fuller read a paper at the twenty-fifth anniversary celebration of *Interpretation: A Journal of Bible and Theology*, the publication of Union Theological Seminary of Richmond, Virginia, a Presbyterian U.S. institution. In his paper Dr. Ladd said:

> If one's view of history is such that he cannot acknowledge a divine plan of salvation unfolding in historical events, then he cannot accept the witness of the Bible. The point we are stressing is that the historical-critical method denies the role of transcendence in the history of Jesus as well as in the Bible as a whole, not as a result of scientific study of the evidences, but because of its philosophical presuppositions about the nature of history. . . . The historical-critical method excludes by definition that which I believe. . . . [12]

Ladd is correct in his assertions that the use of the historical-critical method, to be found among Southern Baptists as well as among Missouri Synod Lutherans, is based on presuppositions that destroy historic orthodoxy. Orthodoxy and the historical-critical method are deadly enemies that are antithetical and cannot be reconciled without the destruction of one or the other.

Before J. A. O. Preus became president of the Synod in 1969, his predecessor, Oliver Harms, constantly defended the seminary at St. Louis and repeatedly assured the denomination that all was well there. Dr. Harms was a well-meaning man whose reassurances were based on statements he had received from the seminary presidents. Since he was not particularly discerning and displayed no particular acuity concerning the issues at stake, he was taken in. He spoke either out of ignorance or lack of understanding, but in any event he served the purposes of the neoliberals in the denomination.

THE JANZOW SURVEY

Walter Janzow, the president of Seward Concordia, earned a doctorate in sociology at the University of Nebraska in 1970. His dissertation entitled *Secularization in an Orthodox Denomination* provided statistical data that show the Missouri Synod indeed has a real problem on its hands. Dr. Janzow made a detailed study of the theological leanings of what he called Missouri's "elite," the laity, and the parish clergy. The results were revealing. Eighty-nine percent of Missouri's laity fell into the upper range of theological orthodoxy; 82 percent of Missouri's parish clergy were found there; only 69 percent of the "elite" (which included people at the head-quarters and at the seminaries and schools) belonged there. Of the "elite," only 51 percent accepted the Bible as the inspired and inerrant Word of God, whereas 65 percent of the parish clergy and 83 percent of the laity did. When the statistics were broken down into age groups, Janzow reported that "members of our elites less than 35 years old, like the parish clergy of this age group, accept inspiration and inerrancy to an even smaller degree; only 35 percent agree with the inerrancy doctrine. Seventy-eight percent (78%) of the lay people, however, in this group accept it."[13]

If history has any lesson to teach, it is that defection from iner-rancy generally takes place in the educational institutions and then spreads from there. In the case of the Missouri Lutherans it appears to have resulted from postgraduate studies pursued by men trained in Missouri schools who then secured doctorates in secular or liberal institutions. They were enamored of the historical-critical method, and numbers of them left their old moorings with respect to biblical infallibility. More frequently than not, men with this kind of training did not go into the parish ministry, but headed for institutions where the possibility existed to disseminate this newfound learning among younger minds that could easily be influenced away from historic Missouri viewpoints. In addition, this kind of mind enjoyed teaching these new and attractive but irregular doctrines through the litera-ture of the denomination. So they became editors and writers for church school materials.

In 1971, *Affirm* reported that in "The Teacher's Manual *The Layman's Bible Commentary* series on the *Gospel According to St. Mark,* Volume 17 (Blue 5-1 Teacher's Kit, 'Countdown to Jerusalem')," the writer said:

"Pages 40-41: The triumphant entry into Jerusalem is 'symbol-ical narrative,' for Mark was not inclined to 'force episode into arbitrary harmony with his *editorial plan*.' "[14]

"Introducing the Bible, Bible I says 'It is not essential that everyone reads the Bible . . . . Do not expect particular blessing from God because you read the Bible . . . . Do not seek answers to the questions in your life . . . . Throwing people into the Bible and telling them to read it is no more sensible than throwing a child into deep water hoping he will swim . . . . You do not need opening and closing prayer . . . . The laws which God's self-disclosure gave to Israel are not

unchangeable and forever valid . . . . God's self-disclosure — particularly in Jesus Christ — is new to every social situation . . . . The writer did not think about himself as writing "Scripture" or Bible. . . ' "[15]

J. A. O. PREUS, MISSOURI'S PRESIDENT

The coming of J.A.O. Preus to the presidency of the Missouri Synod in 1969 was a kind of watershed. It seemed clear enough that the majority of Missouri Lutherans were unhappy about the trend in their church and wanted to do something about it. Dr. Preus knew that the Concordia, St. Louis Seminary was the major source of disaffection. Dr. Tietjen had become president of that institution in a most unorthodox fashion. Once it was known that Dr. Preus might become president of the Synod, the neoliberals worked to secure the appointment of Tietjen as president of the Seminary at St. Louis. He was a minority candidate by far, and protocol was bent to make him president *before* Preus became the titular head of the denomination. Once Preus became president of the Synod, he went to work on the Seminary. Tietjen and his supporters regarded this as persecution, whereas Preus believed he had a mandate to clean up the problem.

When the showdown came at the Seminary in St. Louis, Tietjen was removed from his office. Whatever may have been his objections, the fact remains that he was removed legally and in accord with normal denominational machinery. But Tietjen refused to take his defeat sitting down, nor was he to regard it as final. He established a "Seminary in Exile" ("Seminex") headed by himself, staffed by faculty members who, like him, were supporters of the historical-critical method and were disbelievers in biblical inerrancy. He gained the support of the Association of Theological Schools on the grounds that academic liberty was at stake. This was a charade, for even the Association has always agreed that every denomination has the right to decide what shall be taught at its institutions. To do this is theoretically an "infringement" of academic liberty, but it is the only safeguard that guarantees the integrity of a denomination. Once the spurious claim of "academic liberty" prevails, license then makes possible the propagation of viewpoints opposed to the denomination's standards. The result is suicidal.

Tietjen did what was contrary to Missouri's church order. This was divisive. But the machinery of the liberal-dominated Association of Theological Schools and later the secular machinery of the American Association of University Professors came to Tietjen's aid.

The St. Louis Seminary was put on probation by the Association of Theological Schools and the AAUP castigated the institution. Meanwhile, Tietjen's liberal friends provided housing for his new seminary and a new church organization was set up (ELIM). If the situation had been reversed and the liberals had gained the office of the presidency of the Synod, the creation of a conservative seminary in exile and the setting up of a new church organization would have been roundly denounced by liberals everywhere. And we can be sure that accreditation by the Association of Theological Schools of a new conservative school would never have followed.

Ecclesiological or Theological Struggle?

Tietjen loudly proclaimed that the issue was not so much theological as ecclesiological. It was a struggle for power and control of the denomination. In a sense this was true. He and his followers tried, albeit unsuccessfully, to gain control of the machinery of the church. So did Preus and his followers. Preus succeeded; Tietjen failed. But the effort to control the denominational machinery by both sides was brought about by the theological questions that had become more and more prominent in the life of the Missouri Synod. Bretscher, as we have seen (and he sided with Tietjen), acknowledged that Missouri has a problem. He described the nature of the problem. And he is aware that the issue will be decided at last by whoever controls the machinery of the denomination. History tells us that in the Fundamentalist-Modernist controversy in the '20s the Fundamentalists lost because the Modernists gained control of the ecclesiastical machinery as well as the theological seminaries. It was a decisive combination.

At any time after J. A. O. Preus became president of the Synod, Tietjen and his fellow faculty members could have come to terms with Preus. All they needed to do was to accept without mental reservation the *Brief Statement of the Doctrinal Position of the Missouri Synod* of 1932 that has been in existence for almost half a century. This was the statement that was reaffirmed in 1947. This was the statement on which Preus took his stand. The statement fairly and accurately reflected what has always been the stand of the Missouri Synod. The decision to put it in writing in a more specific way in 1932 highlighted the signs in the Synod of a move away from Missouri's historic position. Preus was not out to change the position of the Synod. He intended to reinforce it, and to see that it was kept honestly by those who were committed to do so in their ordination vows. But neither Tietjen nor the dissident members of the faculty have shown any willingness to assent to the *Brief Statement* and to propagate its teaching in the seminary. This failure in itself is the strongest evidence that Tietjen was beclouding the issue when he argued that it was an ecclesiological and not a theological issue that was at the heart of the matter.

Christianity Today published an article by John Tietjen. In it he accused Preus of using the slogan "They are taking your Bible away" effectively. He called it a smokescreen. But he admitted that there are genuine issues "and they increase in number with each passing month. In fact, the very soul of the Synod is at stake." And with that assessment anyone in and out of the Synod can agree. J. A. O. Preus would also agree with that observation. Tietjen said much the same thing that Bretscher said: "The Word of God is the message of God's judgment and of his promise. Everything in the Bible is either a word of law that condemns or a word of promise that saves. In its proper sense the Word of God is good news about God in action to save. Preeminently the Word of God is Jesus Christ himself."[16] And while all of this may be true in some measure, it is also true that the Word of God is more than Tietjen says it is; it is what Luther proclaimed: the written Word that is wholly inerrant in all its parts. But this is not what Tietjen believes, nor do those associated with him.

WALTER A. MAIER PINPOINTS THE PROBLEM

No one perceived more clearly what the issue was than the late Walter A. Maier. In a short article on *The "Historical-Critical Method" of Bible Study,* written long before Preus became president of the Synod, he said:

> Most of the scholars who use the historical-critical method base their analysis of the Biblical text on certain rationalistic, anti-scriptural presuppositions, anti-supernaturalism, for example. They flatly reject the possibility of divine intervention and miraculous action in human affairs. They also operate with various arbitrary, unwarranted assumptions, such as the unreasonable bias that many Biblical accounts, which purport to, do not really present factual history. As a result, their interpretations often subvert the obvious meaning of clear Scripture passages, and the theological views they express often do not conform to the Word of God. [Then Dr. Maier gave some examples:] (1) When the New Testament evangelists composed their Gospels, they simply took over traditional short stories about Jesus which

had been circulating in Palestinian Christian communities and worked these into running Gospel accounts. Practically all references to time and place. . . are of the evangelists' invention and do not supply authentic information about the life of Jesus. (2) The miracles reported in the Gospels did not actually occur. . . . (3) Many of the sayings attributed to Jesus were never spoken by Him at all. . . . (4) The Gospels contain many legends and myths, pure fabrications, which were given their form "in the interest of the cultus" and for purposes of edification. Mythological and legendary material, which is the product of "pious fancy" and "active Christian imagination," is seen in the following Gospel accounts: the narrative of Jesus' baptism, the narrative of Christ's temptation in the wilderness, the transfiguration narrative, the narrative of the Last Supper, the passion narrative, and the resurrection narrative. Liberal theologians regard it as one of the functions of form critical investigation to help the twentieth-century reader to de-mythologize the New Testament Scriptures and thus get down to "what really happened" at the time of Christ and early Christianity. Additional incredible and, indeed, blasphemous views arising from the modern, scholarly use of historical-critical methodology could be cited.[17]

Walter A. Maier put his finger on the pulse of Missouri's problem many years ago. He was fighting to retain that church's belief in an inerrant Scripture. He knew that in every denomination where this battle had been fought, believers in inerrancy had lost. If he were alive today he would know that the battle that was fought in other denominations decades ago is being fought today in the Missouri Synod. He would know that the issue has been joined and the outcome is by no means assured. But he would also know that, at least for the time being, believers in inerrancy have control of the denomination. Whether they can retain this control and whether they will take the steps necessary to do so, only time will tell. The present struggle in this large and formerly theologically orthodox denomination simply points up the thesis of this book: the Missouri Synod situation is one indication of the existence of anti-inerrancy forces in evangelical denominations and organizations that have traditionally opted for biblical infallibility.

[1] Martin E. Marty, *Lutheranism, a Restatement in Question and Answer Form* (Royal Oak, MI: Cathedral, 1975), p. 8.

[2] Ibid., pp. 10, 11.

[3] *Proceedings* of 1932, p. 1548.

[4] Paul G. Bretscher, *After the Purifying* (River Forest: Lutheran Education Association, 1975), pp. 16, 17.

[5] Ibid., p. 63.
[6] Ibid., p. 101.
[7] Martin Luther, *Weimarer Ausgabe*, 10 III, 162.
[8] *Cresset*, February, 1973.
[9] Tom Baker, *Watershed at the Rivergate* (Sturgis, MI: 1973), p. 18.
[10] Ibid., p. 9.
[11] Ibid., p. 11.
[12] *Interpretation: A Journal of Bible and Theology* (Vol. XXV. No. 1, Jan., 1971), pp. 50, 57.
[13] *Affirm*, June A, 1971, pp. 1, 2.
[14] Ibid., p. 5.
[15] Ibid.
[16] *Christianity Today*, April 14, 1975.
[17] *Affirm*, June A, 1971, p. 9.

5

The Southern Baptist Convention

Through the years, the Southern Baptist Convention, like the Lutheran Church-Missouri Synod, has been numbered among the large denominations that have remained faithful to the Scriptures. The term *Bible Belt* has been applied as a kind of slur to the people south of the Mason-Dixon line. Rather, it should be thought of as a compliment, for probably no other geographical region in the United States has had a better record for belief in the infallibility of the Word of God. And no group has done any better in this regard than the Southern Baptists.

The Southern Baptists were not among those denominations that were seriously affected by the Modernist-Fundamentalist controversy earlier this century. There were a number of reasons why this was so. Not many of their seminary and college teachers had received their doctorates from overseas universities or from liberal institutions in the north. The Southern Baptists were so large that they became a kind of self-contained unit that had all of the educational tools within the denomination. This meant that the outside influences were marginal. As part of the Bible Belt, geographically they were more immune to the liberal forces at work in northern America, forces that were to change the theological landscape. The Southern Baptists were strongly evangelistic, and this provided protection from the inroads of unbelief. And the people who were part of the denominational machinery were themselves theologically conservative and tended to perpetuate conservatism in their appointments to boards and agencies of the denomination. However, significant changes have taken place in recent years that suggest that what happened to other denominations decades ago can happen to Southern Baptists. Seeds of dissent have been planted, and are sprouting in many places among them.

THE CONFESSION OF 1925

Although the Southern Baptists were not seriously affected by the Modernist-Fundamentalist controversy, this did not mean they were unaware of what was happening around them. This we know from what their convention did in 1925. The most complete statement of faith ever considered by Southern Baptists was adopted by that convention. Basically, the statement they voted for was the New Hampshire Confession of Faith that had been in existence for nearly one hundred years. The articles of faith they accepted were later reaffirmed from time to time and still are believed by most Southern Baptists. Among the articles was one on the Scriptures. It reads:

> The Holy Bible was written by men divinely inspired and is the record of God's revelation of Himself to man. It is a perfect treasure of divine instruction. It has God for its author, salvation for its end, and truth, without any mixture of error, for its matter. It reveals the principles by which God judges us; and therefore is, and will remain to the end of the world, the true center of Christian union, and the supreme standard by which all human conduct, creeds, and religious opinions should be tried. The criterion by which the Bible is to be interpreted is Jesus Christ.

Even a cursory reading of that part of the statement on Scripture that says the Bible has God "for its author . . . and truth, without any mixture of error, for its matter" must lead to the conclusion that the entire Bible is free from error. Of that there can be no doubt, either historically, exegetically, or practically. Thus the efforts of some today to limit infallibility to matters of faith and practice so as to exclude historical, scientific, and other items would destroy the obvious meaning and intent of the article on Scripture. Limited infallibility also means that not all of Scripture is infallible, but is mixed with error; and those parts that have errors in them constitute inspired errors allowed by the Holy Spirit, or parts of Scripture that are not inspired at all.

SOUTHERN BAPTISTS HAVE BEEN INFECTED

In this book I am dealing with the question of biblical infallibility and must now produce the hard evidence to enforce the claim that the Southern Baptist Convention has numbers of people in it who deny biblical infallibility. They are challenging the historic position of the denomination and constitute a threat to its future. Not only so, but it will be shown that some who have abandoned biblical inerrancy have also abandoned other cardinal doctrines of the Christian faith so that in any historic sense they have ceased to be Baptists as understood traditionally. Baptists have always claimed that they are not a creedal people and have always taught that all men have the right to believe as they wish. But they have always insisted that if one is to be a Baptist, there are some things that must be believed, otherwise one has ceased to be a Baptist. For example, Baptists do not baptize infants. Anyone who wishes to do so, may believe in infant baptism and practice it as well, but that person is not a Baptist. So also with immersion as the mode of baptism. Anyone may believe that sprinkling and pouring constitute valid baptism, but those who do, have no right to denominate themselves as Baptists. Anyone who wants to believe in episcopacy may do so, but those who so believe cannot be termed Baptists. No one who is truly a Southern Baptist has a right to insist that others *must* believe that the Bible is the inerrant Word of God, but it is consistent to argue that those who do not have really ceased to be Southern Baptists. What evidence, then, can be found to show that the Southern Baptists have in their midst some who deny biblical infallibility?

ROBERT S. ALLEY – UNIVERSITY OF RICHMOND

The first illustration that comes to mind is that of Professor Robert S. Alley. He graduated from the University of Richmond in Virginia and secured a B.D. degree from the Southern Baptist Seminary in Louisville and the Ph.D. degree from Princeton University. At the time he authored his book *Revolt Against the Faithful* he was, according to the book blurb, an associate professor of religion at the University of Richmond and an active member of the Southern Baptist Convention. The university has been a Baptist institution and has consistently received substantial financial support from the Virginia State Baptist Convention. Despite these Baptist connections, neither the Baptists of Virginia nor those of the university where he teaches have taken any action or done anything to indicate their concern that he has abandoned the foundational truths of the Christian faith.

Dr. Alley denies that the Bible is the infallible word of God. He wrote, "While some persons may continue to hold that 'the historic Christian belief in Biblical infallibility and inerrancy is the only valid starting point and framework for a theology of revelation,' such contentions should be heard with a smile and incorporated in the bylaws of the Flat Earth Society. But always we should respect the integrity of a *person* in an argument or debate, though his *position* may indeed be quite ridiculous."[1]

Dr. Alley quotes disapprovingly from the book *Why I Preach That the Bible Is Literally True* by former Southern Baptist Convention president, W. A. Criswell. Dr. Criswell believes in biblical infallibility. Dr. Alley does him the injustice of supposing that he teaches the dictation theory of Scripture. He says, "The idea of verbal inspiration is inconsistent both with human experience and the message of Scripture. . . . It is sometimes argued that there are biblical passages which do support the theory of dictation. . . . What has been presented is the sum total of biblical evidence (i.e. II Timothy 3:16, Rev. 22:18, 19; II Peter 1:20, 21) advanced by literalists to support belief in infallibility and verbal inspiration. How inadequate and unconvincing!"[2]

Later, Dr. Alley says, "Many who promote infallibility of the Bible are simply dishonest. They know better through education and reading but find it advantageous to exploit the uninformed whom they say they have been 'called' to serve and save. They parlay this false doctrine into success, fame and large churches. Such moral dereliction is far too common in many modern public religious activities. . . . To this type of deceit there is no response except contempt and rejection."[3] Elsewhere he says that "Adam, Eve, Noah, Jonah — these were fictitious persons who proclaimed a truth," that the virgin birth is not to be believed, that miracles did not occur, and that the resurrection is not a historical fact.[4]

HOWARD B. COLSON — OUTREACH

A second illustration of how biblical infallibility is denied comes from *Outreach*, a magazine published by the Sunday School Board of the Southern Baptist Convention. The magazine is designed "to provide helps for church staff members, Sunday School general officers, and Sunday School council members." In one issue, Dr.

Howard P. Colson, editorial secretary of the Sunday School Board, published an article entitled "Truth Without Any Mixture of Error." He wrote, "Some people still argue that the Bible is a perfect authority even in scientific matters. But if that were so, how does it happen that the conception of the earth's shape as found in Scripture has been shown not to be a literal fact? The earth as the Bible writers speak of it is flat [which is not true]; yet we know that the earth is actually a sphere. But the purpose of the Bible is not to tell men the shape of the earth. Its purpose is to lead men to God."[5]

Dr. Colson asks, "What is the nature of the error of which the Bible message is completely free? We have said that the truth which constitutes the biblical message is religious or spiritual truth. By a like token, we may now say that the error from which biblical truth is completely free is spiritual error."[6] He is of the opinion that when Southern Baptists say the Bible is "truth without any mixture of error, for its matter" they mean that the "saving truths taught in the Bible are free from all *spiritual* error"[7] (my italics — for herein he denies freedom from historical and other errors even in connection with saving truths).

WILLIAM E. HULL – LOUISVILLE

Dr. William E. Hull was, until the summer of 1975, a long-time professor at the Southern Baptist Seminary in Louisville. *The Baptist Program* published an article of his entitled "Shall We Call the Bible Infallible?" It had been presented first as a sermon at the Crescent Hill Baptist Church in Louisville. At the time, Dr. Hull was dean of the School of Theology at the Southern Seminary. He had received the B.D. and Th.D. degrees from Louisville and had pursued post-doctoral studies at the University of Goettingen, Germany, in 1962-63. In 1968, in his inaugural address as Dean of the School of Theology, he acknowledged his indebtedness to Rudolf Bultmann whose demythologization viewpoint has led him to deny virtually every cardinal doctrine of the Christian faith. The incoming dean made it clear that Louisville should have a curriculum that was not to "be committed either to conservatism or to liberalism, a position which many friends and foes alike find difficult to understand." In his *Baptist Program* article he correctly stated it was not until the post-Reformation period that a doctrine of Scripture was considered integral to a confession of faith. Why this was so, I have already explained. He goes on from there to discuss the article of the New

Hampshire confession on the Scriptures ("truth, without any mixture of error, for its matter") and claims that this always has to do with the saving knowledge of God mediated by the Bible, "never to the historical accuracy of the date and place of every event which is the announced concern of some of us."[8]

Dr. Hull said, "To apply the concept of infallibility to the Bible may do justice to the fact that it was inspired by a perfect God, but it does not do justice to the fact that this revelation was apprehended and written down by imperfect men. If the human writers were limited, as they themselves claimed, then their limitations belong also to a balanced doctrine of Scripture." He also said, "Some contend that a recognition of the human inperfections of the biblical writers leads to a 'low' view of inspiration that is defective or even heretical in comparison with a 'high' view which sees the entire process as infallible. Quite to the contrary, I would insist that the Bible is far *more* miraculous if it conveys the ultimate truth of God by means of ordinary men." "The infallible text [i.e., infallible originals or autographs] is a theory, not a reality. . . . To affirm something about a Bible that does not exist can hardly help but be misleading."[9] He numbers himself among those "who have just as clearly seen the human character of the Bible. They know that its dates do not always agree, that its doctrines develop, that its grammar is sometimes confused. They cannot give up this recognition of the humanity of its writers, for to do so would require them to fly in the face of *established facts* and to repudiate the advances of science in recent centuries" (my italics).[10]

The problems connected with the views of Dr. Hull are obvious. He must decide what Scripture he will trust as truthful and what he will distrust as false. If the assured opinions of science are accurate and they really do conflict with the teachings of Scripture, then science stands in judgment on the Bible rather than the Bible standing in judgment on science. Moreover, if the writers in their humanity were subject to scientific, historical, and other errors, why were they not also subject to theological errors? And if the Holy Spirit could preserve them from theological error, why could not the same Spirit preserve them from scientific and historical errors, too? One is no more improbable than the other.

Dr. Hull left Louisville Seminary to become minister of the First Baptist Church of Shreveport, Louisiana, at the end of the 1974-1975 school year. There were persistent reports that he was edged out of the seminary for his views on Scripture. This was denied by him and others. If it is true that his resignation was not forced and that he could have remained at the Southern Baptist seminary, then it becomes clear immediately that the Seminary is willing to employ faculty members who view the Bible as errant and who would then be free to teach their students that viewpoint. In any event, the seminary made no public statements that could be construed as affirming a belief in biblical inerrancy for the institution or for its faculty members.

THE TOY CASE

Since the Southern Baptist Seminary at Louisville was the institution at which Dr. Hull taught for more than ten years, it may be instructive to go back to its early history to review the famous Toy case. It is important, for it establishes a fact that should not be overlooked in any discussion of biblical inerrancy. The confession of faith that controlled the Southern Baptist Seminary and is still printed in its current catalogs commits the institution to this view of Scripture: "The Scriptures of the Old and New Testaments were given by inspiration of God and are the only sufficient, certain and authoritative rule of all saving knowledge, faith and obedience." Now it can be argued that this statement does not require anyone to believe in biblical inerrancy, although the Convention statement of 1925 does. But the Toy case makes it plain that this statement was understood to mean exactly that, as we shall see.

Crawford Howell Toy studied in Germany after the Civil War and returned to teach on the Louisville faculty. His views on the Bible were criticized and in 1879 he prepared a paper "setting forth his understanding of that doctrine [inspiration of Scripture] and submitted it, along with his resignation, in case his position was not satisfactory, to the Board of Trustees." His resignation was accepted with two dissenting votes. The following is part of what Dr. Toy had to say about Scripture:

> At the outset I may say that I fully accept the first article of the Fundamental Principles of the Seminary: "the Scriptures of the Old and New Testaments were given by inspiration of God, and are the only sufficient, certain and authoritative rule of all saving knowledge and obedience," and that I have always taught, and now do teach in accordance with, and not contrary to it.
>
> It is in the details of the subject that my divergence from the prevailing views in the denomination occurs. The divergence has

gradually increased in connection with my studies, from year to year, till it has become perceptible to myself and others. . . . I find that the geography, astronomy and other physical science of the sacred writers was that of their times. It is not that of our times, it is not that which seems to us correct, but it has nothing to do with their message of religious truth from God. . . . The message is not less Divine to me because it is given in Hebrew and not in English, or because it is set in the framework of a primitive and incorrect geology. . . . I am slow to admit discrepancies or inaccuracies, but if they show themselves I refer them to the human conditions of the writer, believing that his merely intellectual status, the mere amount of information possessed by him, does not affect his spiritual truth. If our heavenly Father sends a message by the stammering tongue of a man, I will not reject the message because of the stammering. . . .

What I have said of the outward form of the Old Testament applies, as I think, to the outward form of the New Testament. I will not lightly see a historical or other inaccuracy in the Gospels or the Acts, but if I find such, they do not for me affect the divine teaching of these books. The centre of the New Testament is Christ himself, salvation is in him, and a historical error cannot affect the fact of his existence and his teachings.[11]

No one can escape the conclusion that Dr. Toy, who was an honest man, and who did not seek to hide his views, understood the statement on Scripture to imply the infallibility of the whole Bible. He offered no arguments to show that his views were in full agreement with the statement on Scripture, or that when he acknowledged the existence of historical or scientific errors, this was in harmony with the seminary's confession. He recognized that what he believed was not really in accord with the statement on Scripture even as he acknowledged that biblical inerrancy was the prevailing view of the denomination. Since the seminary accepted his resignation and the Board approved it, it shows that the institution and its official board understood the statement the same way Toy did. Therefore if any deviation from that earlier understanding is acceptable today, then the statement has been reinterpreted and a meaning attached to it that was unacceptable in Toy's day.

THE CASE OF THE CHRISTIAN INDEX EDITOR

Jack U. Harwell, editor of the *Christian Index*, a publication of the Baptist Convention of the State of Georgia, exchanged letters with

Joe Dunaway of Rome, Georgia. In his letter to Mr. Dunaway, dated December 31, 1974, he wrote,

> I do believe that the Bible is the Word of God. I do not use the word infallible because the Bible is written by men. I would ask you to check very closely the statement "truth without any mixture of error." The statement says that truth is not mixed with error but it does not say that the Bible is not mixed with error. I could cite many, many instances where a literal, absolute, blind acceptance of the Bible without an understanding of human nature leads to all types of contradictions. . . . I do not believe in the plenary verbal inspiration of the Bible. . . . I do not believe that Adam and Eve were one man and one woman. I believe that the terms Adam and Eve represented mankind and womankind. There are volumes and volumes of Biblical scholarship which document this theory many years back. One of the most simple and basic answers to refute the belief that Adam and Eve were one man and one woman is the simple question "Where did Cain get his wife?" If Adam was one man and Eve was one woman and they had two sons named Cain and Abel, who were the parents of the woman that Cain married?[12]

From Jack Harwell's letter we see that one misstep inevitably produces a harvest of errors, or at least more difficult questions than the ones that troubled Harwell in the first place. If Adam and Eve were not one man and one woman, then there could have been no Cain and Abel. And a nonexistent Cain could not have married any woman. So that the question where Cain got his wife has no meaning. More than that, however, it means that the genealogical tables of Genesis and Chronicles are false and this untrue historical material has been carried over into the New Testament. No one can read the genealogical table given in the Gospel of Luke without realizing that Luke believed in a historical Adam. He traced the ancestry of Jesus back from generation to generation, naming men whom we know lived and died. But at the end, if what Harwell says is true, history becomes nonhistory and the tables go from truth to error if Adam is a nonexistent person. What further complicates the problem is that Paul in Romans speaks of the first and the second Adam. Paul speaks of Jesus as the second Adam, but if there was no first Adam the whole point becomes senseless and Paul is guilty of an assumption about the historical Adam who sinned and was lost that is useless as well as senseless. There can be no doubt that Paul believed in a historical Adam as did Luke. Whom then shall we believe? Paul and Luke or Harwell? That is an interesting question.

ASSOCIATION OF BAPTIST PROFESSORS OF RELIGION

Among Southern Baptists, the Association of Baptist Professors of Religion is an organization comprising liberal faculty members in Baptist institutions. Robert Alley, of whom I have spoken, is included among them. On February 23, 1970, *Baptist Press*, the news service arm of the Southern Baptist Convention, issued a release concerning the annual meeting of this association. T. C. Smith, its president and a faculty member of the Baptist school, Furman University of Greenville, South Carolina, delivered an address in which he took issue with Southern Baptists who hold to the traditional view of the Bible. He stated that the view of the Bible of most Southern Baptists is inadequate: "We need to come up with a concept that is more suitable to ourselves, our students and our conventions." He was critical of a Baptist church in Illinois that had dropped from its fellowship a member who did not believe in the infallibility of the Bible. Smith asserted that more freedom (i.e., to move away from infallibility) is essential to a modern understanding of Scripture. Moreover, he asserted that modern Christians should have as much liberty in determining their canon of Scripture (i.e., which books belong in the Bible) as the church fathers had in their time. He said that modern scholarship has more valid criteria for selection of the canon than did religious leaders sixteen centuries ago. He claimed that scholars who employ the historical-critical method (which always denies biblical infallibility; that is, I know of no advocate of the historical-critical method of any note who believes in an infallible Scripture) of biblical research are "following Christ who contradicted the self-assumed authority of the rabbis who accepted no new revelation." It is "the Bible, not God, that we are questioning," the learned professor stated.

At this meeting Professor Alley and W. C. Smith of Richmond reported that members of the Association had been intimidated as a result of a prior action of the group after it had objected strongly to the publicity given to W. A. Criswell's book *Why I Preach That the Bible Is Literally True*. They said that the silence from Southern Baptist theological seminaries on the issue of biblical interpretation was "thundering" and that Duke McCall, president of the Southern Baptist Seminary at Louisville, had become a "champion of biblical fundamentalism" by criticizing the resolution in a widely distributed article.

When anyone begins to examine the literary productions of Bible department professors in institutions normally aligned with Southern Baptists, he will find that numbers of these teachers have already scrapped biblical inerrancy, for this is demonstrated by their critical views of Scripture. An illustration of this can be found in the book *People of the Covenant,* an introduction to the Old Testament, by Robert Wilson Crapps, Henry Jackson Flanders, Jr., and David Anthony Smith. All of these men wrote as members of the faculty of Furman University, a Baptist institution. In this book, they accept the documentary hypothesis of the Pentateuch, giving full approval to the notion of the JEPD theory. The written Yahwistic and written Eloistic histories were taken from oral traditions, "gradually reaching a normative form." Yahwistic written form came around 1000 B.C., the Eloistic written form came later than 1000 B.C. The Deuteronomic history was written later than 587 B.C. and the unified "collections of Israel's traditions from creation to exile" were put together sometime in the exilic or postexilic period.[14]

They said, "The historical narratives in the Old Testament for the most part are not firsthand contemporary records like those found in the inscriptions and records of other ancient peoples." Instead, they are religious works that have gone through a long history of compiling, editing, copying. "Within the Old Testament four major (JEPD) interpretations of the history of Israel are discernible, each of which supplements and complements the others."[15] From this it is easy to discern that the Mosaic authorship of the Pentateuch, affirmed in Scripture, is untrue.

When discussing the prophets in the Old Testament, these scholars assert that in Isaiah 40–66, for example, the prophet's "words and deeds were remembered, recorded, and elaborated by a circle of disciples. . . . Gradually oracles . . . were added to the original core of genuine Isaianic material. The majority of chapters 1–39 had thus been shaped by the time of the exile."[16] "From Isaiah to Second Isaiah . . . although he remains anonymous there can be no doubt [note the nonobjective language] about the tradition in which the unknown prophet of the exile stood. He belonged to the disciples of Isaiah of Jerusalem." But Scripture says that all of Isaiah was written by the prophet, as we shall see in a moment.

When speaking about the Book of Daniel, these writers say that certain factors "suggest that the book was written during the strenuous early days of the Maccabean revolt, or about 168-165 B.C."[17]

Throughout this volume there are constant references to, and recommended bibliographies of, liberal scholars. There is no presentation of the views of historic orthodoxy, nor are there any bibliographic references to evangelical scholars like Oswald Allis, Edward J. Young, Gleason Archer, etc. *The Interpreter's Bible*, a liberal work, is commended highly. And they say that the "introductory articles on the whole Old Testament appear in Volume 1 and are especially helpful" and are, of course, based entirely on liberal critical viewpoints.

C. J. ALLEN AND THE SUNDAY SCHOOL BOARD

All of this provides an interesting background against which to understand a letter I received from C. J. Allen of the Sunday School Board dated June 27, 1972. In it he wrote, "As one who has been involved in the theological thought life of the denomination for more than thirty years, I have yet to discover an iota of responsible concern to endorse and promote 'destructive higher critical views within the denomination.'" Since anyone familiar with the historical-critical method of biblical research as well as form and redaction criticism knows that they all include destructive higher critical views, C. J. Allen can be said to have his head in the sand.

The case of the *Broadman Bible Commentary* is another indicator that points up the prevalence of the problem I am addressing here. Volume 1 was released in January, 1970, by the Broadman Press. Almost immediately the Genesis commentary was pinpointed as theologically aberrant. It was written by G. Henton Davies, principal of Regent's Park College, Oxford, England. There could be no question but that he approached Genesis with the documentary hypothesis in mind, but the objections swung on the question of biblical infallibility. Dr. Davies stated boldly that he did not believe God ordered Abraham to kill his son Isaac but that Abraham's decision "is the climax of the psychology of his life." This was clear enough, but the problem connected with Davies' statement was that it contradicted the biblical account, which claims that God specifically and unequivocally commanded Abraham to slay Isaac as a burnt offering (see Gen. 22). Following a protracted struggle, the messengers of the Southern Baptist Convention voted to have the volume rewritten. It turned out that a rewrite by Davies would not satisfy the demands of the people in the pews so the Genesis commentary was rewritten by Clyde Francisco of whose work it was stated in the *Capital Baptist* and an editorial in *Christianity Today* that it was of similar vintage with Davies' volume so far as its underlying presuppositions were concerned, although it was toned down.

It was in connection with this commentary that I had some correspondence with C. J. Allen of the Sunday School Board, one small part of which is instructive so far as the purpose of this book is concerned. Speaking of the Book of Isaiah, Allen addressed the issue of its authorship. The traditional view has been that the prophet Isaiah penned the whole work of sixty-six chapters. Modern scholars have opted for a dual authorship by two Isaiahs, although others have held to three or four Isaiahs. Generally, modern scholars who hold to the two-Isaiah view think that chapters 1 to 39 were penned by the prophet himself and chapters 40 to 66 were penned by the second Isaiah. Allen has this to say in the words of the writer of the commentary: "In attempting to examine the unity and authorship of Isaiah we are in no way calling into question the inspiration of any part of the book. Nor are we suggesting that the sections judged to be later than Isaiah contain less of the revealed truth of God."[18] Allen adds his own words: "He [the writer of the Isaiah commentary] quotes James Leo Green, with implied full agreement: 'The thing that really matters about any book in the Bible is not who wrote it, but whether the voice of God is heard in it.' Why then any alarm if there were two Isaiahs?"[19] And to this question an answer must be given.

Truly, it sounds good to say that all of the Book of Isaiah is the Word of God, and what really is lost, having said this, if it also is said that the book was written by two people rather than by the prophet Isaiah alone? The answer is that if Isaiah was written by more than one person, inerrancy is nullified. And thus Scripture itself is not free from error, because elsewhere the Bible states that Isaiah did in fact write the second section of the prophecy. Everyone will agree that there are books in the Old Testament about whose authorship we are uncertain. But in those cases nothing in Scripture can be found to lay claim to authorship by this or that or some other person. With respect to Isaiah this is not true. In John's Gospel it is stated specifically that Isaiah wrote the second section of the book. In John 12:38 the Scripture says, translating the Greek literally, "that the word of Isaiah the prophet might be fulfilled which he said: Lord, who believed the report of us? and the arm of the Lord to whom was it revealed?" The quotation, of course, is from Isaiah 53:1, the second section of the book, which according to the higher critics, was not written by the prophet Isaiah. The precision of the Greek in John's Gospel is such that no reasonable exegesis can avoid the conclusion that John believed Isaiah 53 was written by the historical person called Isaiah. So even if one were to claim that all of Isaiah is the Word of God, but deny that Isaiah wrote the entire prophecy, then the result is to call into question the truth of what John wrote when he stated that Isaiah authored chapter 53. If the critics are right, then John is wrong. And if John is wrong, then the Scriptures are not infallible.

THE ARKANSAS BAPTIST NEWS

Another indication of the trend in the Southern Baptist family away from its historic landmarks may be seen in a policy statement that appeared in the April 1, 1971, issue of the *Arkansas Baptist News* magazine. This policy statement is to be found in the minutes of the staff meetings of the executive board of the Arkansas Baptist State Convention, Charles H. Ashcraft, executive secretary. It reads as follows:

> All members of the staff of the Arkansas Baptist State Convention are not only allowed but encouraged to assume full liberty of academic and editorial freedom, to embrace their own beliefs, convictions, viewpoints, concepts and opinions on any and all matters pertaining to the Christian faith; to practice them, preach them, stand for them, defend them, and to live them. However, in the acceptance of full academic and editorial freedom, such must be accorded to all others. It is hereby agreed that every staff member shall have full access to freedom for himself as a person and may assume any theological stance he feels is right; he is not to promote, initiate, or become the part of any organization, conspiracy, movement or fellowship which would deny, impede, harass, disfranchise, or void any other child of God the same privilege.
>
> The staff of the Arkansas Baptist State Convention as a staff will assume no particular theological stance, nor will they promote such. Each staff member may enjoy the full privileges of religious freedom, freedom of press, and speech but is not at liberty to organize others or set in motion an organization or conspiracy to coerce, force or drive others to his particular position. The staff of the Arkansas Baptist State Convention will exercise no option to promote or discredit people with viewpoints at variance or in agreement with theirs. No person in a place of leadership in the convention will be prejudiced in the eyes of any staff person of the convention and shall not be persecuted or promoted because of the presence of or the absence of any particular opinion or viewpoint.

The statement of policy listed above was formed voluntarily by the staff people, under no duress, coercion or pressure from any facet of Baptist life in the Arkansas Convention or elsewhere, and is presented on the initiative of the executive secretary with all staff people in compliance.

This statement is made with the full knowledge of all consequences and is submitted in the general category "For Your Information."

Any actions of any staff member considered in violation of the above stated policy should be directed to the executive secretary.[20]

The implications of the statement are fascinating. Take, for instance, the sentence that reads: "No person in a place of leadership in the convention will be prejudiced in the eyes of any staff person of the convention and shall not be persecuted or promoted because of the presence or absence of any particular opinion or viewpoint." This means that a leader could be an atheist, a Buddhist, a unitarian, an agnostic, or a fundamentalist without jeopardy to his position. No one is to be disenfranchised for any reason having to do with his religious convictions or lack of them. Under this arrangement, freedom becomes license and even the word *Baptist* ceases to have any significant meaning or content. To follow this pattern would be to eliminate Southern Baptists as a distinctive religious entity, for they would become so broad that no one could be excluded from their fellowship or denied admission to their fellowship for any reason whatever.

Anyone who wished to write an entire volume on this subject would have no difficulty finding the material to do so; however, several things stand out starkly. The first is the "thundering" silence, to use Dr. Alley's word, on the part of those who should be defending and propagating the doctrine of biblical infallibility. There is a large body of evidence to show that college and seminary faculty members are opposed to a belief in infallibility. The literature on that subject is substantial. But where is the literature and where are the professors who hold to the historic position of the Convention that the Bible is "truth without any mixture of error"? Why have they not risen to make their voices heard and their writings read by the people in the pews?

How can anyone overlook the fact that the creation of parachurch organizations among Southern Baptists means dissatisfaction with affairs as they stand in the Convention? Why have good men in the Convention started Bible institutes, colleges, and even theological seminaries unless they have reason to believe that the existing institutions are not really doing the job they were created for? Certainly there are in the Convention nonrepresentative elements whose opinions are extreme. Surely there are those who exhibit signs of pathology and strains of paranoia. But when allowances have been made for all of this, the fact remains that some of the Convention's most solid citizens are alarmed at what is happening among the agencies of the Convention. And the evidence for the existence of aberrant viewpoints is sufficient to demonstrate to perceptive people that there is a real problem.

The Southern Baptist Convention is unique, for example, and stands miles apart from any of the large denominations with one or two possible exceptions. As of now, the fuse that could cause a conflagration has not been lighted. The flash point has already come for the Lutheran Church – Missouri Synod. That church is in the midst of a titanic struggle to determine whether the theological conservatives can preserve the denomination's traditional image and organization. But this has not yet happened to the Southern Baptist Convention. And if the kind of struggle that ripped through such groups as the American Baptists, the Methodists, the Northern and Southern Presbyterians, the Episcopalians, the United Church of Christ, and now the Missouri Synod, is not to repeat itself, then the Southern Baptists will have to act with dispatch in the next few years. If they fail to do so, the infection will spread and the time must come when there will be a showdown. And the longer the Southern Baptists wait, the rougher the battle will be, the more traumatic the consequences, and the less obvious the outcome in favor of historic Christianity.

At this moment in history the great bulk of the Southern Baptists are theologically orthodox and do believe that the Word of God is inerrant. At this moment there is no reason for those who support infallibility to give up on the denomination. But if history has any lesson to teach Southern Baptists, it is the lesson that once a denomination departs from a belief in biblical infallibility, it opens the floodgates to disbelief about other cardinal doctrines of the faith. And a little leaven leavens the whole lump. Things will get worse before they get better. But they will not get better if the disease now eating at the vitals of the Convention is not treated and the patient cured.

[1] Robert S. Alley, *Revolt Against the Faithful* (Philadelphia: Doubleday, 1970), p. 167.

[2] Ibid., p. 78.

[3] Ibid., p. 91.

[4] Ibid., pp. 147-158.

[5] *Outreach,* February, 1971, p. 4.

[6] Ibid.

[7] Ibid.

[8] William E. Hull, *The Baptist Program* (Dec., 1970). "Shall We Call the Bible Infallible?" p. 61.

[9] Ibid., p. 17.

[10] Ibid., p. 18.

[11] Robert A. Baker, *A Baptist Source Book* (Nashville: Broadman, 1966), pp. 168-171.

[12] Letter to Joe Dunaway, December 31, 1974.

[13] *Baptist Press,* February 23, 1970.

[14] Robert Wilson Crapps, Henry Jackson Flanders, Jr., and David Anthony Smith, *People of the Covenant* (New York: Ronald, 1963), p. 11.

[15] Ibid., p. 8.

[16] Ibid., p. 306.

[17] Ibid., p. 417.

[18] *Broadman Bible Commentary,* (Nashville: Broadman, 1971), Vol. 5, p. 159.

[19] Ibid., p. 163.

[20] *Arkansas Baptist News,* April 1, 1971.

6

The Strange Case of Fuller Theological Seminary

Fuller Theological Seminary was founded in 1947. It was brought into being through the efforts of Charles E. Fuller of the "Old Fashioned Revival Hour." He secured the services of Harold John Ockenga, then minister of the Park Street Church in Boston, as president of the fledgling institution. The school opened its door with four faculty members: Wilbur Moorehead Smith, Everett F. Harrison, Carl F. H. Henry, and myself. The seminary started with thirty-seven students, and in a few years enrolled three hundred. Faculty members were added, buildings were erected, and endowments were secured.

ONE PURPOSE OF THE FOUNDING

From the beginning it was declared that one of the chief purposes of the founding of the seminary was that it should be an apologetic institution. The son of the founder, Daniel Payton Fuller, had attended Princeton Theological Seminary. Princeton was neo-orthodox at best in its theological stance and had long since abandoned the tradition of biblical inerrancy represented by Charles Hodge and Benjamin Warfield. Charles Fuller wanted a place where men like his own son could receive excellent theological education. He and the founding fathers, including the founding faculty, were of one mind with respect to the Scriptures. It was agreed from the

106

inception of the school that through the seminary curriculum the faculty would provide the finest theological defense of biblical infallibility or inerrancy. It was agreed in addition that the faculty would publish joint works that would present to the world the best of evangelical scholarship on inerrancy at a time when there was a dearth of such scholarship and when there were few learned works promoting biblical inerrancy.

The Fuller Statement of Faith

At its founding, Fuller Seminary had no statement of faith. It was left to the founding faculty to work on, although it was clearly understood that such a statement would encompass the basic doctrines of evangelical faith as held through the ages. Several years elapsed before a doctrinal statement was finished, and in the interim a number of new members had joined the faculty. Among them was Bela Vasady who had come to Pasadena from Princeton Theological Seminary where he had been a visiting professor. It was around the doctrinal beliefs of Bela Vasady that the first theological eruption took place.

As the faculty of Fuller worked its way through the formulation of its confession of faith, it was discovered that Bela Vasady had reservations about an inerrant Scripture. When the faculty completed its work, the following statement on Scripture was adopted by the faculty and by the Board of Trustees of the seminary: "The books which form the canon of the Old and New Testaments as originally given are plenarily inspired and free from all error in the whole and in the part. These books constitute the written Word of God, the only infallible rule of faith and practice."

The statement on the Scriptures was as strong as any ancient or contemporary statement could be. The phrase "free from all error in the whole and in the part" could only mean that all of the Bible and every part of it is free from error. Thus, the statement declared that the Bible is free from errors in matters of fact, science, history, and chronology, as well as in matters having to do with salvation.

The Case of Bela Vasady

The first test of the seminary's determination to be true to this commitment was raised by the response of Bela Vasady to the statement. He made it clear that he could not honestly sign that part of the statement of faith. He was a man of great integrity and was not in the least bit disposed to sign the statement tongue in cheek. In fact, as we shall see later, the catalogs of the school included a preface to the statement of faith to the effect that every member of the faculty signed it every year without mental reservation, and that anyone who could not so sign would voluntarily leave the institution. Bela Vasady left the institution on this basis, and mutually agreeable terminal arrangements were worked out.

THE COMING CRISIS

In or about 1962 it became apparent that there were some who no longer believed in the inerrancy of the Bible, among both the faculty and the board members. One of the key board members, who was later to become chairman and whose wealth helped to underwrite the annual operating budget, was C. Davis Weyerhaeuser. As the situation developed, he was to play a key role in the final outcome. He was clear in his own conviction that the Bible had errors in it. Nor did he hesitate to make his position plain. But he neither chose to resign from the institution nor was forced to resign by other board members.

A second indication of the coming crisis occurred at a faculty meeting when one member of the teaching staff declared that what he was about to say might cost him his job. He said it, but it didn't cost him his job. He made it apparent that he believed the Bible was not wholly free from error. He was joined in this by at least one other faculty member at that meeting. Neither the administration nor the board moved to censure and remove those who could no longer affirm the doctrinal statement of the seminary, at least at the point of inerrancy. The situation was allowed to drift.

A third indication of the coming crisis involved the son of the founder, Daniel Payton Fuller. Following his graduation from Fuller with the B.D. degree, he joined Harold John Ockenga as an assistant at the Park Street Church in Boston. He later went to Northern Baptist Theological Seminary where he earned the Th.D. degree. He then joined the faculty of Fuller Seminary. After he had been there several years, he went to Basel, Switzerland, to work for another doctorate under men like Karl Barth. While Fuller was at Basel, rumors began coming back to America that he had shifted his position on the Scriptures. I personally talked to Charles E. Fuller about this on a number of occasions. In every instance he assured me that there was no truth to the rumors that his son had changed his position. He was wrong, as subsequent events demonstrated.

When Daniel Fuller returned to Pasadena upon completion of his doctoral work at Basel, he was appointed dean of the faculty. I was moved over to vice-president. Edward John Carnell, who had been president, had resigned to return to teaching. Harold John Ockenga again became president *in absentia*. It soon became known that Daniel Fuller indeed had changed his viewpoint. This was pinpointed in two major decisions that were made. The first one had to do with the appointment of Calvin Schoonhoven to the faculty. He was a Fuller Seminary graduate who also had gone to Basel, and was a close friend of Daniel Fuller. When Schoonhoven was examined for a faculty appointment, he admitted that he did not believe in an inerrant Scripture. Other faculty members and I opposed his appointment. We got nowhere. One concession was made, however. Schoonhoven was appointed to a librarian's post with the understanding that he was never to receive a faculty berth in New Testament. This decision was later nullified and he was given a teaching appointment.

The second decision related to the selection of a new president for the seminary. David A. Hubbard was Charles Fuller's candidate and Daniel Fuller's as well. He had the support of C. Davis Weyerhaeuser, too. At the time he was being considered he was on the faculty of Westmont College in Santa Barbara, California. He was teaching in the field of biblical studies, and was embroiled in a controversy with the administration and trustees over a mimeographed Old Testament syllabus he was using in one of his classes. The syllabus was co-authored by him and Robert Laurin, who was then on the faculty of the American Baptist Seminary in West Covina, California. The syllabus contained teachings that were opposed to historic evangelical understanding. They included matters like the nonhistoricity of Adam and Eve, the Wellhausen approach to the Pentateuch, the late dating of Daniel, and other points. The offensive parts had been written by Laurin who, in turn, was defended by Hubbard as an outstanding evangelical. In more recent years Laurin moved farther and farther to the left, and is now dean of the American Baptist Seminary in Berkeley.

Hubbard, one of the brightest students graduated from Fuller Seminary, maintained that his own views were orthodox. But before he was chosen to become president, the office was offered to Harold John Ockenga, who, then and now, was a firm believer in biblical inerrancy. It was agreed by the trustees that if Ockenga did not accept the post it would go to Hubbard. As it turned out Dr. Ockenga did not come and the election of David Hubbard to the presidency followed.

THE CRISIS COMES

It was in the middle of this presidential problem that the developing theological situation came to a head. In December, 1962, a faculty-trustee retreat was held at the Huntington Hotel in Pasadena. On what was called "Black Saturday" by some, the issue of biblical infallibility surfaced. It assumed dimensions that called for a definitive decision with regard to the statement about Scripture as "free from all error in the whole and in the part." Hubbard at that point could have made it clear that if he came as president, he would stand for the inerrancy of Scripture and would carry through on it administratively, removing any faculty members and securing in advance the resignation of any trustees who did not believe in it. He failed to do so.

Stenographers were present at the Black Saturday meeting and every word was taken down in shorthand. From the discussions there could be no doubt that a number of the members of the faculty and board did not believe in an inerrant Scripture. Edward Johnson, president of Financial Federation and a member of the board, focused the issue when he used the term *benchmark* in the discussions. He insisted that once the benchmark (a term used by surveyors having to do with the point from which they take all of their measurements) was changed, the institution would lose its bearing and depart from orthodoxy in other ways. The failure of the board to stand firm on the original commitment of the seminary led Johnson to resign within a month following Black Saturday.

On the Monday following Black Saturday the stenographers began the work of transcribing the records of all that had been said at the retreat. Before they had finished their work, I received a letter from Charles Fuller. In it he wrote, "I think it is best to take the written records of the discussion concerning inspiration and keep them under my personal supervision for a time since the president at the end of the discussion expressed a desire that the discussion be kept within the Seminary family. If copies of the discussion fall into many hands the chances of realizing the president's purpose would not be carried out. Moreover, it might be misunderstood and could hurt the school." The stenographers' notebooks and those parts that had been transcribed were given into the possession of Charles Fuller. I doubt that anyone has seen them from that day to this. Their reappearance would make it clear beyond any shadow of doubt that biblical inerrancy was the key question, and that the faculty and trustees were split over it.

Subsequent Developments

The developments that followed after this episode were interesting as well as indicative of what the new stance of the institution would be. The 1963-64 seminary catalog retained the usual statement about the creed of the school (p. 9). It said, in part, "The Seminary has formulated a statement of faith as expressed in the following propositions, to which each member of the Faculty subscribes at the beginning of each academic year. This concurrence is without mental reservation, and any member who cannot assent agrees to withdraw from the institution." Suffice it to say that every member of the faculty and Board of Trustees signed the statement in September, 1963, including those who indicated they did not believe in inerrancy. Nor did any of them withdraw from the institution as they had agreed to when they had previously signed the statement.

When the 1965-66 catalog appeared, the statement "This concurrence is without mental reservation, and any member who cannot assent agrees to withdraw from the institution" was deleted. It was stated that "every member of the faculty subscribes at the beginning of each academic year." The current catalog reflects a further change from the 1965-66 catalog. "At the beginning of each academic year" no longer appears. This could mean, of course, that once having signed the statement, a faculty member is not required to sign yearly, but I have not inquired concerning the intricacies of the situation since that further change was made.

As time went by, a dark cloud hung over the institution: faculty and trustee board members were signing a statement of faith, one important part of which some of them did not believe. And they were signing with mental reservations at a time when the promotional literature of the institution kept assuring its constituency that all was well and nothing had changed.

Faculty resignations followed on the heels of the change of direction. Charles Woodbridge left first. His departure occurred prior to the Black Saturday episode. Wilbur Smith was the next one to resign after the 1962-63 school year closed. I left the institution at the end of the following school year, and Gleason Archer left several years after that. The departure of all four was directly related to the question of biblical inerrancy. Other members of the faculty who held to a view of biblical inerrancy chose to remain, as did some members of the Board of Trustees.

Fuller acquired additional faculty members when the institution opened its School of Psychology and its School of World Mission and when it began offering a professional and then an academic doctorate. One of the persons joining Fuller was James Daane, with whom I was personally acquainted and with whom I had many theological discussions. He was an amillennialist and did not hold to an inerrant Scripture. When he was interviewed for a professorship, he did not hide any of these things from the institution. He was invited to join the faculty and signed the statement of faith with the consent of the institution with respect to his reservations about Scripture and the institution's commitment to premillennialism.

One of the things I found intensely interesting was what happened during Carnell's presidency in regard to premillennialism. He was convinced that the great creeds of the church left this matter open and that a theological seminary should be broad enough to encompass amillennialism as well. Carnell was a graduate of Westminster Theological Seminary, which was generally amillenarian, and undoubtedly he got his ideas about millennialism there. Westminster, of course, was thoroughly orthodox in its theological beliefs and held strongly to an inerrant Scripture. Carnell had a number of talks with Charles Fuller about this subject and secured from him a written statement that after Fuller's death he could be quoted as approving the deletion of premillennialism from the creedal commitment of the seminary. Charles Fuller himself was a dispensationalist and a premillennialist. His radio broadcast was listened to mostly by people in the same tradition. It would have been catastrophic to the ministry if he had announced a willingness to abandon premillennialism from the seminary's doctrinal statement.

DANIEL FULLER REPUDIATES INERRANCY

In 1968 I covered the World Council of Churches Assembly at Uppsala, Sweden. President David Hubbard of Fuller was there. I asked him when the institution was going to change its doctrinal statement to conform to the realities of the situation. He was not entirely happy with the thrust of the question, but the urgent need to clarify the seminary's ambiguous posture now was apparent in a public sense by what had transpired some months earlier. Daniel Fuller was invited to deliver an address at the annual meeting of the Evangelical Theological Society in Toronto, Canada, in December, 1967. He was not a member of the Society. He delivered a paper entitled "Benjamin B. Warfield's View of Faith and History." So far as I know, this was the first time that a Fuller faculty member went on record in print, declaring that he did not believe the Bible to be free from all error in the whole and in the part.

Daniel Fuller acknowledged that "Warfield, however, inferred from the plenary verbal inspiration unmistakably taught by the doctrinal verses, that all Biblical statements whether they pertain to knowledge that makes men wise unto salvation or to such subjects as botany, meteorology, or paleontology, are equally true. He affirmed 'the complete trustworthiness of Scripture in all elements and in every, even circumstantial statement.' "[1] Daniel Fuller then said he wished to make a slight corrective to Warfield and his view of an inerrant Scripture. He argued that there are two kinds of Scripture: revelational and nonrevelational. Revelational Scripture is wholly without error; nonrevelational Scripture is not.

Dr. Fuller said, "I am sure Warfield would agree that if the doctrinal verses explicitly taught only the inerrancy of revelational matters — matters that make men wise unto salvation — and that if the phenomena bore this out, loyalty to Biblical authority would demand that we define inerrancy accordingly."[2] The "slight corrective" Fuller proposed to Warfield's view "is to understand that verbal plenary inspiration involves accommodation to the thinking of the original readers in non-revelational matters."[3] In other words, nonrevelational Scripture has errors in it; revelational Scripture can be fully trusted.

In analyzing the position of Daniel Fuller, we must make several observations. He said that the phenomena of Scripture show it to have errors. Therefore, whatever the Bible teaches about its own reliability, that teaching must conform to the data of Scripture itself. Thus, because he feels there are errors in the Bible, the Bible itself cannot teach a doctrine of inerrancy in all of its parts. But in all matters having to do with making a person "wise unto salvation" one can trust the Scripture fully, and for those parts it is proper to use the term *inerrant.*

A second point we derive from Daniel Fuller's corrective to

Warfield has to do with the question concerning what parts of Scripture are revelational and what parts are nonrevelational. And who decides which is which? It is conceivable that someone could come to the Bible and declare the virgin birth of Christ to be untrue. This could be argued on the basis of its being a biological problem, buttressed with the claim that it has nothing to do with knowledge that makes us wise unto salvation. Anyone could argue in favor of a dual authorship of Isaiah on the same basis. Again, on the same basis, one could argue that Daniel was written around 168 B.C., rather than the seventh century B.C. as it claims to be. One could argue that Adam and Eve were not historical persons, and affirm this by saying that to believe they were is not necessary to salvation. Anyone can prove anything he wants to when the door has been opened to the distinction the Bible itself does not make: that there are revelational and nonrevelational parts to Scripture. Maybe Daniel Fuller can tell the reader which parts of the Bible to believe and which parts to disbelieve, but then the reader trusts Fuller over the authors of Scripture. And nowhere does Scripture draw the distinction between revelational and nonrevelational parts to the Bible.

GEORGE LADD AND INERRANCY

Professor George E. Ladd stands in the same framework established by his colleague Daniel Fuller. He does not make the distinction Fuller does between revelational and nonrevelational Scripture, but he does come out in favor of errancy in Scripture in the areas of history and fact. In his scholarly and able book, *The New Testament and Criticism,* he has this to say:

> If the Bible is the sure Word of God, does it not follow that we must have a trustworthy word from God, not only about matters of faith and practice, but in all historical and factual questions? "Thus saith the Lord" means that God has spoken His sure, infallible Word. A corollary of this in the minds of many Christians is that we must have absolute, infallible answers to every question raised in the historical study of the Bible. From this perspective, the "critic" is the one who has surrendered the Word of God for the words of men, authority for speculation, certainty for uncertainty.
>
> This conclusion, as logical and persuasive as it may seem, does not square with the facts of God's Word; and it is the author's hope that the reader may be helped to understand that the authority of the Word of God is not dependent upon infallible certainty in all matters of history and criticism.[4]

It is apparent that Dr. Ladd believes in a limited infallibility. In this sense his position does not differ substantially from that of Dr. Fuller. The same questions that Fuller must meet and answer Ladd must face and reply to. The main point made here is that Dr. Ladd at one time signed and professed to believe the first Fuller Seminary statement of faith that the Bible is free from error in the whole and in the part. He no longer believes this.

HUBBARD AND THE FULLER ALUMNI

The matter was further fogged by a letter President Hubbard sent to the alumni during the summer of 1970. In that communication Hubbard said the opposite of what Daniel Fuller had said about Warfield. Hubbard wrote, "And there are those today who even go beyond anything Warfield ever said when they insist that Biblical inerrancy would apply to every scientific, historical, geographical, factual, and theological statement of Scripture."[5] Unfortunately for Hubbard this is precisely what Warfield insisted on. It was this insistence that caused Charles Briggs of Union Seminary in New York to argue that a single proved error in Scripture swept the ground from beneath the feet of Warfield. Daniel Fuller was right in affirming that Warfield believed all of Scripture to be trustworthy. Indeed if Warfield had not believed it, there would have been no need for Fuller to suggest a "slight corrective" to Warfield.

Hubbard, moreover, wanted to do away with the use of the word *inerrancy*. It "is too precise, too mathematical a term to describe appropriately the way in which God's infallible revelation has come to us in a Book." This was equally strange because Daniel Fuller, in an article published in the *Seminary Bulletin*, said, "We assert the Bible's authority by the use of such words as *infallible, inerrant, true,* and *trustworthy*. There is no basic difference between these words. To say that the Bible is true is to assert its infallibility."[6] Again Fuller had the edge on Hubbard, for what he wrote was unquestionably correct. And if inerrancy is too precise, too mathematical a term, how is the situation improved if other words that mean the same thing replaced *inerrancy?* And if none of these words were used to describe biblical authority what other words could be found to do so?

David Hubbard in his letter to the alumni assured them "the faculty and administration have continued to affirm their belief in the divine inspiration of both Testaments. . . ." Since he knew about the views of Daniel Fuller and other faculty members, we can draw

certain obvious conclusions from his statement. "Divine inspiration" could mean no more than what Fuller was saying: some
Scripture is revelational and some is not; some can be trusted and the
remainder cannot. But this must also mean that if both the Old and
the New Testaments are inspired, inspiration is then no guarantee
that what is said is true. Thus, inspiration loses any credible meaning, unless one is ready to say that God inspired error as well as truth.
In that event who can tell what is true and what is not?

FULLER'S NEW DOCTRINAL STATEMENT

It was ten years after the issue of inerrancy had erupted that the
ethical problem was resolved by the adoption of a new doctrinal
statement. Two major changes were made. One had to do with
eschatology. In signing the first seminary statement, the signer made
a commitment to premillennialism. The requirement of this commitment was later eliminated so that men like Daane were no longer
faced with the dilemma of signing, even with administrative and
trustee approval, what they did not believe. The second change was
the statement on Scripture. This was the important one.

Fuller's new statement on Scripture says: "Scripture is an essential part and trustworthy record of this divine disclosure. All the
books of the Old and New Testaments, given by divine inspiration,
are the written Word of God, the only infallible rule of faith and
practice." If it can be assumed that all of the faculty members believe
this and subscribe to it, then it follows that whatever the statement
means, it cannot mean what the former statement meant about being
"free from all error in the whole and in the part." Nor can it mean
what the first statement meant about inspiration guaranteeing all of
Scripture to be inerrant because all of it was inspired. But the key to
an understanding of the new viewpoint is to be found in the words
that the books of the Old and New Testaments "are the written
Word of God, the only infallible rule of faith and practice." It is
where the word *infallible* is placed that makes the difference. Had the
statement said that the Books of the Old and New Testaments "are
the infallible Word of God, the only rule of faith and practice," it
would have repeated in different words what the first statement of
faith had said. But what the new statement does is this: it limits
infallibility to matters of faith and practice. And this is the view
espoused by Daniel Fuller in his address on Warfield. Scripture that
does not involve matters of faith and practice is not infallible.

JEWETT AND THE NEW STATEMENT OF FAITH

More recently Paul King Jewett, a colleague of both Ladd and Fuller, has taken the next step away from a trustworthy Scripture. The seminary statement of faith proclaims a belief in an infallible Bible in matters having to do with faith and practice. But Dr. Jewett now says that it is defective in at least one area having to do with faith and practice.

Dr. Jewett published a book in 1954 entitled *Emil Brunner's Concept of Revelation*. It was an Evangelical Theological Society publication. At that time he was a member of the Society but he no longer is. And at that time, and in this book, he committed himself to a belief in an infallible Bible and accepted verbal inspiration. This can be seen from the following excerpts:

> At the basis of Brunner's rejection of verbal inspiration is the insistence that the Bible. . . . is a human book and as such is laden with imperfections and defects which necessarily attach to all that is human. The Scripture is not just the Word of God, but rather man's word about God's Word, and we must ever keep in mind that while it is divine to forgive it is human to err. . . . Men must first have forgotten what to come in the flesh, to become historical meant, to be able to set up a doctrine of an infallible Bible book. . . . Now if God can reveal Himself in a man who never sinned, and yet is truly human, why could He not reveal Himself in an infallible book which would yet be truly human?[7]
>
> [Jesus'] appeals to Scripture are always final. So far is the Scripture from being laden with the imperfection which Brunner ascribes to all that is human, that for Jesus it is the one thing that cannot be broken. . . . Everywhere Jesus appeals to Scripture, to each part of Scripture and to each element of Scripture as to an unimpeachable authority.[8]

This book which was dedicated to Gordon Haddon Clark, one of Jewett's college teachers and a lifelong advocate of a verbally inerrant Scripture, clearly shows that at that time in history Jewett was committed to inerrancy. But that has now changed as evidenced by his book *Man As Male and Female*. It is true that Jewett's further concession and his departure does not touch on a doctrine that is essential to salvation, but he signs a statement that declares in favor of biblical infallibility on matters of faith and practice. And in this book the subject he treats is distinctly a matter that has to do with the Christian faith and the practice of that faith by Christians.

The nub of Jewett's argument is that the apostle Paul erred on the matter of the subordination of a wife to her husband, which is taught in 1 Corinthians and Ephesians. Paul gives a rabbinic view that contradicts the first creation account in Genesis and he also is in disagreement with his own teaching that there is neither male nor female in Jesus Christ. But let Professor Jewett speak for himself.

> Furthermore, in reasoning this way, Paul is not only basing his argument exclusively on the second creation narrative, but is assuming the traditional rabbinic understanding of that narrative whereby the order of their creation is made to yield the primacy of the man over the woman. Is this rabbinic understanding of Genesis 2:18f. correct? We do not think it is, for it is palpably inconsistent with the first creation narrative, with the life style of Jesus, and with the apostle's own clear affirmation that in Christ there is no male and female (Gal. 3:38).[9]

> Finally, all of the Pauline texts supporting female subordination, both those that are directly from the apostle's pen and those that are indirectly so, appeal to the second creation narrative, Genesis 2:18-23, never to the first.[10]

> Because these two perspectives — the Jewish and the Christian — are incompatible, there is no satisfying way to harmonize the Pauline argument for female subordination with the larger Christian vision of which the great apostle to the Gentiles was himself the primary architect. . . . For one thing, in the very passage where he most emphatically affirms female subordination he makes an interesting parenthetical remark. . . .[11]

> [Jewett approves of Gen. 1:27 being] understood not as a literal piece of scientific reporting but as a narrative which illumines the ultimate meaning of Man's existence in the dual form of male and female. The narrative in Genesis 2:18-23 is commonly classified by scholars as a religious "myth" or "saga" in the sense that it clothes the truth about the origin of man and woman in poetic or parabolic form.[12]

> We have rejected the argument for female subordination as being incompatible with (a) the biblical narrative of Man's creation, (b) the revelation which is given us in the life of Jesus, and (c) Paul's fundamental statement of Christian liberty in the Epistle to the Galatians. . . . The problem with the concept of female subordination is that it *breaks the analogy of faith*.[13]

It can readily be seen what Jewett's conclusions are. First, he says that Paul *did* teach female subordination. The second conclusion is that Paul used Genesis 2:18-23 to support this view and followed the traditional rabbinic understanding of that passage. But this understanding cannot stand up under the teaching of the first creation narrative in Genesis 1:27. Therefore what Paul taught about female subordination is wrong. Third, he says that what Paul taught in 1 Corinthians and Ephesians goes against the revelation given us in the life of Christ and contradicts Paul's own teaching in Galatians 3:28. So Paul was teaching two different viewpoints and his subordination viewpoint was also contrary to the revelation in the life of Jesus. Thus the Bible is in error and this sort of error definitely has to do with matters of faith and practice. But Jewett signed the Fuller statement of faith that declares in favor of what he now denies — that the Bible is "the infallible rule of faith and practice."

In this same book Dr. Jewett has a striking paragraph on Scripture that is worth perusing.

> While the theologians have never agreed on a precise theory of inspiration, before the era of critical, historical study of the biblical documents, they tended, understandably, to ignore the human side of Scripture and to think of divine inspiration in a way that ruled out the possibility of any human limitations whatever in the Bible. The Bible, for all practical purposes, was so immediately dictated by the Holy Spirit that the human writers were more secretaries than authors. Historical and critical studies of the biblical documents have compelled the church to take into account the complexity of the human level of the historical process by which the documents were produced. Instead of the simple statement, which is essentially true, that the Bible is a divine book, we now perceive more clearly than in the past that the Bible is a divine/human book. As divine, it emits the light of revelation; as human, this light of revelation shines in and through the "dark glass" (I Cor. 13:12) of the "earthen vessels" (II Cor. 4:7) who were the authors of its content at the human level.[14]

It is apparent that Professor Jewett does not believe in an infallible Bible and that this in turn has led him to abrogate what he himself says is the clear teaching of the apostle Paul about female subordination. I am not entering here into the current discussion having to do with the liberation of women. That is worthy of a tome of its own. I simply am pointing out that Professor Jewett's conclusion that Paul is wrong in his teaching about subordination shows that he has attributed error to the apostle in a matter having to do with faith and practice and thus has invalidated the new Fuller Seminary statement of faith.

Lest it be supposed that I have misunderstood or misinterpreted Professor Jewett it would be well to consider the review of his book by the Rev. Tom Stark of the University Reformed Church in East Lansing, Michigan. Writing in the magazine of the Reformed Church in America, *The Church Herald,* he says this:

> . . . (Jewett) proceeds to reject systematically many of the teachings of Scripture. Perhaps Dr. Jewett's key statement is "The traditional teaching of Judaism and the revolutionary new approach in the life and teaching of Jesus contributed each in its own way to the Apostle's (Paul) thinking about the relationship of the sexes." He proceeds to say that Paul's two perspectives are incompatible and cannot be harmonized, and that Paul speaks in such a way that he probably has "an uneasy conscience." It is all done very calmly, but the reader should be clear — Dr. Jewett believes that the traditional understanding of what the Apostle Paul is teaching is a correct understanding of what the Apostle Paul taught and thought, but he is rejecting almost all of those passages, except for Galatians 3:28.
>
> . . . my further problem is that his doctrine of inspiration allows him to set himself as a judge of the Apostle Paul, and to discard many verses in Scripture, ostensibly on the basis that they contradict one verse of Paul (Gal. 3:28), and the life-style of Jesus. Dr. Jewett reveals in his book a clear break from an evangelical view of the inspiration and authority of the Bible.

There are many other things that could be said to provide more background relative to the changed situation, but though they are interesting, they are not essential to the main point this book addresses — the current slide with regard to biblical inerrancy. In fairness it should be stated that, so far as I know, no member of the faculty has denied any of the other theological essentials of the Christian faith up to this point. But neither can one be left comfortable, since for ten years there were faculty and board members who did not believe what they were then affirming. And with this sort of background it would not be difficult to imagine that a similar situation could exist at this moment. Once a trust has been breached, especially when the official standards of the institution were being claimed as the viewpoint of all when actually they were not, it is difficult to regain the confidence that has been lost by such action.

The question must be asked: Is the change of doctrinal commitment from an inerrant to a partially errant (in nonrevelational parts) Scripture one that is incidental and not fundamental? This question is asked on the basis of the assumption that Fuller Seminary is still faithful to the other fundamentals of orthodox Christianity. It is the thesis of this book that biblical inerrancy is a theological watershed. Down the road, whether it takes five or fifty years, any institution that departs from belief in an inerrant Scripture will likewise depart from other fundamentals of the faith and at last cease to be evangelical in the historical meaning of that term. This is the verdict of history. And Fuller Seminary has taken the first step that will bring about this untoward result unless it proves to be the first exception in history, or unless the institution reverses its stance and returns to its original commitment to biblical inerrancy in principle and in fact.

Now Dr. Jewett has taken the second step, a step that could not be taken if the original commitment to inerrancy had been kept and enforced. Will Fuller Seminary do anything about Jewett and any other faculty member who may have breached the new statement of faith on the same plane that Jewett has, although it still may not have touched upon one of the essential doctrines of a salvatory nature? It has taken only five years since the revised statement of faith was promulgated, for the institution to reach stage number two. How long will it be before it reaches that stage in which the atonement, the resurrection of Jesus in the same body, or the Second Coming are challenged?

Dr. Jewett also lists himself as the Dean of the Young Life Institute in his book. The importance of this connection cannot be overlooked. He has the responsibility for the theological training of many people connected with Young Life. These people, in turn, are found in the high schools of America where they have a formidable influence on minds still in formation. The percolation of Dr. Jewett's views is a significant matter under these circumstances. Perhaps his influence in this area is more important than his influence in a theological seminary where other scholars who hold another view can articulate that view strongly in their classrooms.

[1] Evangelical Theological Society *Bulletin*, Vol. II, No. 2, Spring 1968, p. 80.

[2] Ibid.

[3] Ibid., p. 82.

[4] George Ladd, *The New Testament and Criticism* (Grand Rapids: Eerdmans, 1967), pp. 16f.

[5] Unpublished letter to the Alumni, Summer, 1970.

[6] *Fuller Theological Seminary Bulletin* Issue, Vol. XVIII, No. 1, March, 1968.

[7] Paul King Jewett, *Emil Brunner's Concept of Revelation* (London: Clarke, 1954), p. 164.

[8] Ibid., pp. 166-168.

[9] Paul King Jewett, *Man As Male and Female* (Grand Rapids: Eerdmans, 1975), p. 119.

[10] Ibid.

[11] Ibid., pp. 112, 113.

[12] Ibid., p. 122.

[13] Ibid., p. 134.

[14] Ibid., p. 135.

7

Other Denominations and Parachurch Groups

So far I have been talking about the stresses and strains over infallibility among some people in the Southern Baptist Convention and the Lutheran Church–Missouri Synod. I then traced the same development at Fuller Theological Seminary. In this chapter I will enlarge the picture to include the North Park Theological Seminary, the only theological school of the Evangelical Covenant Church of America. From there I trace the beginnings of erosion in the Evangelical Theological Society and the American Scientific Affiliation, followed by the Wenham Conference on Scripture, and then the Free University at Amsterdam.

The design is to show that biblical inerrancy is under attack and disavowed in places where one would hardly expect it to happen. The case studies here are not intended to be complete, nor should the absence of any particular group or denomination lead to the conclusion that other groups do not have a similar problem.

Richard Quebedeaux in his book *The Young Evangelicals* (some of whom he has identified as such, have repudiated his designation and dissociated themselves from this new categorization) has flatly asserted that wherever young evangelicals are found, a trend away from inerrancy exists.[1] Donald Dayton of the North Park Seminary in Chicago agrees with this. He said that Quebedeaux

> probably understates the case. Some NAE colleges are to the left of

Fuller Seminary in their use of critical methodologies, and a growing community of younger evangelical scholars refuses to understand the Scriptures in terms of the doctrine of inerrancy as spelled out by the Evangelical Theological Society. The meaning of all this, however, is not yet clear. Quebedeaux slights the extent of Ladd's [George E. of Fuller Seminary] developments. In *Interpretation* (January 1971) Ladd stated that he no longer assents "to the older orthodox view . . . that 'revelation, in the biblical sense of the term, is the communication of information.' " For Ladd "revelation moves in the dimension of personal encounter. . . . God reveals *himself*." These comments imply a shift to a largely neoorthodox position and raise again for evangelicals basic questions about the nature of revelation and inspiration as well as the hermeneutical issues discussed above.[2]

No one connected with any group not mentioned in these pages should imagine that his group is therefore immune from the problem. At the same time, it would be folly to claim that no institution or denomination is free from it. I rather doubt that groups on the far right of the spectrum have any present difficulty over inerrancy. The General Association of Regular Baptist Churches certainly do not appear to have such difficulty. Nor do some institutions in the middle, such as Moody Bible Institute, Wheaton College, or seminaries like Dallas, Trinity, Bethel, the Conservative Baptist seminaries at Portland and Denver, Gordon Conwell, Westminster, the Reformed Seminary at Jackson appear to be struggling with the problem at the present time.

We must remember it is possible for people to harbor disbelief in inerrancy without letting it be known. History shows that there are always those who are ready to leap to the support of an issue when aggressive leadership is provided. How many evangelicals are mute, not because they believe in inerrancy, but because they choose not to speak out against it, no one knows. And it is improper to charge anyone with holding an anti-inerrancy viewpoint when there is no data to back it up. There is enough concrete evidence to support the thesis of this book without having to resort to innuendo or unproven assertions.

THE EVANGELICAL COVENANT CHURCH OF AMERICA

The Evangelical Covenant Church of America (hereafter referred to as the Covenant Church) has a membership of less than 100,000. Its membership is composed primarily of people of Swedish descent, although patterns of change are evident. The denomination traces its origins to immigrants who came to America from Sweden in the nineteenth century. These people had left the Lutheran Church of Sweden for a nonstate or free church in their native land. When they came to America, they brought their pietistic faith with them — a faith that was in reaction to a sterile intellectual Lutheranism. Their "creed" was the Bible and their chief emphasis was on the "new Life" in Christ "that is continually nourished and nurtured by the sacred Scripture, Old and New Testaments. . . . Always the Bible has been regarded as sovereign over all creedal interpretation and expression." Until the 1960s "it has been adequate for us simply to acknowledge the Bible as the Word of God and the only perfect rule for faith, doctrine, and conduct."[3] This denomination traditionally has been a Bible-believing people, although little attention was given to the theological content and meaning of the phrase "the Bible as the Word of God."

In recent years the Covenant Church has encountered difficulties over the Scriptures that have grown increasingly important in the thinking of numbers of its people. It has come about by what might almost be termed an accident of history. The Covenant Church has its own theological seminary in Chicago, the North Park Theological Seminary. As higher education was emphasized increasingly, faculty members and graduates of the seminary were faced with an educational impasse. The seminary itself offered no doctoral work beyond the basic theological degree. It was a small school whose students generally came from Covenant churches, and its educational offerings were limited. Anyone who wished to pursue graduate training had to go outside the denomination to do so. Unlike the Southern Baptist seminaries, most of which offer work for the doctorate, North Park has no program for the pursuit of the doctoral degree. Since the school is located in Chicago, it was not unnatural for faculty members of the seminary to seek graduate degrees in that city. The divinity complex at the University of Chicago was the most prestigious institution in the area. North Park teachers wended their way to the University of Chicago.

I can recall the process from personal experience and from marriage into a Swedish family with deep roots in the denomination. I was teaching at the Northern Baptist Theological Seminary in Chicago, a school that had been founded to offset the theological liberalism of the Divinity School at the University of Chicago. The Chicago Baptist Association included in its membership faculty members from both institutions. Men from Northern and from Chicago would come up for examination for ordination, and pitched battles were fought over every candidate. Those candidates who came from the Northern Baptist Seminary were worked over hard by the men from the Divinity School at Chicago. And when Chicago men came up for examination, they were given a hard time theologically by the Northern Baptist people. I recall distinctly the remark made by the well-known Peder Stiansen, one-time dean of Northern Baptist Seminary, when a Chicago graduate came up for ordination examination. When the graduate had been queried as to his theological convictions, he was so vague and so uncertain that Stiansen said, *sotto voce,* "This brother might just as well be up for ordination for the Buddhist priesthood." And he was not far from the truth, for the candidate by his own testimony was no more Christian than a confirmed Buddhist.

At this time (1944-1947) I had contact with faculty, students, and lay people of the Covenant denomination. It was clear then that a theological change was taking place and it was due largely to the educational training received by North Park faculty members at the University of Chicago. One could have predicted with certainty even then, that in due time the seminary would be greatly influenced by teachers who would reflect the theological viewpoints of the Divinity School at Chicago. And this is precisely what happened, although the erosion was gradual. By 1965 the situation had reached a point where the Board of Directors of North Park College and Theological Seminary recommended that the denomination appoint a representative committee to study the seminary of the church. This was done. Two years later the report of the eight-member committee was presented to the 1967 annual meeting of the Covenant Church and the report was adopted in its entirety.

The committee that studied the seminary reported some of its findings about the denomination at large. The first and most important finding was that two divergent views about biblical inspiration prevailed in the denomination. One held that the Scriptures partake of "salvational reliability," "which regards the scriptural authority as extending only to matters of faith, doctrine, and conduct. Covenanters holding this position have not felt that it was necessary for the authority of the Scriptures to be extended to scientific literalism in order for it to be a creditable and authoritative book."[4] On the other hand, the committee found that "through the years of our life as a church there has been a vital segment of our constituency that has held to a position of verbal inerrancy as regards the scriptural authority. These Covenanters have held to the trustworthiness of the scriptures in all subjects it addresses."[5]

The report followed up this second viewpoint by stating that at the heart of the matter is the reliability of the Bible "in statements of fact, history, science, and chronology." Whatever may have been the other matters that surfaced for discussion, the key issue found and isolated in the Covenant Church was the inerrancy of the Word of God.

The investigating committee focused on some of the concrete issues involved in the inerrancy question. Those who held to infalli-bility insisted on belief in the Mosaic authorship of the Pentateuch, the unity of Isaiah, the historicity of Jonah and Daniel — in other words, the common problems that always divide those who believe in inerrancy from those who do not. On the basis of these distinc-tions, the committee sought to discover the degree of differences about these matters among the faculty members and the students. The results were startling to say the least.

First, it was discovered that not a single member of the biblical faculty believed in an infallible Scripture. Not only so, the atmos-phere at the seminary was hostile toward those who held to iner-rancy. The committee reported that "the climate of the seminary is not always congenial to the second [i.e., the inerrancy] position and that students of a more conservative persuasion who enter the semi-nary feel themselves increasingly at odds with the prevailing ap-proach."[6]

The second fact the committee adduced came from its survey of the senior students nearing the completion of their course work in June of 1966. As a result of interviews with these students, the committee reported "that no one held to this second view [i.e., to an infallible Scripture] and that in varying degrees the students were inadequately informed of this position and/or opposed it."[7] It is almost impossible to suppose that with a large constituency that believes in biblical infallibility all of these students started out disbe-lieving the viewpoint. Rather, it is fair to conclude that whatever students began their seminary education believing in inerrancy were disabused of that notion and were influenced to discard it. Of course, these graduates could be expected to carry their theological opinions with them into the parish ministry, and it takes no prophet to predict that the churches in time would become what the seminary students themselves had become — disbelievers in inerrancy.

The committee said, "We must recognize a particularly serious breakdown in understanding and communication between North Park Theological Seminary and substantial segments of our Covenant family today. The imbalance in the biblical field at the seminary coupled with what at times has seemed to be a settled indifference toward positive and enlightened scholarship adhering to the second view of Scripture [i.e., biblical infallibility] have made it difficult for many to identify with their own school."[8] From the report, when read between the lines, some conclusions can be drawn. Biblical inerrancy had gotten short shrift at the seminary, the tone and atmosphere of the school was hostile toward such a viewpoint, and students were being systematically won over to the anti-inerrancy position.

The recommendations of the committee called for "the fostering of a spirit of acceptance and respect for divergent views within the context of our historic commitment."[9] And this recommendation was followed up by one that called for appointment to the biblical faculty of "a fully trained and qualified teacher who holds to the more conservative position on Scripture."[10] The report was adopted and the seminary did seek out and add to its faculty Dr. Donald Madvig, who fulfilled the requirements. Apparently the seminary could not find a Covenant scholar who filled the bill. Mr. Madvig was a Baptist. He has since taken a position elsewhere and has been replaced by a new faculty member who believes as he does.

In the years since the 1967 report the presidency of North Park has changed hands, but the disproportion of faculty members who favor the view of an errant Scripture remains. This is due no doubt to tenure, plus the fact that the denomination itself voted to live with two contradictory viewpoints about Scripture, pleading for mutual respect, tolerance, and brotherly love. Some students have preferred to pursue their theological studies in seminaries committed to an infallible Bible. The rule of thumb of the denomination that those ordained to the Covenant ministry must study at least one year at North Park has rendered their educational pursuit more difficult but not impossible. Some students take all of their important theological and biblical studies elsewhere, coming to North Park for their senior year, concentrating on the practical disciplines.

It remains to be seen if the Covenant denomination will be able to carry water on both shoulders perennially, or if one side or the other will prevail. Up to now there can be no doubt that, so far as the seminary is concerned, the balance is weighted heavily in favor of those who believe that Scripture is errant. Whether faculty members on retirement will be replaced by those who hold to the inerrancy viewpoint cannot now be predicted. But whichever way things go, the local congregations have been infiltrated by scores of young clergymen over the past twenty-five years who believe and can be expected to preach and teach that the Bible cannot be trusted beyond matters having to do with faith and practice.

By way of a postscript, I add several quotations from a letter I have in my possession written by a current member of the North Park faculty. He wrote, "I almost never use the word 'evangelical' to describe my own position — though it may be in the future, as the word gains new connotations, that I will find the word more congenial. . . . I must clearly state that my own agenda within my own constituency has two high priorities: to use whatever influence I may have to encourage a greater sense of social responsibility and to resist the impact of the Evangelical Theological Society's view of Scripture [i.e., of inerrancy] and certain elements of *Christianity Today*'s style in favor of a greater openness to such issues as biblical criticism." This is a University of Chicago man whose statement does not suggest the "fostering of a spirit of acceptance and respect for divergent views" as advocated by the committee that investigated North Park Seminary.

THE EVANGELICAL THEOLOGICAL SOCIETY AND THE AMERICAN SCIENTIFIC AFFILIATION

A quarter of a century ago (1949, to be exact) the Evangelical Theological Society came into being. It was created by evangelicals who believed in biblical inerrancy. The Society adopted a doctrinal statement for itself that comprised one assertion: "The Bible alone, and the Bible in its entirety, is the Word of God written, and therefore inerrant in the autographs." This has been the basis of its fellowship across the years. Today approximately one thousand scholars are on the roster of this organization. Should not one expect that an organization so created would be preserved from the inroads of modern biblical criticism that has led to a repudiation of inerrancy? But it is not so. Even the ETS has felt the impact of the age and has found in its midst those who hold to biblical errancy.

Perhaps it would be appropriate here to link the American Scientific Affiliation with the discussion. This can be done for several reasons. One is that this organization was also created by evangelicals who were thoroughly convinced that Scripture is infallible and that there is no real conflict between science and Christianity. The purpose of the organization was to relate science to the Christian faith and to demonstrate the reliability of the Bible by better understanding the limitations of science and by offering explanations to harmonize the apparent discrepancies. Since some of the persons whose opinions I shall quote have been connected with both organizations, it will serve to demonstrate the point I wish to make: both of these groups have people in them who deny inerrancy. Thus, these organizations have been infiltrated by viewpoints at variance with what the organizations originally believed and set out to do.

I will not spend much time showing that inerrancy has surfaced even in groups especially touchy regarding it. Several illustrations will suffice and I can go on to discuss other groups that have been penetrated by the errancy viewpoint.

Richard H. Bube is a professor at Stanford University. He is a member of the ETS and has been editor of the *Journal of the American Scientific Affiliation.* He authored a book entitled *The Encounter Between Christianity and Science.* Professor Bube has become an articulate spokesman in support of biblical errancy.

In his book Bube discusses the creation of Adam and Eve from the biblical as well as the paleontological evidences. He asks whether Paul's reference to the first Adam in Romans requires us to believe that "there was a unique first man by the name of Adam who experienced the events of Genesis in a natural historical sense."[11] His answer is no. He says that "Paul's reference to Adam as the head of the human race, as well as the words of Jesus in Matthew 19:4-9, may be taken as a revelational presentation of the truth of God inherent in the Genesis account, without necessarily giving sanction to the literal historicity of the details of that account . . . there is no information in the Bible, for example, that is either in favor of or opposed to theories of organic evolution."[12]

"If it is assumed," says Bube, "without due biblical support, that every statement of a biblical author on a 'technical detail,' whether it is related to an apparent pronouncement about astronomy, geography, geology, or any other topic not directly involved in the revelational purpose of the author, must be taken as scientifically objective fact, then it is virtually impossible to speak about the absence of errors in the Bible."[13] Bube goes so far as to say that the authorship of the Pentateuchal books by Moses "is actually neither affirmed nor denied by the statement of Jesus. This question is simply not relevant to His statement. No conclusion can be drawn from it about the authorship of Leviticus."[14]

An article by Bube appeared in *The Christian Reader*. It was a reprint of a 1963 article that first appeared in the *Journal of the American Scientific Affiliation*. It was part of a pro and con series. Dr. Charles Ryrie of Dallas Seminary wrote the *pro* article in favor of biblical inerrancy. Bube wrote the *con* article that opposed it. His argument, in its simplest terms, was that Scripture can be trusted in revelational matters, that is, in matters having to do with God and salvation. He objects to earlier models of inerrancy that left one feeling "as if there were only one kind of inerrancy imaginable — a kind of all or nothing inerrancy." He then advocates a partial inerrancy, an inerrancy limited to those things he thinks to be necessary. The purpose of the authors was to supply mankind with knowledge about God and Christ, and all that the writers intended to convey about these matters was conveyed without error. We are urged not to examine the Bible on the basis of criteria the books of the Bible were not written to satisfy.[15] Unfortunately, these criteria do not turn out to be more than Bube's criteria and his criteria are neither better nor worse than mine. The only criteria are those laid down by the Scriptures and Bube makes no case for biblical criteria.

In the first issue of the *Journal of the American Scientific Affiliation* that Bube edited an article by Paul H. Seely appeared. Seely said that

> the Bible assumes that the universe consists of three stories. . . . The earth is presumably, but not necessarily flat . . . but we do not believe that Christians are bound to give assent to such a cosmology, since the purpose of the Bible is to give redemptive, not scientific truth. The relationship of science to Scripture is this: The Bible gives redemptive truth through the scientific thoughts of the time without ever intending that those scientific thoughts should be believed as inerrant. . . . The aim of the Bible is to give redemptive truth. It never intended to teach science; nor does it ever claim to be "inerrant whenever it touches on science." It does not correct the errant science of the times in which it was written, but rather incorporates that pre-scientific science in its redemptive message. . . . To insist that the Bible be inerrant every time it touches on science is to insist on an *a priori* doctrine that has been read into the Bible. This doctrine not only leads to intellectual dishonesty about such matters as the three-

storied universe and to fighting against God as He is working through men called to be scientists, but it destroys faith in Christianity by implying that only obscurantists can be Christians.[16]

I do not need to belabor the issue further. The American Scientific Affiliation and the Evangelical Theological Society have in them people who do not believe that the Bible is free from all error in the whole and in the part. The disease with which we are dealing, then, is not limited to denominations like the Southern Baptists, the Lutheran Church–Missouri Synod, and the Evangelical Covenant Church. The infection has spread into parachurch organizations that were created for the purpose of maintaining full belief in biblical infallibility. And this leads us to the Wenham Conference on Scripture.

THE WENHAM CONFERENCE ON SCRIPTURE

The Seminar on the Authority of the Scripture convened at Gordon College and Divinity School campus in Wenham, Massachusetts, from whence comes the name "Wenham Conference." Fifty-one biblical scholars spent ten days in intensive discussion of the authority and inspiration of the Bible. The committee that headed up the conference comprised Harold John Ockenga, Russell T. Hitt, and Frank E. Gaebelein. A grant made the conference possible, although the source of the funding was not made public.

The participants came from six European countries as well as from Australia, Korea, Canada, and the United States. Among the denominations represented by the conferees were the Anglican, Reformed, Lutheran, Baptist, Methodist, Congregational, Free Church, and independent bodies. In order to insure openness, none of the sessions was taped and there was no stenographic reporting. (This no doubt came out of Dr. Ockenga's experience in connection with Fuller Theological Seminary, discussed in an earlier chapter.) No observers were admitted to the sessions. This meant the press was excluded. No releases were to be given outside the meetings save for those made by the group itself.

Papers were presented and among those who contributed them were Donald Wiseman, professor of Assyriology at the University of London; Herman Ridderbos, professor of New Testament at the Theological Seminary of the Reformed Churches, Kampen, the Netherlands; James I. Packer, warden of Latimer House, Oxford; Oswald C. J. Hoffmann, preacher on the "Lutheran Hour"; and

Kenneth Kantzer, dean of Trinity Evangelical Divinity School. Some of the greatest stalwarts who have consistently defended biblical inerrancy backed out of the conference. They felt that their presence would serve no useful purpose and that little was to be gained by discussing inerrancy with those in attendance whose minds already had been made up against it. The conference indeed was called precisely to air the two opposing viewpoints that existed among those who were generally thought to be evangelical in everything, at least apart from inerrancy.

Wenham made one thing clear. A deep cleavage over inerrancy existed among the evangelicals present. The numbers of those representing the two sides would be impossible to state precisely, but no one's mind was changed as a consequence of the conference. In the wide-ranging discussions the same old story came to light. Some held to inerrancy as an essential biblical doctrine. Others did not. All of them agreed on the complete truthfulness of the Bible and its authoritativeness as the infallible rule of faith and practice. None of the participants affirmed the errancy of the Bible. They only refused to accept inerrancy! The communique issued by the conference spoke of the truthfulness of Scripture, but it was plain that the statement reflected the obvious ambivalence but in no sense affirmed inerrancy. To the untutored in theological dialogue it might seem that the words "the Scriptures are completely truthful and are authoritative as the only infallible rule of faith and practice" meant that all of Scripture is errorless. But it did not. The statement released by the group meant only those parts of Scripture are completely truthful that have to do with matters of faith and practice.

The division that existed and exists today among neoevangelicals about biblical infallibility was clearly manifested at Wenham. What it did not do is equally important. It did not discuss in depth the consequences flowing from a limited inerrancy that, in effect, denies inerrancy. Nor did it make clear what the boundaries are for those who believe the Bible to be completely trustworthy only in matters of faith and practice. The question of who determines which parts of Scripture can be trusted and which parts have nothing to do with matters of faith and practice was left unanswered. The participants who opposed inerrancy did not claim that inerrancy was not the historic view of the church — only that they did not believe it. Wenham provided further evidence to support the contention of this book that the historic view of the church is not the view of some of those in the neo-evangelical tradition who profess to be heirs of the orthodoxy of the centuries since Pentecost.

Those who denied inerrancy have allied themselves with the larger denominations of Christendom in America and around the world who discarded the doctrine of biblical infallibility before, during, and after the Modernist-Fundamentalist controversy. The battle being fought today is the same battle that was fought and lost by those who held to inerrancy decades ago. The Presbyterians, the Methodists, some of the Lutheran denominations, the United Church of Christ, and the Episcopal Church capitulated during the earlier struggle. Now the same war rages over the same issue and the same question remains: Which side will win? This time around, the battle involves the few large denominations that did not surrender in the earlier struggle, as well as smaller and generally more evangelical denominations, many of which are to be found in the membership of the National Association of Evangelicals.

One need only travel to the campuses of colleges connected with the smaller denominations as well as the larger ones to discover that some of these institutions that have been distinctively evangelical, are now confronted with the same problem that the larger denominations faced years ago. Numbers of their faculty members have taken doctoral work in the hard and the soft sciences without the benefit of theological training, indeed without an awareness that what they have learned in secular universities has implications for their Christian faith. Numbers of these professors teach one thing in the classroom, and believe something else in church on Sunday morning. They never put two and two together. Many of them have no conscious awareness that there is a dichotomy between what they believe in their hearts and what they teach from their heads. But almost inevitably they have been conditioned in such a way that the so-called "certainties" of their doctoral disciplines cause them to test Scripture against these "certainties" rather than testing their presuppositions and conclusions against biblical revelation.

I am saying that there are really two problems. One has to do with neoevangelicals who are theological seminary graduates and whose teaching is in the biblical disciplines. They are caught up in the struggle over biblical infallibility. But there are multitudes who, though they neither teach in the biblical areas nor are instructed in Christian theology, are nevertheless caught up in the same battle. My own conversations with faculty members in a number of different

institutions has led me to conclude that theologically naive or untutored teachers present no less of a challenge to the historic notion of
biblical infallibility than do teachers in the biblical and the
philosophical fields.

The problem is compounded by the students in these institutions,
too. They come for instruction without sufficient background training, having been raised often in evangelical churches that have not
provided the kind of biblical training they needed. Exposed to non-
Christian or anti-Christian teaching in the secular high schools of
America, they hit the Christian college campuses illiterate, with a
kind of mental grid that makes them easy prey to aberrant beliefs.
Some of them have built up a resistance to anything that smacks of
authoritarianism not only in conduct but also in the thought life.
Steeped in a relativistic thought pattern, they find it difficult if not
impossible to accept a view of Scripture that is absolutistic and
demands the submission of mind, body, and life to its world view.
They are not helped by teachers in the biblical disciplines who either
do not believe in an infallible Scripture, or who teach it without
passion and conviction just because it is part of the institution's
doctrinal commitment. They are given no help from teachers outside
the biblical disciplines, either because they have nothing to offer
their students since they are theologically deficient, or they are
damaged further by attitudes that subject Scripture to the conclusions of the secular subjects rather than testing the conclusions of the
secular subjects on the basis of what Scripture teaches.

This is happening not only in institutions connected with denominations that turned away from biblical infallibility years ago. It is
happening under our eyes in institutions that are still committed to
Scriptural infallibility in principle but are deficient in practice. And
we shall note later that this means that numbers of our evangelical
schools that at one time were on a platform now are on a slope. And a
slope soon becomes a slide, and it does not take long for people and
institutions to hit the bottom.

THE FREE UNIVERSITY AT AMSTERDAM

The Christian Reformed denomination has been thought of as a
theologically orthodox church. It had its origins in the settlers who
came to America from Holland. The denomination has maintained
intimate connections with the Free University at Amsterdam. This
institution has had a long and honored history as a theologically

orthodox university. The unhappy fact is that the Free University has begun to move away from its historic moorings and at the heart of the slippage lies a departure from the belief in inerrancy. Although there are problems at the Free University, the matter of biblical infallibility has surfaced in the General Synod of the Reformed Church in the Netherlands. In that body, the question relates to the latitude allowed with respect to teaching in the church and this in turn is at the heart of the inerrancy dilemma.

The RES *News Exchange*, a publication of the Reformed Ecumenical Synod, reported that at a meeting of the Reformed Church Synod Professor G. C. Berkouwer asked the question: "Is there room in the Reformed Churches for persons — and I reckon myself among them — who at this stage of their reflection have great hesitations concerning the historicity of Adam?" The Synod gave no answer to the question posed by Berkouwer's statement. Professor J. H. Velema wrote in *de Wekker* concerning the consequences of the declarations of the General Synod saying, "The Reformed Churches have taken an important step in the direction of the Netherlands Reformed Church in that they tolerate latitude in teaching in fact and in the declaration. This entails that the Reformed Confessions (which include inerrancy) are no longer safe with the Reformed Churches which a half century ago swore to hold the heritage of Kuyper."[17]

Berkouwer has certainly been the leading theologian at the Free University. The admission that he now has reservations about the historicity of Adam is indicative of his shift. He was a contributor to the Current Religious Thought Column of *Christianity Today* for some years. When readers raised the question about his belief in biblical inerrancy, I wrote to him for clarification. Despite extended correspondence, I could get no answer from him either affirming or denying inerrancy. When a man refuses to reply to a direct question about his continued acceptance of inerrancy, the only conclusion that can be drawn is obvious. In the translation of Berkouwer's book *Holy Scripture* into English, it is now possible to discover what his views are with regard to inerrancy. Geoffrey Bromiley in a view of the English translation had this to say:

> His reactions to some forms of fundamentalism, his lack of coherence in treating inerrancy, and his misdirected approach to time-relatedness weaken the total impact of what is for the most part a strong and positive statement. They do this, unfortunately, at the very time when the normativity of Scripture seems to be dissolving in a sea of relativism and the distinctiveness of the Christian "transforming"

of life and thought is apparently being lost in the blur of secular "conforming." Berkouwer himself believes that in the long run his understanding will strengthen the authority of Scripture. We hope he is right, but gravely fear that he is wrong.

Even more revealing is the stance of H. M. Kuitert of the Free University. Bernard Ramm chose to list him among the great theologians of our times. In his review of Kuitert, Ramm says that when his book *The Reality of Faith* "was translated into English and published in 1968 it received more approval from nonevangelical journals than any other book I can think of in the past two decades. One of the reviewers said that if evangelicals could write this kind of theology then real conversations could be had with them."[18] What the reviewer really meant was that Kuitert had made such concessions to nonevangelical theology that of course he was acceptable to them because he was writing on their own wavelength. The book that illustrated Kuitert's departure from biblical infallibility is entitled *Do You Understand What You Read?* And incidentally it was Kuitert who was a major speaker at a minister's colloquium of the Christian Reformed Church just a few years ago. I happened to follow him the year after he had been there, and it was plain from the reaction that my own adherence to infallibility was accorded a mixed reception: those who held it were delighted; those who were opposed to it were unhappy. Fortunately, or unfortunately, I was not aware that Kuitert had been there the year before me, but it was apparent that within its leadership the Christian Reformed Church is also struggling with the inerrancy issue.

Kuitert forthrightly declares there are historical discrepancies in Scripture, and offers the weak solution that if we understood the purpose of each writer we would not focus our attention on the contradictions. He says, "To insist that everything happened precisely as it is read in the Bible is to read the Bible badly indeed, or at least superficially . . . some things are reported that simply did not happen the way they are told."[19] Kuitert does not read Genesis 1-11 as real history. He says, "Even as faith does not ask us ever to call white black, faith does not demand that we dig in our heels, and contrary to all scientific evidence, insist that the original human couple of Genesis is a literal and historical pair of people."[20] He argues that nothing is lost if we read the story of Jonah as fiction and not history.[21]

Kuitert's view of the Bible is further expanded when he says, "The sheer fact that certain events are reported in the Bible does not guarantee that they occurred. . . . We do not insist that the resurrection of Jesus really happened just because the Bible says it did."[22] "Whenever anyone asks the question, 'Do you believe in Adam and Eve?' he exhibits a misunderstanding of the Christian faith."[23] That, of course, may be true. But how a man answers that question can tell me quickly whether he does or does not believe in biblical inerrancy.

Ramm observes that Kuitert "thinks that a purely verbal understanding of inspiration and a purely propositional notion of revelation are both untrue to Scripture. Revelation is more in terms of events, images, and models." Then Ramm concludes, "I also find it somewhat contradictory for a book to attack revelation as propositional by using propositions to do it! If propositions can do this service, they can't be all that bad."[24]

A lot more can be said about Kuitert, Berkouwer, and the churches that fall within their orbit, but it is unnecessary. The point has already been made. Here are groups long known for their staunch adherence to an infallible Scripture who have leaders in their midst who are cutting away at their foundations. These evangelical groups are confronted with the same kind of problem to which we are addressing ourselves.

SUMMARY

In conclusion, we can say that the evidence tells its own story. In all of the case histories I have written about, changes are taking place. In every instance the changes reflect a basic movement away from an infallible Scripture. This, in itself, shows that the prevailing viewpoint they are abandoning is inerrancy. And it is inerrancy that is under attack. No matter how guardedly the case against inerrancy is presented, the logical outcome is always in favor of an errant Scripture. It would be wrong at this stage to make a generalization saying that those evangelicals who oppose inerrancy have also scrapped some or all of the other foundational truths of the Christian faith. Some so-called evangelicals have gone further; others have stopped short by rigidly insisting upon an errancy limited to data outside matters of faith and practice.

Evidence exists to show that some people in the groups we are talking about have gone far beyond a mere denial of biblical inerrancy. A classic illustration of this is Professor Alley of the University of Richmond and a member of a Southern Baptist Convention church. But this is a far-out case. Other cases could be cited, but they represent a minority. The majority would still be committed to a view of the Scripture that takes seriously the basic doctrines of a soteriological nature. Within this range there would be differences, of course, and no one can suppose that all or most of the people we are referring to would fit into one specific classification.

If I could venture a generalization about the battle being fought among people who call themselves evangelical, it would be this. At this moment there are two prevailing views, roughly speaking, and most evangelicals would fall into one or the other of these two camps. The first is that of the believer in biblical inerrancy. The second comprises those who do not believe in biblical inerrancy, but who have some elements of inerrancy in their theological position. It is framed differently, depending upon which adherent you refer to, but the differences are more marginal than substantive. Among most evangelicals who object to inerrancy there is a belief in the Bible as infallible in matters of faith and practice. Men like Daniel Fuller speak about revelational and nonrevelational Scripture. Revelational Scripture for them includes those things that have to do with faith and practice. Nonrevelational Scripture has to do with all other matters. Others speak of Scripture as the revelation of God set in a human context bearing evidences of fallible humanity, but with the message of God shining through the human errors. However stated and however limited, the difference between the two views at present is that some of Scripture, but not all, comprises the revelation of God, and that portion of Scripture that does this can be trusted and is true and free from error.

The errancy camp is divided, and can be expected to be divided, over questions that may or may not bear upon matters of faith. Does the belief or disbelief in a historical Adam and Eve have anything to do with the "infallible rule of faith"? Does the acceptance of Jonah as a novella rather than history, the non-Mosaic authorship of the Pentateuch, the nonhistorical character of the first eleven chapters of Genesis, the theory of two Isaiahs, the late dating of Daniel, the non-Pauline authorship of books like Ephesians and the Prison Epistles, and the non-Petrine authorship of 2 Peter relate to nonrevelational matters or do they involve the "rule of faith"? Who is to decide, and on what basis, what constitutes the material that is to be trusted and that which is not to be trusted? Does it make any difference whether one believes in the virgin birth of Christ and the physical resurrection of Christ from the dead? No one can escape these questions, and answers must be provided to them by those who deny inerrancy.

At least one other question must be decided also. Is the term "evangelical" broad enough in its meaning to include within it believers in inerrancy and believers in an inerrancy limited to matters of faith and practice? At this stage, no one is apt to argue that the refusal to accept inerrancy means that the person who does this is outside the Christian faith, i.e., unsaved. Are all, then, who have been regenerated by the Holy Spirit, entitled to be labeled "evangelicals"? The answer to the question depends on the definition given to "evangelical." As some define it, there is room for both under that label. As others define it, there is not. The problem from my perspective becomes important for another reason. I am contending that once biblical inerrancy is scrapped, it leads inevitably to the denial of biblical truths that are inextricably connected with matters of faith and practice. History bears this out as we shall see, and nowhere is there any example of a group that has proclaimed a belief in the truthfulness limited to those matters having to do with faith and practice where further defection has not occurred.

It seems to me that those who believe in inerrancy are left with little choice except to stand for a definition of "evangelical" that includes in it the notion of biblical inerrancy. This is especially true if inerrancy is really a watershed that determines where one ends up. This need not be taken to mean that those who hold to a limited inerrancy are excluded from the household of faith. But it does mean that there is a real difference that should not be obscured, for the dangers inherent in the limited-inerrancy viewpoint are too important to be overlooked.

For me to so define "evangelical" may appear divisive, and it may seem to present a threat to the unity of faith. We are always confronted with the dilemma of having to choose between truth and unity. Where truth is not at stake and there is disunity, it is not only unfortunate, it is also wrong. But where unity must be foregone because of adherence to truth it is a different matter. The absence of unity does not require anyone to isolate himself so that there can be no interchange, or so that there is an end to discussion. If it is possible to dialogue with people of other faiths and of no faith, it surely must be possible to dialogue with those who profess some form of the Christian faith. Nor does it necessarily imply that those who believe in inerrancy must separate themselves from groups and denominations that fail to support the viewpoint. So long as the believer is not called upon to renounce his convictions at this point, and has the freedom to propagate what he believes, he may find it within the will of God to have a ministry in such a group or denomination. In principle, there is no reason why an evangelical believer could not accept a post on the faculty of the Harvard Divinity School however distasteful some of its theological opinions might be, so long as he is not required to compromise his own convictions.

Now we must go on to show what has happened to those denominations and groups that have abandoned inerrancy. This is the next step on the program.

[1] Richard Quebedeaux, *The Young Evangelicals* (New York: Harper and Row, 1974), pp. 74ff.

[2] *The Other Side,* March-April, 1975, pp. 34, 35.

[3] *The Covenant Companion* (Vol. LVI No. 22), November 3, 1967, "The Report of the Seminary Study Committee," p. 3a.

[4] Ibid.

[5] Ibid.

[6] Ibid., p. 4a.

[7] Ibid.

[8] Ibid., p. 5a.

[9] Ibid.

[10] Ibid.

[11] Richard H. Bube, *The Encounter Between Christianity and Science* (Grand Rapids: Eerdmans, 1968), p. 96.

[12] Ibid., p. 97.

[13] Ibid., p. 100.

[14] Ibid., p. 96.

[15] *The Christian Reader,* August-September, 1964, pp. 54ff.

[16] *Journal of the American Scientific Affiliation,* Vol. 21, No. 1, March, 1969, pp. 18ff.

[17] RES *News Exchange,* January 19, 1971.

[18] *Eternity,* June, 1972, pp. 36-38.

[19] H. M. Kuitert, *Do You Understand What You Read?* (Grand Rapids: Eerdmans, 1970), pp. 14, 15.

[20] Ibid., p. 101.

[21] Ibid., pp. 104, 105.

[22] Ibid., p. 82.

[23] Ibid., p. 67.

[24] *Eternity,* June, 1972, p. 38.

8

Deviations That Follow When Inerrancy Is Denied

Before taking the next step, I remind the reader of what I have done so far. Three things should be mentioned. The first is that, following the introduction in which the biblical doctrine of inerrancy was shown to be the centerpiece of evangelical difficulty today, I defined what is meant by inerrancy. Then came a detailed study of the evidences from history to show that the doctrine of biblical inerrancy has been normative since the days of the apostles. It was not until the last century and a half that the opponents of inerrancy, or whom we might call believers in errancy, have become a dominant force in Christianity. I alleged that the church in history paid scant attention to biblical inerrancy for a simple reason. It was not seriously challenged since the New Testament was written, any more than the inerrancy of the Old Testament was challenged before and during Jesus' day.

In the United States, and this book deals mostly with this country, the real struggle was fought in three periods of recent history. The first real battle started in the 1880s and the chief protagonists were Warfield, Hodge, Briggs, and Smith. The second battle was fought during the 1930s and the name that stands above all others is that of J. Gresham Machen. The third battle is the one being fought right now.

In today's Christian world there are a substantial number of

141

mission boards, denominations, and parachurch organizations that have been noted for their commitment to an inerrant Bible. Within these groups will be found those who currently challenge the doctrine of infallibility while remaining within the fellowship of groups committed to it. Thus the third objective was to provide evidences to demonstrate that there is rising opposition to biblical infallibility among evangelicals. It was not my purpose to do this at great length or in depth, although it would have been easy. There is enough documentation for anyone who wishes to take the time to look for it and to read it. All I hoped to do was alert the reader to the existence of the problem, and to offer sufficient documentation to sustain the charge. No allegations have been made for which there is no hard evidence. I now go on to the next step.

WHAT HAPPENS WHEN INERRANCY IS ABANDONED

The fourth step is to sketch what happens when biblical inerrancy is scrapped and errancy is accepted. It is my contention that once biblical infallibility is surrendered it leads to the most undesirable consequences. It will end in apostasy at last. It is my opinion that it is next to impossible to stop the process of theological deterioration once inerrancy is abandoned. I have said that it is a theological watershed just as the Continental Divide is the watershed for the United States and Canada. The water that flows on one side of the divide ends up in the Atlantic Ocean. The water that flows on the other side of the divide ends up in the Pacific Ocean. But once the water starts down one side or the other, it continues until it reaches its oceanic destination. Errancy and inerrancy constitute the two principles, and which one a person chooses determines where he will end up.

No matter how sincere a man may be, and however carefully he guards against further theological concessions, they are inevitable once inerrancy is given up. Francis Schaeffer has told conferees at L'Abri that "the generation of those who first give up biblical inerrancy may have a warm evangelical background and real personal relationships with Jesus Christ so that they can 'live theologically' on the basis of their limited-inerrancy viewpoint. But what happens when the next generation tries to build on that foundation?" I am saying that whether it takes five or fifty years any denomination or parachurch group that forsakes inerrancy will end up shipwrecked. It is impossible to prevent the surrender of other important doctrinal teachings of the Word of God when inerrancy is gone.

I am not saying that belief in inerrancy guarantees the continued pristine purity of churches or parachurch organizations or institutions. Nor am I saying that belief in biblical infallibility will automatically prevent them from going astray. But I am saying that without a belief in inerrancy any group is bound to go astray. With inerrancy it may or may not defect, depending on how the group carries out the implications that are inherent in this belief. The Roman Catholic Church did not go astray because it surrendered a belief in inerrancy. We have seen that the church indeed, until recently, always believed and taught the doctrine of inerrancy. But it did not follow through on the implications. The hearts of men are deceitful and wicked. Thus it is always possible for anyone to deny in practice what he affirms in principle, even though principle and practice should go hand in hand. But when the principle is lost, there is no hope for true survival, for no one does in practice what he denies in principle. A belief in inerrancy makes *possible* the unsullied continuance of the group that holds it, whereas the surrender of this principle virtually guarantees that such a possibility does not exist.

There is another question that must be faced, but whether there is an answer to it I do not now know. Is it possible for a denomination or a parachurch organization to recover a belief in inerrancy in principle and practice once it has been lost? Perhaps the reason why this question cannot be answered is the recency of the movement away from inerrancy in Christendom. Had churches and parachurch organizations defected from inerrancy six or seven centuries ago, the passage of time would have given us evidences on which to draw some conclusions. But the flowering of disbelief in inerrancy has covered less than two centuries. Insufficient time has elapsed, therefore, to say flatly that recovery is either possible or impossible. In any event, the time has come for me to state the facts that support my contention that the surrender of inerrancy produces further concessions and a more marked departure from belief in other basic doctrines of the Christian faith.

THE UNITARIAN UNIVERSALIST DEFECTION

The Unitarian Universalist denomination is the grossest illustration of how far a group can depart from historic Christianity when the full trustworthiness of Scripture is discarded. The Unitarian defection in New England began early in the last century. The

Unitarian denomination was formed from the Congregational churches in New England. Basically the schism occurred over Christology. The Congregational churches that did not defect remained Trinitarian; the Unitarian churches did not. The latter denied that Jesus Christ is God and they repudiated the person of the Holy Spirit as the third member of the Godhead. This defection resulted from a denial of the plain teachings of the Bible. In due season it led to the denial of other cardinal doctrines of Christianity. The bodily resurrection of Jesus Christ from the dead was denied. The vicarious blood atonement of Jesus and the virgin birth were no longer believed. Gradually the denomination became humanistic.

The Universalist denomination had an earlier history in New England. One of its chief beliefs was universal salvation, the notion that all men will be saved. When the Unitarian and Universalist denominations joined to form the Unitarian Universalist Association in 1961, the merger was one that brought together two church groups of similar beliefs, or should I say unbeliefs? Today the consequences of the denial of biblical infallibility are apparent to all. This denomination has gone beyond humanism into agnosticism and atheism. Everyone is free to believe anything he chooses, or nothing at all. There is no basic doctrine of the Christian faith that is held by this denomination. It is thoroughly and completely apostate, with no belief in either heaven or hell. For this organization the Bible is truly irrevelant, the gospel an anachronism, and the worship of God a travesty. It is difficult to see how any denomination could go beyond the place where the Unitarian Universalist Association now stands.

So renegade is the Unitarian Universalist denomination and so far outside the pale of anything that resembles Christianity, that it is not even a member of the National Council of Churches. But what is strange is that numbers of these churches and clergymen are members of local councils of churches in the major cities around the United States. It is easily understandable why evangelical councils of churches have come into being in many cities. Conscience could not permit them to remain as members of local church councils in which Unitarian Universalist churches also held membership. But what does that tell us about those churches that permit this to happen and do nothing about it even now? Does not this kind of stand represent a betrayal of Christian faith and a denial of biblical teaching that truth and error should not fellowship together?

THE 1967 POLL OF NCC DELEGATES

Newsweek magazine ran an article entitled "The New-Time Religion." In that article it said:

> Conservative critics frequently complain that the National Council of Churches is too liberal to represent mainstream American Protestantism. Are they right? Last week the NCC released a survey of 521 clergy and laymen who attended the council's 1966 General Assembly in Miami Beach. Based on responses from 37 percent of the voting and alternate delegates, plus 298 consultants and "accredited visitors" at the assembly, the survey does indeed reveal a *modest* liberal stance [my italics].
>
> To be sure nearly two-thirds firmly believe in God [this means that one third do not], and more than half — 58 percent — confidently regard Jesus as divine. Thus on at least two fundamental points — together with the 22 percent who temper their beliefs with only occasional doubts — the survey shows that NCC representatives are as traditional as most American churchgoers.
>
> But in other specific areas, NCC assemblymen seem to have jettisoned much of the old-time religion. Only one in four accepts Biblical miracles — such as the virgin birth of Christ — as literally true. In fact, a third of the respondents believe such miracles can be explained by natural causes. The devil "definitely" does not exist for one in three, and only 15 percent believe that children are born into the world already guilty of sin — a doctrine basic to reformers Martin Luther and John Calvin. Finally, with something less than triumphant optimism, barely 62 percent look forward with "complete certainty" to a life after death.[1]

Does not this survey provide convincing evidence of what happens once biblical inerrancy is scrapped? Since the people polled here come from the major denominations in the United States, it is safe to say that they are fairly representative of what is believed or disbelieved among the clergy, professors, and laypeople of these groups.

It is not unfair to allege that among denominations like Episcopal, United Methodist, United Presbyterian, United Church of Christ, the Lutheran Church in America, and the Presbyterian Church U.S. there is not a single theological seminary that takes a stand in favor of biblical infallibility. And there is not a single seminary where there are not faculty members who disavow one or more of the major teachings of the Christian faith. And what is true of denominational schools is true also of nondenominational schools such as the Chicago Divinity School, Harvard Divinity School, Yale Divinity School, the Pacific School of Religion, and the Union

Theological Seminary in New York. This is not to say that there are no faculty members in any of these schools who hold to an inerrant Scripture. But the number, when compared to those who do not, is inconsequential. And the writings of the professors from these institutions demonstrate beyond question that multitudes have departed from the clear teachings of Scripture. One need only recall names like Harvey Cox, Paul Tillich, Reinhold Niebuhr, Henry Pitney VanDusen, Shirley Jackson Case, and Henry Cadbury to illustrate the fact that they have gone far beyond a mere rejection of biblical infallibility to a denial of major doctrines of Christianity.

THE BISHOP PIKE CASE

The case of the late Bishop James A. Pike highlights how the abandonment of inerrancy leads to the progressive departure from other biblical truths. In his book *If This Be Heresy* (which it was) Bishop Pike includes statistics taken from a survey made by the Survey Research Center at the University of California at Berkeley. These statistics indicate how many so-called Christians have defected from major biblical teachings. Pike says, "Higher but not impressively so are the number of those believing in Jesus Christ as Savior as absolutely essential for salvation: Congregationalists, 38 percent; Methodists, 45 percent; Episcopalians, 47 percent; Disciples, 78 percent; United Presbyterians, 66 percent; Lutherans, 77 percent; American Baptists, 78 percent; Lutheran–Missouri Synod, 97 percent; Southern Baptists, 97 percent; Roman Catholics, 51 percent."[2] Bishop Pike reported that the statistics for his own church showed that "61 percent of Episcopal laymen cannot affirm as historical the Virgin Birth and 53 percent will not affirm the doctrine of sole salvation through Jesus. . . ."[3]

Bishop Pike was not hesitant about denying his belief in the doctrine of the Trinity, the virgin birth of Christ, and the bodily resurrection of Jesus from the dead. Of course, he denied biblical inerrancy. He was so blatant in his views as bishop that the Episcopal Church was forced to act in his case. The Roman Catholic magazine, *Triumph,* had this to say: "The Episcopalians appointed an Advisory Committee on Theological Freedom and Social Responsibilities with instructions to study 'the theological situation faced by the Episcopal Church,' and concretely, to answer the question: 'What is heresy? How should the Church define, detect, and deal with it?' The Committee's verdict was that the word 'heresy' should be abandoned. 'It too often conjures up a picture of a static fortress of propositional theology that requires to be, and can be defended by appeal to the letter of a theological statement. It presumes to a measure of theological pre-judgment (that is a belief that the Bible is true and can prejudge doctrinal views) which is inappropriate to the mature Christian community. It too often implies a set of theological categories unconditioned by their historical and cultural period' " — in other words, such an approach refuses to use and apply the historical-critical methodology that always ends up denigrating Scripture. *Triumph,* speaking of this and the fact that ninety Episcopal priests in New York in a meeting at the Cathedral of St. John the Divine had stated that homosexuality is neither right nor wrong, said, "These two incidents in the recent history of the Episcopal Church unavoidably raise the question whether the body is tending toward an official position of neutrality on matters of faith and morals — whether, that is, Episcopalians are capable of loving Truth sufficiently to recognize its opposite."[4] Does anyone need more evidence to show that the departure from biblical inerrancy in the Episcopal Church has led to further departure from basic biblical orthodoxy?

THE CHURCH OF ENGLAND

The Church of England has been noted for its Thirty-nine Articles of Religion, which have been the backbone of Anglicanism across the centuries. The Religious News Service reported the action taken by the 1968 Lambeth Conference in London: "Assent to the 39 Articles — the Church of England's code of doctrine — is no longer to be required for clergy ordination. . . . The decision was taken when the 460 Bishops — not without some division — approved an amendment to a resolution moved by Bishop George Luxton of Huron, Canada. He called assent to the Articles 'theological smog' and 'double talk.'" Archbishop Michael Ramsey, titular head of the Church, said he was "very glad" that the Conference had endorsed the "valuable report" drawn up by the Commission and that he, himself, "took a rather more radical line than the report did."[5] So the action of the Church of England also indicates how far one can stray from the most holy faith once the doctrine of biblical inerrancy is forsaken.

LUTHERANS IN THE UNITED STATES

What has happened among Lutherans in America demonstrates

how much they have slidden down the slippery slope to an ever-increasing departure from the faith of their fathers. The slide has occurred in concert with an increasing rejection of the Bible as inerrant. Dr. Raymond Surburg wrote an article in *The Springfielder*, a theological journal published by the faculty of the Concordia Seminary at Springfield, Illinois. In the article Dr. Surburg reviewed the contents of the book *A Study of Generations*, which was assembled by four specialists. The project was funded by the Lutheran Brotherhood, and the book was published by Augsburg. Surburg stated that "this volume is based on over seven million pieces of data from 4745 persons out of 316 congregations of the Lutheran Church in America, the American Lutheran Church and the Lutheran Church–Missouri Synod. It gives a religious profile of six million confirmed Lutherans belonging to 15,000 congregations." The study "seems assured of becoming a classic" according to *Time* magazine. Dr. George Elford, Research Director of the National Catholic Educational Association, claims that the book "is the best piece of religious research ever done. . . . Dr. James E. Dittes of Yale University wrote in the Foreword: 'Lutherans can be assured that their portrait has been drawn here sensibly and responsibly by a skilled team. The first thorough denominational portrait has set high standards for others to follow.' "[6] The results of the study show how far Lutherans have departed from their confidence in the Bible — a departure that flows from a disbelief in the truthfulness of the Scriptures.

According to this book, "about 33% of Lutherans do not believe in Biblical miracles as described in the Bible. The creation of the world by fiat command, the deliverance of Israel by the miracle of the parting of the waters of the Red Sea, the miracles of Elisha and Elijah, the incarnation of God as man, the resurrection of Christ, the ascension and second return could all be involved. 82% of the members of LC–MS believe the miracles the way they are said to have happened in the Bible, as compared with 69% in the ALC, and 61% in the LCA."[7] This, of course, indicates that the Missouri Synod people are definitely more committed to biblical reliability than its two sister denominations.

"Three out of every ten Lutherans do not believe in a life after death. For these individuals the grave is the end of man's existence. This also means no heaven or hell. Seven out of ten Lutherans believe that all religions lead to the same God, while four out of ten agree that all religious are equally important to God. . . . The Devil is described in Holy Writ as the demonic personality who tempted Eve in Eden, that caused David to number the people, who tempted Jesus in the wilderness and who is active tempting and seducing people to sin. . . . According to the *Report* 75% of the members of the Missouri Synod believe in the Devil's reality, while only 50% of the ALC, and 33% of the LCA."[8]

Lutheran Christology has changed for the worse also. In his article on *A Study of Generations* Surburg observes:

> Two of the ecumenical creeds of Christendom confess the Virgin Birth of Christ. Two Gospel passages set forth the truth that Mary became pregnant because the Holy Spirit brought about this condition in her womb. According to the *Report* only 40% of Lutherans agreed with the statement: "Jesus was conceived by the Holy Spirit and born of the Virgin Mary" (p. 379). Historic Lutheranism has held to and confessed its belief in the deity of Christ, who is depicted in the New Testament as possessing the attributes of omniscience, omnipresence, and omnipotence. 56% of Lutherans reject Christ's omnipresence. According to John 1:3, Colossians 1:16 and Hebrews 1:2 Christ is set forth as the Creator of all that exists. Yet 54% of Lutherans who are supposed to draw their doctrines and beliefs solely from the Holy Scriptures, deny that Jesus Christ created everything.
>
> A vital part of Christian doctrine is the correct understanding of the nature and purpose of Christ's death. One of the statements to which responses were requested was: "Jesus died for sinners. As a substitute, he suffered the just penalty due to us for sins in order to satisfy the wrath of God and to save guilty men from hell" (p. 379). Only 37% would strongly agree with this statement. Only 24% would assert about those people who deny the substitutionary death of Christ or disbelieve the Pauline statement about the nature of Christ's atoning death that they are not true Christians. . . . 44% believe that "Salvation depends upon being sincere in whatever you believe" (p. 369). 31% contend that "If I believe in God and do right, I will get to heaven" (p. 369).[9]

THE UNITED PRESBYTERIAN CHURCH

Another instance of a large denomination that has moved farther and farther away from commitment to biblical infallibility is the United Presbyterian Church. The General Assembly of what was then the Presbyterian Church in the U.S.A. adopted the famous "five points" in 1910. By this adoption the church committed itself to the following beliefs in an official sense: (1) the inspiration and inerrancy of the Holy Scriptures; (2) the virgin birth of Jesus Christ; (3) the vicarious and substitutionary atonement of Jesus; (4) the bodily resurrection and subsequent ascension of the Lord Jesus; and (5) the reality of the miracles of our Lord. In the 1920s the denomination was faced with a revolt against this sort of teaching. The Auburn Affirmation was put together and signed in 1924 by clergymen who decried the necessity for any ordinand who wished to be ordained to the Presbyterian ministry having to assent to these five fundamentals. All of these are taught in Scripture and all of them appear in the Westminster Confession of Faith. And every Presbyterian clergyman was required to assent to the system of doctrine contained in the Confession, not to mention his assent to the belief that the Scriptures are wholly truthful. The Presbyterian Church took the fateful step when its General Assembly decided that it was no longer necessary for a prospective clergyman in the denomination to assent to these propositions. Thus the denial of biblical infallibility opened the door wide to a denial of other basic doctrines of the faith and to further defection from the truth.

In the late nineteenth and early twentieth centuries no denomination stood more strongly for biblical inerrancy than the Presbyterian Church in the U.S.A. and particularly Princeton Theological Seminary. B. B. Warfield and Charles Hodge were stalwarts in defense of that doctrine. The action of the General Assembly in 1910 was due to the sustaining influence of men like those. But this was all swept away. In the 1930s J. Gresham Machen was defrocked because of his refusal to disassociate himself from the Independent Board for Presbyterian Foreign Missions. He founded Westminster Theological Seminary, which was designed to stand in the tradition of Warfield and Hodge. The church became increasingly inclusivistic, and was ready for the next step away from its heritage in the proposed Confession of 1967 that was finally adopted by the denomination. The late Oswald T. Allis, an old-fashioned evangelical, wrote about the proposed confession and its true meaning, a meaning that escaped even some of the most orthodox clergymen in the church. He mentioned the statement put forth by Dr. Edward A. Dowey, Jr., about the reasons why a new Confession was considered necessary. Dr. Downey said, "Church theology should not reflect every ripple of history and every wind of doctrine. But it must respond when it crosses over a major watershed such as the eighteenth century. It must be ready to respond again in the future to yet unknown but certainly profound changes that lie ahead."[10] Dr. Allis in his critique observed, "The obvious meaning of these words is that the church must accept evolution, higher criticism, development in theology as essential elements of modern culture. It must recognize that in doing so, it is taking only the first step toward a changing creed for a changing world. It is in this light that the New Confession should be regarded by the officers and members of the Presbyterian Church."[11]

Dr. Allis, in his appraisal of the New Confession, gives examples of Old and New Testament views that do violence to the doctrine of biblical infallibility. At the conclusion he observes:

> The above quotations [i.e., those referring to disavowals of what Scripture clearly affirms] are all taken from books published by the Westminster Press under the authority of the Board of Christian Education of the Presbyterian, now United Presbyterian Church in the U.S.A. They have been cited for the purpose of illustrating the meaning and implications of the words of the proposed Confession of 1967: "The church, therefore, has an obligation to approach the Scriptures with literary and historical understanding," which means, according to Dr. Dowey, to restate and interpret it in terms of evolution, of higher criticism, and of development in theology. Such teachings as these are in conflict with the Scriptures and with the doctrinal standards of our Church. It is the manifest purpose of the proposed Confession so to change our standards that such radical teachings will no longer be in conflict but in harmony with the Standards of the Church and be authorized and approved by them. In this way the forces which make for change, radical change in the doctrinal position of the Church will be greatly strengthened and the authority and trustworthiness of the Scriptures, on which our present Confession is wholly based, be correspondingly weakened and undermined. Do we wish our faith to rest on the changing opinions of men or on the unchanging and infallible Word of the living God? That is the issue which the Confession of 1967 sets before the Presbyterians of today.[12]

The United Presbyterian Church of late years has failed to produce any high-caliber evangelists, its overseas missionary force has shrunk by more than 50%, its Sunday school enrollment and its membership statistics for the church at large have begun to decline. What vigor there is springs from the faithful remnant of evangelical believers who labor on despite the existence of what one of their historians, Lefferts Loetscher, calls "the broadening church," which is nothing more or less than an inclusivist church that has in it all shades of theological opinions that are mutually contradictory. If the United Presbyterian Church were to lose its evangelical remnant, it is easy to predict that it would have a future similar to that of the Unitarian Universalist Association. At any rate the rejection of biblical infallibility by the church has produced a marked decline in the last half century.

THE UNITED CHURCH OF CHRIST

The United Church of Christ, a combination of the Congregational-Christian Churches and the Evangelical and Reformed Churches, adopted a statement of faith when its General Synod met in Oberlin, Ohio, July 8, 1959. John M. Morris wrote his reaction to the confession in *The Unitarian Register*. He said:

> Although we properly distrust such "creeds" on principle, liberals will find the new statement more unitarian than any theological pronouncement yet to come from an "orthodox" denomination.
>
> To be sure the unitarianism is largely negative. The trinity is not mentioned. Jesus is not called God or Saviour, but he is called Lord. God is an Infinite Spirit who is Jesus' father, but he is also the father of all men. Jesus is called a man. The Bible is not mentioned.
>
> In short, aside from the Madison Avenue language of the thing, there is nothing to roil the liberal Christians and much to annoy the conservative Christians in the United Church. It might, in fact, have been adopted by any Unitarian church of a century ago.
>
> If the statement does represent the current theology of the United Church, it makes one gesture of some of its members a little ridiculous. In view of the omission of the formula "God and Saviour," why do they remain so arrogantly self-righteous in approving exclusion of Unitarian and Universalist churches from the various Councils of Churches — for refusing to use those very words?[13]

The situation in the United Church of Christ is such that nothing more than this is needed to show how far that denomination has moved away from biblical inerrancy and how diluted its theology has become over the years. When Unitarians find themselves so much at home with their statement of faith, it should be no surprise to evangelical believers that when denominations adopt new statements of faith, they reflect the theological deterioration of the church and the movement away from basic Christian doctrines. In the words of the late William Culbertson, former president of the Moody Bible Institute: "The root from which all heresy springs is a faulty view of the inspiration and the inerrancy of the Word of God."

THE UNITED METHODIST CHURCH

The United Methodist Church probably is as far to the left in the theological spectrum as the United Church of Christ. This denomination does not have a single theological seminary that could be considered close to being evangelical. The Asbury Theological Seminary is an evangelical school, but it is not directly related to the denomination and is looked upon with suspicion by the denomination. The theological seminaries of the church have little use for Asbury. There is a small group of evangelicals who are emerging in this church, but they represent a remnant.

One of the signs of the times in Methodism is how far to the left some of its seminaries have gone. The Atlanta *Constitution*, on March 19, 1975, reported what was happening at the Candler School of Theology, which is a part of Emory University. This is the institution that had Thomas Altizer on its faculty. Altizer was the atheist intimately connected with the Death-of-God school of theology. The president of Emory defended him when questions were asked. Since then Altizer has left and was last teaching at the State University of New York at Stony Brook.

A Candler student for a doctorate, the Rev. K. Richard Robinson, filed a complaint with the Civil Rights Division of the Department of Health, Education and Welfare, charging violations of his civil rights and of his religious freedom. His story was graphic and enlightening. One of his professors, he stated, began every new class by saying, "Ladies and Gentlemen, I am an atheist." And then he would explain why he was. Another professor, according to Robinson, had as his only requirement for the course a term paper. He told the students that anyone holding to a fundamental belief in God could not get higher than a C minus. Another professor made some reference to the snake in Genesis and said, "The whole thing was just somebody's idea of a sexual hangup." When Robinson protested and offered a biblical viewpoint, he was told, "Why don't you go to Asbury where all the conservatives are?"[14] Some of his professors accused him of being mentally ill because he believed in God.

The *Constitution* stated that "a student friend of Robinson's, the Rev. Charles Stopford, who is married, has six children and pastors the Redan United Methodist Church, said he believes Robinson has received a 'raw deal' at the theology school. 'However,' he said, 'I disagree with Dick that the faculty must all be professing Christians.'" Robinson thinks the problem at Candler comes from younger faculty members who have come to the school from Yale.

Candler seems to have a preference for Yale men, according to Robinson, and the Yale men believe "there is no God except when people love one another — that's God — there's nothing after death." Robinson also said that when he told one of his professors he believed that all of the Bible was salvation history from Genesis to Revelation, the professor looked at him and said, "You know, you represent a brand of Southern fundamentalism that I thought had died out sixty years ago."[15]

It was at Emory that Altizer launched his contribution to the Death-of-God school of theology. When friends of Emory University asked questions about this, since the institution was supposed to be Christian, the president of the university defended Altizer. He believed and taught that the "death of God is an historical event, that God has died in our cosmos, in our history, in our Existence." He and William Hamilton joined in writing a book in which they said that the new theology hoped "to give support to those who have chosen to live as Christian atheists."

All of this is quite different from what historic Methodism has stood for, and John Wesley would be dismayed at what has transpired in the church he founded and the institutions that rose from the church. He would be astounded at the attitude of all too many clergymen and teachers toward the Bible he believed in and held to be without error.

I have said that once biblical infallibility is discarded it quickly leads to concessions that have little or nothing to do with error if we think of it as mistakes in dates, numbers, names, or scientific facts. Once inerrancy is lost, men go far beyond this kind of error and open the Bible wide to destructive tendencies that are of a different order entirely. This can be illustrated without difficulty outside of Methodism as well.

WILLIAM BARCLAY

William Barclay has written a commentary of the New Testament. He does not hold to biblical infallibility. In his discussion of the virgin birth in Matthew's Gospel Barclay says this: "It is a doctrine which our Church does not compel us to accept in the literal and physical sense . . . There is much more in this chapter than the *crude* fact that Jesus Christ was born of a virgin mother" (my italics).[16] Whether any church requires its clergy to accept the virgin birth or not is immaterial. Churches can and do err. And the record of the virgin birth has nothing whatever to do with error in the sense mentioned above. It is a story that purports to tell us how the birth of Jesus came about. From a scientific, biological standpoint the virgin birth *seems* impossible, but no reputable scientist can say that the virgin birth *is* impossible. Science is based on observation. The *most* that a true scientist can say about the virgin birth is this: "I do not know of any instance where it has occurred." What he cannot say is: "There can be no virgin birth." For him to make the latter statement would be to get outside the realm of science and into the area of the metaphysical. The scientist has no business going from science to metaphysics without telling his listener what he has done. He has ceased being a scientist as soon as he gets into metaphysics.

Moreover, the virgin birth involves the miraculous. Once miracles are denied, then, of course, the virgin birth becomes an impossibility. But even here a scientist can do no more than say, "I do not know of any evidence to support miracles." He cannot say that miracles are impossible without getting into metaphysics and out of science. Undoubtedly Matthew is saying clearly enough that he believes in miracles and that the virgin birth is a miracle. Here there is no textual or transmissional error in the common meaning of that term. It is a statement of fact. If Barclay wishes to deny this fact, he is free to do so, but he denies the miraculous at the same time. And to call the virgin birth "crude" exhibits a bias that tells us a great deal about his presuppositions.

ARCHBISHOP TEMPLE

Take the statement made by the late archbishop William Temple in his book *Nature, Man and God:* " . . . the atheist who is moved by love is moved by the spirit of God; an atheist who lives by love is saved by his faith in the God whose existence (under that Name) he denies."[17] This statement has nothing whatever to do with biblical infallibility, but it is the logical outgrowth of a denial of infallibility. Temple denies what the Bible affirms. Scripture teaches that the man who says he is an atheist is a fool. And there is salvation in none other than Jesus Christ. Yet Temple asserts that an atheist who denies Jesus can be saved. Temple's opinion judges that what Scripture teaches is untrue, and then writes his own Scripture in place of what has been denied.

THE BARCLAY-BRUCE COMMENTARY

Morton S. Enslin, in a commentary series edited by William Barclay and F. F. Bruce, wrote one volume entitled *Letters to the Churches* (1 and 2 Timothy and Titus). Speaking of the authorship, Enslin says, "Since he [the unknown author] is writing in the name of Paul, convinced that were Paul alive this is what he would have said, it is not surprising that he has adopted the innocent device to personal recipients. . . . To style the author a 'forger' is nonsense."[18] Enslin takes great liberties with Paul's letters to Timothy. First, they were written after Paul was dead; second, he says that this writer supposes that this is what Paul would have written if he were alive; third, the man who did this is not a forger. We must remember again that this has nothing whatever to do with error. Error is not in question here. What is in question is whether there was deception, fraud, and plain lying.

If Paul's letters to Timothy were penned by someone else who wanted to make people think they came from the apostle, it is nothing else than false witness. If it had been done in such a manner that the readers would know it was not Paul who wrote it, then the device was unnecessary. Whichever route one chooses to go, it turns out that if Paul did not write the letters, then they were written with the intention to deceive. In 2 Timothy Paul claims to be alone with Luke. He longs to see Timothy and asks that he bring Mark with him when he comes. He asks for his cloak, as well as his books and parchments. All of this makes the book incredible, if it indeed was written by someone other than Paul. It is exceedingly far-fetched to suppose that one writing in the name of Paul *after* his death would have Paul ask for cloak and books, and for Timothy to visit him. To accept the idea that someone else wrote it takes a credulity that is incredible. It is far easier to believe that it came from the pen of Paul, unless one adopts the naked unbelief and the darkness of spiritual intellect displayed by Enslin in this commentary.

What is perhaps most distressing of all is that William Barclay and F. F. Bruce are listed as the editors of this commentary series. That their names should be attached to a vehicle through which Enslin can infect others, and send forth this kind of pseudo-scholarship to the detriment of men's souls, is unfortunate.

In the same commentary series edited by Barclay and Bruce, Thomas Kepler authored a volume entitled *Dreams of the Future*

(Daniel and Revelation). Kepler says that the Book of Daniel "reinterprets history from the time of Nebuchadrezzar until the time of Judas Maccabeus and Antiochus IV, and written in 165 B.C. fits better into the scheme and purpose of Daniel than if the book were written in the period of Nebuchadrezzar, predicting history for the next 450 years. . . . In true apocalyptic fashion he puts himself and his message as though it was before 400 B.C., not to defraud but to impress people with his message which he feels is inspired by God to encourage the people of his day. . . . Who the writer of Daniel is we cannot know."[19]

Kepler here is not talking about error at all. He is not saying that the Book of Daniel has incorrect information, that its chronology is wrong, or that the writer got his sequences mixed up. He has gone far beyond the question of error. He has decided that the Book of Daniel was not written by Daniel although it claims to be and Jesus attributes the book to him. He is saying that by writing the book *after* the events took place rather than before makes it a better book. He says that the writer did not intend to defraud the people, only to impress them with the message "he feels is inspired by God," not a message he is sure is inspired by God.

Clearly if the book was written by someone other than Daniel, the writer, by using Daniel's name, thought he gained an advantage the book would not have had if his own name had been attached to it. He was telling lies for a good purpose. Since his intention was laudable, we can overlook the fraud. In other words, let us sin that grace may abound. Or to further the work of God by deceit and lying is legitimate, so long as the intention is good. Despite the disclaimer of the commentator that we cannot know who the author of Daniel was, there is another possibility. It was written by Daniel as the book itself claims and as Jesus attests. Why should we believe Kepler more than Scripture and regard him as a better commentator than Jesus Christ whom Scripture tells us was omniscient? In any event, Kepler has gone far beyond the realm of error as we think of it, which always happens sooner or later when biblical infallibility is abandoned.

One other illustration will suffice for our purpose here. Yet we must remember that it is possible to produce hundreds of illustrations that show that once biblical inerrancy is scrapped, those who no longer believe it go on from there to entertain opinions that eat at the heart of both revelation and inspiration, making both a shambles. George A. F. Knight wrote the volume *Prophets of Israel*

(1) Isaiah as part of a series edited by William Barclay and F. F. Bruce. He outdoes those who believe in two Isaiahs. He believes in three Isaiahs! In the introduction to his volume Knight says:

> 1. Chs 1-23, 28-34 are substantially from the hand of the prophet whose name we know as Isaiah, and who lived in Jerusalem in the second half of the eighth century B.C.
> 2. Chs 40-55 come from an anonymous prophet who . . . was alive about 540 B.C. as the exile in Babylonia drew to a close. We call him Second-Isaiah for convenience.
> 3. Chs 56-66 are the work of one or more unknown servants of God who belonged to the generation that returned to Jerusalem between 537 and about 515 B.C. . . . For convenience, once again, we call this section by the name Third-Isaiah, even though it is not from a single hand.

Knight goes on later to make this interesting observation:

> We need not hesitate to call the whole 66 chapters of our book by the name "Isaiah." The latter half of Isaiah is, we remember, anonymous. . . . In consequence we do not need to hesitate about agreeing with the words used by the disciple Philip (Acts 8:27-35). At the moment when he heard the Ethiopian eunuch read aloud from Isaiah 53 the words: "He was led as a sheep to the slaughter," Philip we are told, understood he was "reading Isaiah the prophet."[20]

Whatever Knight may say, if it is true that Isaiah did not write the latter half of the prophecy that goes under his name, then the time has come for us to give it another name by which the reader would know that it was not Isaiah who wrote it. What I have already said in my correspondence with Dr. Allen of the Southern Baptist Convention pertains here too. Many scholars have written other commentaries on Isaiah and they have said that Isaiah wrote the entire book. Why do we need to accept what Knight wrote and not what evangelical scholars have written when they favor the unity of the prophecy of Isaiah? Somehow liberal scholarship that denigrates and degrades Scripture seems more attractive to younger men and students who are not mature in the Christian faith. Somehow the spirit of unbelief seems to prevail when the choice must be made between what the Scripture itself declares and what scholars who disagree with Scripture say. Once again I draw attention to what really happens: liberal scholarship stands in judgment on Scripture and on God to the disadvantage of both.

RECAPITULATION

The time has come to recapitulate what has been said. This book is not about denominations and parachurch groups that are well along in their journey away from biblical inerrancy. It is written about the present struggle over inerrancy as that struggle is being fought among those who lay claim to the name "evangelical," "conservative," "conservative-evangelical," or even "neo-evangelical." The purpose of this chapter has been to show how the situation grows worse when infallibility has been surrendered. This was illustrated by examples of people affiliated with groups that abandoned inerrancy decades ago. The signs are there for all to read.

Evangelicals who have given up on biblical infallibility must be brought to see what follows after a denial of inerrancy. No doubt many of them really believe they will never surrender their belief in any other major doctrines of the Christian faith. Probably many of them would protest that they would never do what the people I have used for illustrations have done. But the abandonment of inerrancy opens the door wide to such deviations, and multitudes of others who felt the same way at one time have made these further concessions. And it has always been attended by a decline in Christian zeal and evangelistic outlook as well as in one's ethical life.

I do not deny that many of those who have given up infallibility are truly regenerated. In that sense they are my brethren. They are to be found among my former colleagues at Fuller Seminary for whom I have the deepest affection. They are in the Missouri Synod, the Evangelical Covenant Church, the Southern Baptist Convention, the Evangelical Theological Society, and the American Scientific Affiliation. They are to be found in other evangelical denominations, Christian institutions, and parachurch groups. I truly believe that many of them would rather die than repudiate biblical truth having to do with salvatory data and with Scripture that involves matters of practice. But the weight of history and all the evidence it supplies leads me to no other conclusion than that even if these friends are able to stop at this point, those who follow after them will not stop where they have stopped. The second generation will follow through on the implications contained in the abandonment of inerrancy and will make concessions on questions that pertain to matters of faith and practice as well as to matters of history, science, and chronology. When inerrancy goes, it opens a small hole in the dike, and if that hole is not closed, the levee will collapse and the whole land will be overrun with the waters of unbelief not unlike that exhibited by Bultmann and theological liberalism.

[1] *Newsweek,* June 26, 1967. Copyright 1967 by Newsweek, Inc. All rights reserved. Reprinted by permission.

[2] James A. Pike, *If This Be Heresy* (New York: Dell, 1969), p. 72.

[3] Ibid., p. 73.

[4] *Triumph,* January, 1968.

[5] *Religious News Service,* August 30, 1968.

[6] *A Christian Handbook on Vital Issues* (New Haven: Leader, 1973), p. 78.

[7] Ibid., p. 79.

[8] Ibid.

[9] Ibid.

[10] Oswald T Allis, *The Proposed Confession of 1967* (Philadelphia: The Presbyterian and Reformed Publishing Co., n.d.), p. 1.

[11] Ibid.

[12] Ibid., pp. 11, 12.

[13] *The Unitarian Register,* November, 1959. Reprinted in *A Christian Handbook,* p. 624.

[14] *The Atlanta Constitution,* March 19, 1975.

[15] Ibid.

[16] William Barclay, *The First Three Gospels* (Philadelphia: Westminster, 1967).

[17] William Temple, *Nature, Man and God* (Toronto: Macmillan, 1934), p. 416.

[18] Morton S. Enslin, *Letters to the Churches* (Nashville: Abingdon, n.d.), p. 34.

[19] Thomas Kepler, *Dreams of the Future* (Nashville: Abingdon, 1963), pp. 33, 34.

[20] George A. F. Knight, *Prophets of Israel* (Nashville: Abingdon, 1961), p. 38.

9

Discrepancies in Scripture

I do not wish to dismiss the questions that critics have raised about errors in Scripture with a casual wave of my hand. However, I do not think the problem areas constitute a threat to biblical infallibility nor do I think that there are any insoluble difficulties. This does not mean that I can provide a ready solution to every datum raised by those who oppose inerrancy. I can say, however, that a multitude of what formerly were difficulties have been solved, so that the detractors have had to back water again and again. But as each apparent discrepancy is resolved, another objection is raised. Although in hundreds of cases criticisms of Scripture have been shown to be unfounded, those who refuse to believe in inerrancy never seem to be satisfied. Why is this so? Does it not constitute a frame of mind that *wants* to disbelieve? Does it reflect a viewpoint that says in effect, "I will not believe what the Scripture teaches about itself until *every* objection has been answered to my satisfaction"? Does not this tell us something about the nature of man who, though he may be regenerated, yet retains strong characteristics of the old nature so that unbelief crops up again and again? May not the real difficulty be a want of biblical faith rather than a want of evidence?

How do people like myself who believe in inerrancy answer the claims of those who espouse errancy when they say we need inerrancy as a security blanket and that we believe that to give up this notion would be to scrap the entire Christian faith? I do not know anyone who believes in inerrancy who says that if one error were found in Scripture, he would then give up the Christian faith in its entirety. Nor do I know any evangelical believer in inerrancy who uses it as a security blanket. He accepts it, not because it makes him feel comfortable, but because it is taught in Scripture, just as the deity of Christ, the virgin birth of Jesus, and the bodily resurrection of our Lord from the dead are taught in Scripture. Moreover, he has the witness of the Holy Spirit to which, for example, the Westminster Confession makes reference: "Yet notwithstanding, our full persuasion and assurance of the infallible truth and divine authority thereof, is from the inward work of the Holy Spirit bearing witness by and with the Word in our hearts."

ADOLPH SAPHIR ON THE VERACITY OF SCRIPTURE

I cannot deal with the whole range of alleged discrepancies or errors in the Bible, nor do I need to. But there are a few points that can and should be made so that believers in inerrancy can know they have a strong case, not a weak one. The first point that should be made concerns past history. Adolph Saphir in his book *The Divine Unity of Scripture* says, "The evidence for the accurate veracity of the history of the Bible is accumulating day by day, and comes to us from all sources, and, if I may say so, from independent and impartial and, oftentimes, hostile sources. I believe that it is all actual history. . . . At the same time I must confess that it is difficult — that it is impossible — to realize it, unless there is given to us grace. The Scripture history does not demand credit merely. The Scripture demands faith."[1] There were those who thought that Abraham was a mythical figure or, if historical, he came from a backward and uneducated people. Saphir observes, "Professor Sayce before the Victoria Institute in 1889 said 'How highly educated this old world was we are just beginning to learn. . . . It has long been tacitly assumed by the critical school that writing was not only a rare art in Palestine before the age of David, but was practically unknown. . . . But this assumption can no longer be maintained. Long before the Exodus, Canaan had its libraries and its scribes, its schools and literary men."[2]

Skeptics once believed that the census of Cyrenius who was governor of Syria was an error on the part of Luke. Now we know that he was accurate. The 1967 *New Catholic Encyclopedia,* which was quoted earlier, says flat-footedly, "Darius the Mede did not succeed Balsas-sar" (i.e., the Belshazzar of Daniel 5:30). Recent evidence indicates that Darius the Mede can be identified with Gubaru whom Cyrus appointed as governor of Babylonia after the death of Ugbaru, who survived his brilliant capture of Babylon by only three weeks. Gu-baru the Mede (Darius) continued in office until 521 B.C., although Cyrus himself seems to have assumed the title of king of Babylon within two years after Gubaru's appointment.

There was a time when the skeptics doubted what the Bible said about the Hittites. It was not believed that such a people ever existed. Today no one in his right mind would make this kind of statement. But how was it possible for "scholars" to have asserted this in years gone by? Two things may be said. First, there was no evidence at the time for their existence external to the Bible itself. Second, it shows that the skeptics did not believe the Bible unless what the Bible said could be supported by external evidence. This meant that the Bible was not looked upon as a reliable source of information. It demonstrated the fact that such people came to the Bible with a predisposition to disbelieve what could not be dem-onstrated outside of Scripture. Thus another authority was set above the Bible and became the critic of Scripture instead of letting Scrip-ture sit over other authorities.

ALLEGED ERRORS BY ROBERT MOUNCE

A recent example of alleged discrepancies in the Bible by an evangelical may be seen from the article "Clues to Understanding Biblical Accuracy" written by Robert H. Mounce, a former student of mine who was at that time, but is no longer, an associate professor of Biblical Literature and Greek at Bethel College, St. Paul, Min-nesota. He authors the column "Here's My Answer" for *Eternity,* which published the article. Dr. Mounce cast his vote in favor of limited inerrancy. His conclusion is indicative of this: "Are there errors in the Bible? Certainly not, so long as we are talking in terms of the purpose of its authors and the acceptable standards of precision of that day. . . . It is a counsel of despair to hold that all such variations (as e.g. the 23,000 and the 24,000 of 1 Cor. 10:8 and Num. 25:9) did not also exist in the autographs. For the purpose that Paul had in mind it simply made no difference. His concern was to warn against immorality, not to give a flawless performance in statistics."[3] What Dr. Mounce is saying should be clear enough. Paul was using this incident to make a spiritual point. The use of the statistic was incidental to the point he was making. The fact that he was wrong in the use of the number constitutes no problem. It was not a flawless performance to be sure, but the truth shines through the error.

JESUS AS DAVID'S SON

Dr. Mounce cites four examples of error in the Bible. One can only suppose that he has chosen these four because he thinks they are foolproof. In the interest of my thesis, we should take a look at his allegations. The first one is taken from the life of Jesus in the Synoptic Gospels where He engages in a discussion with the Pharisees about David's Son. He specifies Matthew 22:42 where, according to Matthew, Jesus says, "What do you think of the Christ? Whose son is he?" "Luke places a different set of words in Jesus' mouth; 'How can they say that the Christ is David's son? (Luke 20:41).' From a strictly literal standpoint Jesus must have said one or the other or neither." And he concludes that "literalistic inerrancy has already begun to shade off into a divine adequacy in terms of the purpose of the author."[4]

Unfortunately, Dr. Mounce has failed to do justice to the Scripture in this case. His argument that "Jesus must have said one or the other or neither" leaves out an alternative. Jesus could have said both of these things without there being any problem. Let me illustrate it by bringing the Scriptures into harmony at this point. The solution is that both what Matthew writes and what Luke writes were part of the total conversation. And much more than appears in either or both accounts may have been said. But what is said by both authors does not contradict each other. "Now while the Pharisees were gathered together, Jesus asked them a question, saying, 'What do you think of the Christ? Whose son is he?' They said to him, 'The son of David' " (Matt. 22:41). "But he said to them, 'How can they say that the Christ is David's son?' " (Luke 20:41).

It becomes apparent that Matthew is quoting one part of the conversation and Luke another. The part quoted by Luke follows closely after the words of Jesus in Matthew. Then each writer goes on from there and makes the clinching point with the quotation from the Psalms, "The Lord said to my Lord, Sit at my right hand, till I make thy enemies a stool for thy feet." Thus there is no error, no incongruence, no real problem of any kind, at least not in the words of Scripture.

THE CASE OF THE MOLTEN SEA

The measurements of the molten sea as described in 2 Chronicles 4:2 is the second problem that bothers Mounce. He writes the following: "The molten sea is said to be 'round, ten cubits from brim to brim . . . and a line of thirty cubits measured its circumference.' Since the circumference of a circle is pi x D (3.14159 times the diameter), it would be impossible for a *round* vessel to have a diameter of ten and a circumference of thirty. . . . The rough measurements of antiquity do not have to conform to space age requirements. In the culture of that day the measurement was not only adequate, but also 'inerrant.' In our determination of what constitutes an error we must judge the accuracy of Scripture according to the prevailing standards of the time."[5] I must say that in the culture of that day, or of any day, the figures are wrong if the Scripture is giving us this information the way Dr. Mounce understands it. Two and two make four, and they did in Solomon's time, just as they do in Mounce's time. To say that two and two make five and then excuse it because it was said three thousand years ago in a different culture hardly makes good sense. Now how do we respond to Mounce's allegation?

First, let us agree that the people of that day may have been ignorant of that branch of mathematics called algebra. I am not saying this was so. I merely grant it for convenience' sake. Thus they did not know about *pi* or its value. But I cannot agree with the implication contained in the phrase "the rough measurements of antiquity." A cubit was a cubit was a cubit. It had a specific length. And any carpenter who wanted to lay out a cubit five times or ten times or a hundred times would have produced as accurate a measurement as any carpenter who has a yardstick in his possession is capable of doing today. I can only conclude that those who constructed the molten sea were capable of measuring what they had constructed. And they measured the diameter as well as the circumference. And what they recorded was absolutely accurate — not just a rough measurement. How could this have come about?

A cubit is equal to eighteen inches. A handbreadth is equal to four inches. These are the significant data. Ten cubits equal 180 inches. Thirty cubits equals 540 inches. But we must remember that the wall of the molten sea was a handbreadth in thickness. This means that it was four inches wide from the exterior of the vessel to the interior where the liquid filled it. What happened was simple indeed. When the diameter was measured, the measurement was taken from the outside perimeter. And it was ten cubits or 180 inches. But when they used their measuring instrument for the circumference, they did not measure it from the outside but from the inside. It measured 30 cubits, or 540 inches. Now see what this does. If we allow for the eight inches for the two sides of the molten sea, it means that the diameter was 180 inches, less eight inches, or 172 inches. And when 172 is multiplied by 3.14 (the value of pi) the result is 540.08, which is quite accurate. In other words, when diameter is measured the same way the circumference was measured, there is no discrepancy at all. Dr. Mounce is wrong and Scripture is right. And we should expect that it would be, for they had adequate measuring instruments so that nothing was left to chance or to guesstimate. The diagram below will make the computation plain.

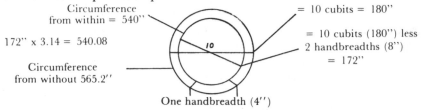

Circumference from within = 540"

$172" \times 3.14 = 540.08$

Circumference from without 565.2"

= 10 cubits = 180"

= 10 cubits (180") less 2 handbreadths (8") = 172"

One handbreadth (4")

DAVID AND ABIATHAR THE HIGH PRIEST

Dr. Mounce's third example of error is adduced as follows: "In Mark 2:26 Jesus refers to David entering the house of God and eating the bread of the Presence 'when Abiathar was high priest.' But in I Samuel 21:1ff. it is Ahimelech, the *son* of Abiathar who was priest at that time. Most explanations of this 'mistake' are highly fanciful and much harder to accept than the more obvious possibility that no greater degree of precision should be required."[6] Dr. Mounce is mistaken at several points, and the difficulty he alludes to lies in his own imagination. In the first place, he is mistaken when he says that the Ahimelech of 1 Samuel 21:1 was the son of Abiathar. The reverse is true. Abiathar was the son of Ahimelech, who was the son of Ahitub. Abiathar succeeded his father as high priest after Ahimelech had been murdered. Abiathar did have a son named Ahimelech. The son was named after his grandfather, the father of Abiathar. But to confuse the first Ahimelech with the grandson is an error. Mark 2:26 does not say that Abiathar was present when the incident involving his father occurred. He may have been. Like some other commentators, Matthew Henry suggests this concerning Mark's account: "This, it is said, David did in the days of *Abiathar the High-Priest;* or *just before* the days of Abiathar, who immediately succeeded Ahimelech his father in the pontificate, and, it is probable, was at that time his father's deputy, or assistant, in the office; and he it was who escaped the massacre, and brought the ephod to David."[7]

Haley says that the expression in Mark "may denote merely that Abiathar was acting as his father's sägan or substitute. Or, since Abiathar was, from his long association with King David, much more famous than his father, his name, although he was not yet high-priest, may be used here by a kind of historical anticipation."[8] Robertson suggests that "Apparently Ahimelech, not Abiathar, was high priest at this time. It is possible that both father and son bore both names (I Sam. 22:20; II Sam. 8:17; I Chron. 18:16), Abiathar mentioned though both involved."[9]

Mark 2:26 *does not* say that David dealt with Abiathar. It can be read that the incident occurred during the times of Abiathar who was high priest. But his identification as high priest in this manner does not mean that he was high priest when the event took place. It is not uncommon to say, for example, that a certain event took place during the times of John F. Kennedy who was president of the United States. But this does not mean that the specific incident referred to happened *while* Kennedy was president. The words "president of the United States" do no more than identify the man who was president and speak of his times, not necessarily of the period when he was president. To call the various explanations "fanciful" and "harder to accept than the obvious possibility that no greater degree of precision should be required" tells us that Mounce is looking hard to find an error, and if this is the best he can come up with, his case is weak indeed. If there is any possible alternative, the Word of God should be given the benefit of the doubt.

THE CASE OF THE MISSING THOUSAND

The last problem Dr. Mounce mentions is the difference in numbers where Paul in 1 Corinthians reports that "23,000 fell in a single day" while the account in Numbers 25:9 says "24,000." Mounce argues, "We need not make ourselves ridiculous by following the suggestion that the other fatalities took place during the night. It is a council of despair to hold that all such variations did not also exist in the autographs." In plain English, he is saying he has found a demonstrable error in which one writer reported a figure that was a thousand less than the other. How do we handle this one?

First, I think we can assume that there are no manuscript problems here. C. I. Scofield does suggest in this connection the possibility of a scribal error involving transmission, since the Hebrew numbers can be easily confused because of the way they were written. It is also Scofield who suggests the possibility that Paul gives the number of deaths in "one day," a possibility that Mounce discards by suggesting it is ridiculous. There have been more difficult problems resolved by such "ridiculous" possibilities. But there are other answers that are very satisfactory. One of them comes from the pen of John Calvin:

> But although they differ about the numbers [i.e., between the Pauline account and the Mosaic account], it is easy to reconcile their statements. For it is not unheard of, when there is no intention of making an exact count of individuals, to give an approximate number. For example, there were those whom the Romans called the *Centumviri*, The Hundred, when, in fact there were one hundred and two of them. Therefore, since about twenty-four thousand were destroyed by the hand of the Lord, in other words, over twenty-three thousand, Moses gives the upper limit, Paul the lower, and so there is really no discrepancy. This story is to be found in Numbers 25:9.[10]

Calvin, of course, is saying what we all know to be common today. Let's suppose the actual number of people who died was about 23,500. It would be both easy and correct for one to use the 24,000 figure and the other the 23,000 figure, since both were speaking in round numbers. And indeed there is no error unless Mounce wants to insist that the writers of Scripture should not use round numbers; or for him to impose his own intentions on them by saying that Paul was mistaken in using the 24,000 figure simply because more than 23,000 died is self-defeating.

Leon Morris, a respectable scholar, provides still another possibility that neatly handles the problem. He says that "judgment came in the form of a plague, and twenty-four thousand people perished (Nu. xxv. 9). Paul speaks of twenty-three thousand. Obviously both use round numbers, and in addition Paul may be making some allowance for those slain by the judges (Nu. xxv. 5)."[11] A careful reading of the account in Numbers makes this a distinct possibility. But whether one chooses Calvin's or Morris's solution, there is an answer to the problem that will satisfy anyone who is willing to look at it fairly and will recognize that it was something that we could easily do today without any intention of making an error or being thought of by those who read us as having made an error. The error appears only to those who read the account superficially and have not probed into the real possibilities.

DANIEL FULLER AND THE MUSTARD SEED

In an earlier chapter I mentioned the views of Professor Daniel Fuller of Fuller Theological Seminary. In his public lectures, one of the examples he constantly injects to show that there are errors in the "nonrevelational" portions of Scripture is found in Matthew 13:31, 32. Jesus says, "The kingdom of heaven is like a grain of mustard seed which a man took and sowed in his field; it is the smallest of all seeds. . . ." Dr. Fuller alleges that botanically we know that there are smaller seeds than the mustard seed. And that is true. Then he argues that Jesus accommodated Himself to the ignorance of the people to whom He was speaking, since they believed this.[12] But it constitutes an error, and the presence of one error invalidates the claim to biblical inerrancy. The *American Commentary* says of this passage that it was popular language, and it was the intention of the speaker to communicate the fact that the mustard seed was "the smallest that his hearers were accustomed to sow."[13] And indeed this may well be the case. In that event there was no error. If the critics of Scripture wish to use the intention of the writer, this is one place it can be used in favor of inerrancy.

Matthew Henry in his commentary has it read, the mustard seed "which is one of the least of all seeds." From the Greek it is not clear that Jesus was saying that the mustard seed is the smallest of all the seeds on the earth. He was saying it is less than all the seeds. What must be determined is what the words "all the seeds" mean here. If Jesus was talking about the seeds commonly known to the people of that day, the effect of His words was different from what they would have been if He was speaking of all seeds on the earth. When the possibility exists for a translation that fulfills the intention of the speaker and does not constitute error, that passage is to be preferred above one that does the opposite. And when two possibilities exist, why should not the benefit of any doubt be given in favor of the one that fulfills what the Scripture teaches about inerrancy? To choose the other route leaves behind the implication that one is seeking out error and trying to establish it on flimsy grounds.

DEWEY BEEGLE ON INERRANCY

I turn now to the work of Dewey N. Beegle entitled *Scripture,*

Tradition, and Infallibility, published by the William B. Eerdmans Publishing Company. This is the same publishing house that printed Kuitert's book, *Understandest Thou What Thou Readest?* which constitutes a frontal attack on biblical infallibility, as does Beegle's book. Beegle has an evangelical background, but his commitment to the fallibility of the Bible has become a passion for him, and he wants to share this insight and to convince everyone he can that the Bible is indeed errant. Even a most casual reading of the book shows that Beegle is out for the kill. But in fairness it must be admitted that this volume, which is a revision, is a substantial improvement on his earlier book, *The Inspiration of Scripture.* In approaching the new work we should remember that the first book drew impassioned criticism from some sources and enthusiastic praise from others. The heart of Beegle's argument is that inerrancy and infallibility apply only to God and to His Son, Jesus Christ. Inasmuch as Scripture has been given, transmitted, and interpreted through human agencies, it is bound to bear the marks of that humanity. Nevertheless, God is not restricted by this self-imposed limitation. Dewey Beegle puts it this way: "Difficult though it may be to understand, God chose to make his authority relevant to his creatures by means that necessitate some element of fallibility."[14] Despite this, Scripture is sufficiently accurate and trustworthy to accomplish the divine purpose because the Holy Spirit drives home God's message with authority.

It is worth our time to pause to reflect on Beegle's unique statement that constitutes the heart of his viewpoint. He says that God communicated "by means that necessitate some element of fallibility." In other words, it was impossible for God to communicate infallibly. If God could not communicate infallibly, then He could not do so on those matters having to do with salvation either. There must be theological error along with theological truth. But if God could communicate infallible theological truth, why is it necessary that there be some element of fallibility in the other parts? Why could He not secure the other parts of Scripture from fallibility just as He did the parts that are infallible?

Moreover, Beegle says that "God *chose* to make his authority relevant" by this fallible means. Patently, if God is sovereign and God chose to do this, then God could have chosen *not* to do this. He could have chosen to do it through a Scripture that is entirely infallible. Beegle is saying that God, who had choice, chose to make Himself known fallibly and thus God chose to include in Scripture that which is in error. But nowhere does Beegle tell us what evidence he has for his assertion that God chose to make Scripture fallible unless he is saying, that because he thinks there are errors in Scripture, he must then define inspiration and infallibility based on the phenomena of Scripture. If he does this, he is faced with the uncomfortable datum that the phenomena of Scripture include the assertion that all Scripture is profitable. And if error is profitable, we are talking nonsense. Logically and epistemologically, Beegle doesn't have a leg to stand on.

Professor F. F. Bruce gives the book this commendation: "Dr. Beegle's first edition was largely a demolition job. Here he has rearranged and amplified his material, given the work a new and more comprehensive title, and struck a more positive note. I endorse as emphatically as I can his depracating of a Maginot-line mentality where the doctrine of Scripture is concerned."[15] Apparently F. F. Bruce thinks that for one to hold to biblical inerrancy is to display a "Maginot-line mentality."

Beegle neatly hits J. I. Packer over the head with a meat cleaver as well as all others who believe in inerrancy. He says, "Packer's sentiments are commendable (in his book *'Fundamentalism' and the Word of God*), but he and his fellow inerrancists have so completely fused their emotions and sense of mission with their definition of God's honor that they find it impossible to admit an error when the evidence clearly points in that direction."[16] He himself is not exactly without bias, and it could be said that his own emotions and sense of mission so dominate him that he is incapable of clear thinking. One of the most illuminating of Professor Beegle's many statements about errors in Scripture has to do with Pekah in the Old Testament. But before we look at this particular case study, a word of background is in order.

THE FAMOUS CASE OF PEKAH

Marcus Dods in his book *The Bible: Its Origin and Nature* states, "Professor Sayce, one of the most conservative living critics, tells us that 'Assyrian inscriptions have shown that the chronology of the book of Kings is hopelessly wrong.'"[17] Dods quotes this approvingly and is in agreement with this opinion. It is true that the chronology in the *Kings* was a problem for many years. It appeared impossible to reconcile the difficulties arising from a comparison of the records that came from the archives of Judah and of Israel. In addition, it seemed impossible to reconcile these with the records of the secular kingdoms of the days. Edwin R. Thiele wrestled with this problem in his doctoral dissertation. In 1951 his book *The Mysterious Numbers of the Hebrew Kings* was published. It brought order out of chaos as Thiele managed to reconcile the chronologies in such a way as to enforce the claim to accuracy of the biblical texts. Unfortunately, he ran into an apparently irresolvable problem in the case of Pekah. It is this one that Beegle uses as a *cause célèbre* in his latest work, and from it he argues strongly that he has found the most positive proof of errancy in Scripture. So we should take a hard look at this problem to see whether it is really as damning as Beegle claims it to be. We do so with the statements of Beegle in mind: "Moreover, it should be noted that Thiele's revised theory does not lessen the problem for the inerrancists. 2 Kings 15:27 states quite unambiguously that Pekah reigned in Samaria twenty years after he became king of Israel, and this is precisely what did not happen."[18] "There is no other way out but to admit that the erroneous details of 15:27, 32; 16:1 were in the original compilation of 2 Kings."[19] I should add that I met with Dr. Beegle in his apartment at the Biblical Seminary years ago and was informed by him that Thiele at that time confessed that the problem connected with Pekah constituted an error in Scripture. Beegle had this in writing from Dr. Thiele according to his testimony.

Since that time Edwin R. Thiele has published an article entitled "Coregencies and Overlapping Reigns Among the Hebrew Kings" in the *Journal of Biblical Literature*. In this article Dr. Thiele has given the key to the Pekah problem. And Beegle's claim that Scripture has erred falls to the ground. Scripture assigns a twenty-year reign to Pekah. Where Beegle went wrong was to assume that 2 Kings 15:27 was intended to mean that Pekah reigned twenty years in Samaria. At first glance, it appears to say that. But ironically the key to the problem falls in line with one of the claims of the historical-critical school, which argues that we must ask what the writer intended to say.

Thiele lays down this principle with respect to the reigns of some of the kings as given in the Book of Kings. He says, "The synchronism for the accession is that of the commencement of the sole reign, but the datum for the length of reign covers both the years of sole reign and also the overlapping years with another king."[20] This was true not only in the case of Pekah, but it was also true of Omri (1 Kings 16:23), Jehoshaphat (1 Kings 22:41, 42), and Jeroboam (2 Kings 14:23). We know that Pekah actually reigned in Samaria for eight years. We know that his successor was Hoshea who reigned nine years before Israel was overthrown by the king of Assyria in 722 B.C. Thus, the reign of Pekah ended 732/31 B.C. This is important, because if Pekah began his reign in Samaria and if the reign lasted twenty years, then he was king until 720 B.C. and this was two years after the kingdom of Israel had been taken captive. This would have allowed no time for the reign of Hoshea under whom the kingdom was taken away by the Assyrians. And if Beegle's arguments are correct, then indeed there is a serious chronological error in Scripture.

We know that when Pekah began his sole reign over Samaria in 740 B.C., he overlapped Menahem ten years and Pekahiah two years. This means that the year 752 B.C. was the beginning date for Pekah, who overlapped two kings for twelve years and was sole ruler for eight more years after that. When the writer of the Book of Kings set down the chronology he did two things: first, he gave as the accession date for Pekah the year he became sole ruler; second, he gave the total number of years for Pekah's reign as twenty, and included the twelve years when he was coregent with Menahem and Pekahiah. This was no extraordinary procedure, nor did it comprise an error. It was the same style used in connection with the other three kings we mentioned above.

Thiele concludes that there are no longer any problems connected with the chronology of the Kings and that the biblical data are shown to be accurate. He writes, "An understanding of the application of these principles in these instances, and a recognition of the overlapping reigns thus called for, clears up the once seemingly irreconcilable contradictions in the regnal data, and provides a pattern of reigns which can only be recognized as constituting the original arrangement of years for the rulers of Israel and Judah at this period."[21] All of this is particularly interesting because Beegle is quite critical of Clark Pinnock who, in his book *Biblical Revelation — The Foundation of Christian Theology*, said, "The supposedly 'incontrovertible' evidence for biblical errors is, upon careful scrutiny, not that at all. Without wishing to minimize any of them, we regard none of them as insuperable...." Then, in speaking of Pinnock, Beegle adds his *coup de grace:* "In his chapter on the phenomena of Scripture he ignores the Pekah problem entirely, but had he considered it, still the evidence would not have been 'insuperable.'. . . . While admitting that 'minor imperfections' in our present Bibles 'do not obscure the message of Scripture,' Pinnock feels constrained to add, 'But unless we wish to blame God for man's mistakes, we have an obligation to try to show that these discrepancies are not original errors.' With this basic premise there is no possibility of honestly facing the evidence. The issue has been settled beforehand, and thus it is pious rhetoric to talk about 'careful scrutiny' and being 'open to all facts'."[22] And to all of this, it may be added that it is now time for Beegle to look at the facts and admit that he was mistaken.

PETER'S DENIAL OF JESUS

Beegle, among the other examples of biblical errors, uses the one about Peter and his denial of the Lord Jesus. This illustration is important because it is an incident that is spoken of in all four Gospels. Had the question arisen only in connection with one gospel account, it would take on a different dimension. But when one has to reconcile four different accounts, it becomes far more complex. Beegle correctly states that in Mark 14:30 Jesus says to Peter, "Truly, I say to you, this very night, before the cock crows twice, you will deny me three times." Then in verse 72 of the same chapter the fulfillment is recorded: "And immediately the cock crowed a second time. And Peter remembered how Jesus had said to him, 'Before the cock crows twice, you will deny me three times.' " However, both Matthew's account (26:34, 74, 75) and Luke's account (22:34, 60, 61) report that Jesus said, "Before the cock crows you will deny me three times."[23] From Mark's account there had to be two crowings of the cock. From the accounts of Matthew and Luke the words "twice," "second time," and "twice" are omitted. Beegle asks the question: "But what essential difference is there if the other Gospel writers, Matthew and Luke, follow the general tradition of the cock's crowing just once? (whereas Mark says the cock crowed twice). All three Gospels contain the historical features necessary to convey the truth of the matter: the prediction of denial and Peter's boast, the fulfillment of the prediction, and Peter's remorse on remembering the words of Jesus."[24] It is the same old story: never mind the details that are in error; what the writers intended to say comes through despite the errancy of the divergent accounts. How do we respond to this challenge?

In 1965 I was in touch with J. M. Cheney of Oakland, California. This man had labored long and hard to reconcile problems connected with some of the apparent discrepancies in the New Testament. He provided me with the answer to this particular problem. I will reproduce only a portion of the material he sent me. He stated that Peter received two different warnings about denying Jesus and in each warning he was to deny Jesus three times. The first crowing of the cock would occur after the first three denials and the second crowing of the cock would occur after the sixth denial. He then wove together the accounts of the four Gospels to show how they fit and to conclude that there are no errors.

Here is the story from the beginning, the superscript numbers identifying the various Gospel writers (with [1] for Matt., [2] for Mark, [3] for Luke, [4] for John).

[4] The maid who kept the door said to Peter, "Are not you also one of this man's disciples?" He said, "I am not."

Now the servants and officers, because it was cold,[3] had kindled [4] a charcoal fire [3]in the middle of the courtyard, [4]and they were standing and warming themselves. Peter also was with them, standing and warming himself [2]at the fire, [3]and when they sat down together, [1]he sat [3]among [1]the guards to see the end.

. . . [4]Now Simon Peter [1]was sitting [2]below, in the courtyard [1]outside, [2]and [4]standing and warming himself. They said to him, "Are not you also one of his disciples?" He denied it and said, "I am not."

[3]Then [2]one of the maids of the high priest, seeing Peter warming himself, [3]and gazing at him as he sat in the light, said, "This man also was with [1]the Galilean." And [2]she [3]came up to him, and said, "You also were with [2]the Nazarene, Jesus." [1]But he denied it before them all saying, [3]"Woman, I do not now him: [2]I neither know nor understand what you mean." And he went out into the gateway; and the cock crowed.

YET THREE DENIALS MORE!

[1]And when he went out to the porch [3]a little later, [1]another maid (RSV says *maid*, Greek says only *female* [Matt. 26:71] saw him, and she said to the bystanders, "This fellow was with Jesus of Nazareth." [3]And someone else saw him and said, "You also are one of them!" But Peter [1]again denied it with an oath, [3]"Man, I am not! [1]I do not know the man."

[2]And the maid saw him, and began again to say to the bystanders, "This man is one of them!" But again he denied it.

[3]And after an interval of about an hour still another insisted,

saying, "Certainly this man also was with him; for he is a Galilean." [4]One of the servants of the high priest, a kinsman of the man whose ear Peter had cut off, asked, "Did I not see you in the garden with him?" [2]And again the bystanders [1]came up and said to Peter, "Certainly you are also one of them, [2]for you are a Galilean — [1]your accent betrays you."

[2]But [1]then [4]Peter again denied it, and [1]began to invoke a curse on himself and to swear, "I do not know [2]this man of whom you speak. [3]Man, I do not know what you are saying!"

And immediately, while he was still speaking, the cock crowed [2]a second time. [3]And the Lord turned and looked at Peter. And Peter remembered the word of the Lord, How [2]Jesus had said to him, [3]Before the cock crows today, you will deny me three times". . . . [2]"Before the cock crows twice you will deny me three times." And he broke down, and went out and wept bitterly.

The longest paragraph in the above gathers together all the material related to the final denial in all four accounts. But none of it is incompatible; the accounts only supplement each other. A number of accusers evidently surrounded Peter at the climax. Note also that denials four and five are credibly accounted for and make the seeming contradictions in the Synoptics understandable.

WHAT THEN IS PROVED?

Certainly, to begin with, the honesty and accuracy of all four evangelists. Their testimony agrees with a completeness and precision that never marked the word of four witnesses in a courtroom. Yet it is plain they were not coached in that testimony, as is also the fact that they testified independently of each other.

BEEGLE AND ESSENTIAL MATTERS OF FAITH

Now I return to Beegle and the issue of biblical discrepancies. Previously I alleged that once biblical inerrancy is scrapped, it inevitably leads to further concessions that strike, at last, at the heart of the Christian faith. Beegle has stated that "in all essential matters of faith and practice, therefore, Scripture is authentic, accurate, and trustworthy."[25] But by claiming there are errors in Scripture he has gone beyond that and has denied that in essential matters Scripture can be trusted. Earlier in his book he quotes Machen in regard to the virgin birth. Machen said, "One thing at least is clear: even if the belief in the virgin birth is not necessary to every Christian, it is certainly necessary to Christianity. And it is necessary to the corporate witness of the church." Then Beegle adds his own conclusion: "Machen has shown the impossibility of prescribing a minimal core of biblical events to which assent must be given before saving faith is possible. God recognizes the sincere doubts of men and he undoubtedly saves men who do not have enough faith to believe certain teachings of Scripture."[26] Unfortunately, Beegle does not list the "certain teachings of Scripture" that men can doubt and still have saving faith. Nor does he list what the "minimal core of biblical events" are "to which assent must be given before saving faith is possible." But surely the resurrection of Jesus Christ from the dead must be considered one of the essentials of saving faith if 1 Corinthians 15:1-5 tells us the truth and if the Acts of the Apostles, which majors on the resurrection, is valid.

THE RESURRECTION AND WILLI MARXSEN

Beegle treats the case of Willi Marxsen, professor of New Testament at the University of Munster, West Germany. Marxsen was charged with heresy by the Evangelical Church of Westphalia. Marxsen himself wrote, "There is no doubt that the authors of the New Testament [or, to be accurate, the authors of some of the books of the New Testament] were convinced that the resurrection of Jesus actually took place on the third day after the crucifixion. Anyone who says that this was not a real event is therefore saying something different from what these writers thought." Then Beegle adds, "But Marxsen cannot accept *their* view literally because of the numerous contradictions of details in the various accounts."[27] Later he adds, "Marxsen's sincerity is evident throughout the book. He is absolutely convinced that Jesus of Nazareth is living and calling him to faithful service, but he is equally certain that belief in the physical resurrection of Jesus is unfounded. Accordingly, he feels compelled to express his conviction honestly and openly. . . . This writer concurs with him acknowledging that the biblical passages dealing with the resurrection *swarm* with difficulties, some details of which cannot be harmonized, but such contradictions do not cancel out the historical core of the accounts"[28] (my italics — and what a loaded word!). Then Beegle arrives at his odd but interesting conclusion: "Neither this writer nor any other Christian has the authority to declare that Marxsen cannot possibly have genuine faith because he cannot bring himself to believe in the bodily resurrection of Jesus."[29]

It is imperative for us to note what Beegle is saying and what the implications are. Marxsen admits that the New Testament writers believed in the bodily resurrection of Jesus from the dead and so taught. He is not arguing, and neither is Beegle, that there are errors in the accounts about the fact of the bodily resurrection so far as the apostles are concerned. And Beegle has stated that on essential matters of faith, Scripture can be trusted. Clearly and unequivocally, Scripture teaches that belief in the resurrection of Jesus Christ from the dead is essential to saving faith. Paul says, "If you confess with your lips that Jesus is Lord and believe in your heart that God raised him from the dead, you will be saved" (Rom. 10:9). The converse of any proposition is true. Thus, "If you do not call Jesus Lord and do not believe in your heart that God raised him from the dead, you will not be saved."

It can be established beyond question that when Paul talked about Jesus being raised from the dead he was talking about a bodily resurrection. In John 12:9 this is made plain: "When the great crowd of the Jews learned that he was there, they came, not only on account of Jesus but also to see Lazarus, whom he had raised from the dead." And the same Greek word for "raised" is used here that was used in Romans 10:9. If Lazarus was raised from the dead in bodily form, then Jesus was raised in bodily form. And the Scripture states that anyone who does not believe that God raised Jesus from the dead cannot be saved.

Marxsen may be sincere and may express his conviction honestly and openly about Jesus and the Resurrection. And Beegle may be just as sincere and just as honest and open when he says that no one "has the authority to declare that Marxsen cannot possibly have genuine faith because he cannot bring himself to believe in the bodily resurrection of Jesus."[30] But both of these sincere men are wrong. And Beegle cannot honestly face the facts nor can he honestly say that Scripture can be trusted on essential matters of faith and at the same time adjudge that Marxsen is a Christian. For the apostle Paul declares that no one can be a Christian who does not believe that God has raised Jesus from the dead, and even Marxsen agrees that Scripture is speaking of a bodily resurrection. Logically Beegle, then, has to be claiming that Paul is wrong about this essential matter. This means that his doctrine of biblical errancy has gone far beyond the question of incidentals on matters of science, fact, and chronology. His errancy teaching has brought him to the place where he overtly denies one of the most important teachings of the Scriptures, the teaching by Paul that no one can be saved who denies the bodily resurrection. And if Beegle can do this, then there is no reason why he cannot also go beyond that and assert that an atheist who is sincere and expresses his convictions honestly and openly can be saved too. And the one who does not believe that Jesus is God can be saved. And whoever is sincere, honest, and open but does not believe in the Holy Spirit as the third person of the Trinity can be saved.

Beegle's adherence to a fallible Bible, we now can see, has taken him far beyond the simple claim that there are incidental errors. His book gives ample proof of my assertion that once inerrancy goes, it inevitably leads to further concessions, and sooner or later it leads to a denial of basic theological truths about which there can be no compromise. But more than that, Beegle's position puts him as an authority over the apostle Paul who has declared that what Beegle claims cannot be true. So we are faced with the problem of having to choose between Beegle and Paul. For Beegle to sit in judgment on Paul is arrogant, unless Beegle has the truth and Paul does not. In that contingency Paul ceases to be a conveyer of theological truth, despite his claim that he was led by the Holy Spirit in inditing Scripture. But Beegle does not claim to be led of the Holy Spirit to indite new Scripture that corrects the errors of the New Testament.

Beegle is wrong at one other point. He says that no Christian has authority to declare that Marxsen cannot possibly have genuine faith. If Paul says that such a man does not have genuine faith despite his sincerity, honesty, and openness, then any Christian has the right to agree with Paul and to pronounce Paul's, not his own, judgment: no one who denies the bodily resurrection of Jesus Christ from the dead can be a Christian — unless the Bible has told us what is false, and if it is false at that point that is so important, of what value is it for anything else?

In another place Beegle tells us that "very many people have held correct doctrinal views without possessing genuine faith."[31] I suspect that no one will disagree with that statement. The Scripture itself tells us that the devils believe and tremble (James 2:19). They know and accept all the doctrinal truths of Scripture, but they are not saved. It should be patent that these people of whom Beegle speaks must have held the essential doctrines of the Christian faith, but they did not have genuine faith. They were unsaved. And yet Beegle, in the case of Marxsen, states that this man is saved even though he denies essential doctrine. It would be fascinating to know how Beegle is able to discern who is saved while not holding correct doctrine, and who is lost even though he does hold correct doctrine. He must have some other criteria that are indefectible and infallible, or he possesses a prescience equal to that of the angels who know the saved from the lost and will separate the wheat from the chaff at the end of the age — if there is an end of the age, and a judgment, and a separation of the sheep from the goats!

In another way Professor Beegle strays far beyond the question of apparent errors in Scripture. He assures us that some of the writings of post-Reformation people would have found their way into sacred Scripture. He says:

> From the standpoint of *theological interpretation* the canon has never been closed. For this reason there is no basis in considering all of the biblical writers and editors as qualitatively different from post-canonical interpreters. Some of the psalms are simply an exhortation to praise God because of his dealings with Israel. . . . Some of the great hymns evidence the same kind of inspiration. Had Isaac Watts, Charles Wesley, Augustus Toplady, and Reginald Heber lived in the preexilic centuries of David and his successors and *been no more inspired than they were in their own day,* there is little doubt but that their hymns (which would have been different, of course, because the revelation of Jesus was still in the future) would have found their way into the Hebrew canon."[32]

Beegle seems to be saying that the same kind of inspiration that the writers of Scripture experienced has been and may be experienced by men today. And what they have written and are writing could be in the canon of Scripture. This will sound wild to those who believe that the writers of Scripture were chosen vessels through whom God elected to reveal Himself in a special way and for the special purpose of inditing Scripture. Not even these people were rendered free from error outside of that special task of inditing Scripture. No evangelical will allege that Christians cannot write things that are fully in accord with the revelation of God. But that is something quite different from saying that what they write, even though true, could be thought of as canonical, or as inspired in the same way as that term is used with respect to Scripture.

Beegle's statement is of special interest from another perspective. The people he has chosen for his illustration represent a special class of people: what they wrote is harmonious with the divine revelation we now have. With regard to the essentials of the Christian faith, they are impeccable. Now if Beegle is correct in stating that there is no basis for considering all of the biblical writers and editors as qualitatively different from postcanonical interpreters, then he surely would have to include men like Karl Barth, Emil Brunner, John Baillie, William Temple, Reinhold Niebuhr, Hans Küng, and Willi Marxsen. If these people are not qualitatively different from the biblical writers and editors, how can it be that they have embraced viewpoints that are opposed to the doctrinal viewpoints of the writers of Scripture? And how come they also have written things that plainly contradict those of Watts, Toplady, Heber, and Charles Wesley? Beegle evidently has in mind a kind of inspiration in which different writers, equally inspired, can write the opposite of each other. And if this kind of inspiration exists, it is a strange kind of inspiration and something we can afford to do without. If all inspiration guarantees to us is that we get viewpoints that are contradictory, which ones are we to believe and how are we to know who is right and who is wrong? Or in these days of existential nihilism can we now say that Christ is God and that Christ is not God and that both statements are true? Thus Beegle again demonstrates that he has gone far beyond the question of errors in Scripture. He has wandered into a wasteland filled with quicksand from which there is no escaping. Having scrapped inerrancy, he has fallen into this quicksand, a fate that could not have befallen him if he had stayed with inerrancy and followed through on its implications. This note must be emphasized again and again. Those who hold to inerrancy will not fall into the inconsistencies that characterize Beegle's position.

Now I return to Beegle's claim that Scripture contains errors of various kinds. I have discussed two of the illustrations he has adduced and have shown that there are answers to his allegations of error. I have acknowledged that some of the so-called discrepancies do involve intricate problems, such as Peter's denial of the Lord Jesus. I do not claim to have answers to all of the objections raised by Beegle and other critics of Scripture. But I have satisfied myself that a multitude of the problems surfaced by critics of former ages have already been answered and no longer constitute problem areas. I am satisfied that some of the difficulties mentioned in this chapter posed by men like Mounce and Beegle have solutions. What about the problems that remain?

It is my judgment that many of the so-called discrepancies will be resolved as evangelical scholars give their attention to them. It would be foolish for me or for anyone else to assert that all of the difficulties will be answered this side of eternity. They may, or they may not be. But the absence of a solution for even a single remaining problem is no reason to suppose that there is no solution. The fact that there have been dogmatic assertions made about the certainty of this mistake or that only to have the miasma dispelled by a solution suggests the need for critics to be very tentative in charging error against Scripture.

Professor Beegle concurs with Marxsen "that the biblical passages dealing with the resurrection swarm [a very strong word] with difficulties, some details of which *cannot* be harmonized . . ."[33] (my italics — a word that gives evidence of a dogmatic conclusion). I recall that my friend Cheney years ago worked out the resurrection narratives and did for them what he has done for Peter's denial, which is discussed in this chapter. I do not know what has happened to his material since his death, but I am confident that if it can be found it will provide a satisfactory response to Beegle's claim that the accounts "swarm" with difficulties.

All of this leaves us with this question: Since everyone admits that there are problem areas for which there are no present answers, why then believe in an inerrant Scripture? There are two possible answers to this question, and perhaps both of them should be used in tangent. The first is that God is the author of Scripture and He cannot lie. This is the presuppositionalist's claim and looks at the problem deductively. It hardly strains the imagination to suppose that if God used erring human beings through whom to convey theological truth, it is no less difficult and appropriate for Him, consistent with His nature, to preserve them from historical, factual, and scientific errors as well. He could have done this while respecting their human-ity, using their own literary styles, and preserving their personhood and integrity. This mystery is no less profound than that of the two natures of Christ in one person, a human nature and a divine nature, operating coordinately so each functions properly and there is no violation of each nature. But the mystery remains.

The second answer to the question is that Scripture itself claims to be inerrant. This represents the inductive approach and is derived from an examination of the phenomena of Scripture. If we cannot trust what Scripture says about itself, there is no reason to trust Scripture at all. If Scripture claims to be inerrant and we find that there are places that call this claim into question, then we must choose between those Scriptures that claim inerrancy and those that purportedly are in error. If we opt for error, then we must conclude that the claim of Scripture to inerrancy is an error too. But if we opt for the claim of Scripture to inerrancy, then we must conclude that the problem areas are not erroneous and that when all the facts are in, adequate solutions will be found for them.

Perhaps a third possibility should be explored — namely, that the Holy Spirit bears witness with our spirits that this is the Word of God that can be trusted. But this presents its own difficulty, since there are those who claim to be Christians who would say that the Holy Spirit has not witnessed to them that way. And some might even claim that the Spirit has witnessed to them that there are errors in the Word of God. There is one last word that needs to be said, however.

God's great adversary is Satan who seeks to defeat the work of God at every point. He is forever active and he clouds the minds of men through sin. There is no Christian who has ever had a normal mind since Adam fell in the Garden of Eden. All men's minds, even those that have been converted by the grace of God, still bear the imprint of their old nature. We all see through a glass darkly and we know only in part. If we were truly normal, we would all see things the same way so far as truth is concerned. But we are not, and these important differences will persist until every believer has been glorified and we then have the mind of Christ in all of its purity and truth. Until that time comes, Christians should be valiant for the truth. And from my perspective, God is glorified by the mind-set that attributes perfection to Scripture, rather than by that mind-set that attributes error to the written Word of God and always leads to further concessions until at last, if not halted, it leads to a full falling away from the holy faith.

[1] Adolph Saphir, *The Divine Unity of Scripture* (London: 1892), p. 259.

[2] Ibid., p. 6.

[3] Robert H. Mounce, "Clues to Understanding Biblical Accuracy," in *Eternity*, June, 1966, p. 18.

[4] Ibid.

[5] Ibid.

[6] Ibid.

[7] Matthew Henry, *Commentary on the Whole Bible* (New York: Revell, n.d.), Vol. V, p. 463.

[8] John W. Haley, *An Examination of the Alleged Discrepancies of the Bible* (Nashville: Goodpasture, 1951), p. 320.

[9] A. T. Robertson, *Word Pictures in the New Testament* (Nashville: Broadman, 1930),

Vol. I, p. 273.

[10] John Calvin, *Calvin's Commentaries: The First Epistle of Paul the Apostle to the Corinthians* (Grand Rapids: Eerdmans, 1960), pp. 208f.

[11] Leon Morris, *Tyndale New Testament Commentaries. The First Epistle of Paul to the Corinthians* (Grand Rapids: Eerdmans, 1958), p. 143.

[12] Daniel P. Fuller, Unpublished paper delivered at Wheaton College, Wheaton, Illinois.

[13] John A. Broadus, *Commentary on the Gospel of Matthew* (Philadelphia: American Baptist Publication Society, 1886), p. 296.

[14] Dewey M. Beegle, *Scripture, Tradition, and Infallibility* (Grand Rapids: Eerdmans, 1973), p. 299.

[15] Ibid., p. 10.

[16] Ibid., p. 267.

[17] Marcus Dods, *The Bible: Its Origin and Nature* (1895), p. 146.

[18] Beegle, *Scripture, Tradition, and Infallibility*, p. 182.

[19] Ibid., p. 184.

[20] Edwin R. Thiele, "Co-regencies and Overlapping Reigns Among the Hebrew Kings," *Journal of Biblical Literature* (Vol. 93, No. 2, 1974), p. 195.

[21] Ibid., p. 200.

[22] Beegle, *Scripture, Tradition, and Infallibility*, p. 268.

[23] Ibid., p. 192.

[24] Ibid., p. 193.

[25] Ibid., p. 308.

[26] Ibid., p. 65.

[27] Ibid., p. 60.

[28] Ibid., p. 61.

[29] Ibid., p. 63.

[30] Ibid.

[31] Ibid., p. 45.

[32] Ibid., pp. 308f.

[33] Ibid., p. 61.

10

How Infection Spreads

History affords us notable examples of institutions and denominations that have gone astray. At times it is not easy to perceive *how* this happened. The trend away from orthodoxy may be slow in movement, gradual in its scope, and almost invisible to the naked eye. When people awaken to what has happened, it is too late. In medicine, thousands of people die unnecessarily because the cancers that kill them have been diagnosed too late. The cancers existed long before the diagnoses, and they grew and spread until the situations, when diagnosed at last, were hopeless. Theological aberration, like cancer, begins as a small and seemingly insignificant blemish, but when it is left to itself it grows and spreads. One of the classic cases of a theological disease that overtook an institution is that of the liberalism that took over Union Theological Seminary in New York City.

UNION SEMINARY AND CHARLES AUGUSTUS BRIGGS

The Union Seminary case study centers around the personality of Charles Augustus Briggs, an Old Testament scholar who was noted for his battle with B. B. Warfield. Warfield was a professor at Princeton Seminary and was a solid defender of biblical inerrancy. Briggs was to become a professor at Union Seminary in 1874 but before this, as a result of his studies in Germany, he was already

185

moving away from biblical orthodoxy. In 1889, two years before the delivery of his installation address in connection with a new chair that had been created and endowed for him at the institution, he published a volume entitled *Whither? A Theological Question for the Times*. In it he went hammer and tongs against biblical inerrancy. In his opening chapter he stated that the "religion in Great Britain and America is at present in a very unsatisfactory condition."[1] He went on to castigate the churches for their failure to evangelize the masses in the great cities. Then he made an observation about the work of certain evangelists such as Moody. Of him and his ministry he said:

> Another strong effort has been put forth by Mr. Moody and other so-called [sic] evangelists who have pursued his methods. Great combinations are made with great effort and great noise for a little while here and there, and much good was accomplished, but with the cessation of the special efforts everything goes back to the former state of things. There is nothing permanent about these evangelistic labors. Moreover, Mr. Moody and his followers are crude in their theology, they pursue false methods in their interpretation of Scripture, and therefore they spread abroad not a few serious errors, and on the whole work disorganization and confusion. They do not edify the Church of Christ, they do not organize and train the awakened and converted. The churches ought to do all this work of evangelization and vastly more that is left undone.[2]

This statement by Briggs shows where he stood and what his attitude was toward men like Moody, who had been singularly blessed by God and whose labors we now know produced results for good almost beyond imagination. Briggs' labors were to produce results for evil that exceeded his wildest expectations.

BRIGGS VERSUS PATTON, HODGE, AND WARFIELD

Briggs went to work on Hodge, Warfield, and Patton over inerrancy. "It is claimed," he said, "by President Patton [of Princeton] that inerrancy of Scripture is essential to the inspiration of the Scriptures, and Doctors Hodge and Warfield go so far as to say that 'a proved error in Scripture contradicts not only our doctrine, but the Scripture's claims, and therefore its inspiration in making those claims.'"[3] Briggs claimed that the doctrine of inerrancy was a new theory despite the fact that there is extensive documentation to the .contrary. He argued that "the doctrine of inerrancy of Scripture not only comes into conflict with the historical faith of the Church, but is also in conflict with biblical criticism."[4] He was wrong in his first assertion, but right in the second. There is no doubt that inerrancy is in conflict with biblical criticism. The learned professor went on to say later that if anyone can "find any comfort in verbal inspiration and the inerrancy of the Scriptures, we have no desire to disturb him, provided he holds these errors as private opinions and does not seek to impose them upon others. But fidelity to the truth requires that we should state that they are not only extra-confessional, but that they are contrary to truth and fact, and that they are broken reeds that will surely fail anyone who leans upon them, and that they are therefore positively dangerous to the faith of ministry and people."[5]

BRIGGS AND HIGHER CRITICISM

Toward the end of his book Dr. Briggs says, "There can be no doubt that recent criticisms have considerably weakened the evidences from miracles and predictive prophecy. To many minds it would be easier to believe in the inspiration of the Scriptures and the divinity of Jesus Christ if there were no such things as Miracles and Prediction in the sacred Scriptures."[6] And the learned doctor came to the end of his book with a statement that any evangelical could agree with: "The more conflict the better. Battle for the truth is infinitely better than stagnation in error. Every error should be slain as soon as possible. If it be our error we should be the most anxious to get rid of it. Error is our greatest foe. Truth is the most precious possession."[7] I'm sure every evangelical would agree that the foremost error of this generation is the one that discards biblical inerrancy, and it should be slain as soon as possible.

Briggs took his doctorate at the University of Berlin, working under A. I. Dorner, the professor of higher criticism. Carl E. Hatch, in his book *The Charles A. Briggs Heresy Trial,* to which I will be making extensive references, says it was the University of Berlin "that turned the New Yorker into a fiery apostle of German theology." His conversion to modern theology was "complete before returning to America. . . . He caustically remarked that the Americans were far behind the times. He added he now knew that his mission in life was to return to America and modernize theological studies in his own country. This he would attempt to do by disseminating German critical methods through American seminaries."[8]

Briggs joined the Union Seminary faculty in 1874. By 1890 "he was inwardly burning with discontent . . . he had not yet found the proper means to advertise the modern German approach to the Testaments. . . . Other conditions at Union increased his ill-humor. In 1870, Union entered into an agreement with the General Assembly of the Presbyterian Church. . . . the official Presbyterian position was staunchly opposed to German theology."[9]

Hatch notes that the majority of the faculty members at Union were overt or covert adherents to the Wellhausen documentary hypothesis. But Briggs had to tread cautiously, for the Presbyterian Church could cancel his appointment to the faculty. His writings were "studded with guarded qualifications."[10] He was successful in getting the executive board of Union to institute a new department of higher criticism with himself at its head. But it was entitled "Department of Biblical Theology" to avoid the criticism that would be sure to rise from the use of the words "higher criticism." Charles Butler, a long-time friend of Briggs and a director of the seminary, endowed the new chair with a gift of $100,000, earmarked solely for the Department of Biblical Theology.[11]

BRIGGS DROPS HIS BOMB

On January 20, 1891, Charles Briggs dropped his bomb on Union. Adams Chapel was filled to capacity as Briggs delivered his inaugural address. But before delivering the address, he "was requested to submit to the pledge required of newly appointed or transferred teachers at all Presbyterian seminaries. This involved making a public declaration of belief in the Holy Scriptures as the only infallible rule of faith and practice. Little did the unsuspecting assembly realize that in less than five minutes, all that had been professed would be repudiated."[12]

Briggs stated that four barriers kept people from the Bible. The first one was superstition. "The Bible," he said, "has no magical value in it, and there is no halo enclosing it. . . . It will not keep off evil spirits any better than a cross. It will not guard a home from fire half as well as holy water. The Bible, as a book, is paper, print, and binding — nothing more."[13] The students broke out with loud applause.

"The second barrier keeping men from the Bible is the dogma of verbal inspiration. . . . There is nothing divine in the text — in its letters, words, or clauses." The students again gave him a great ovation. Then he went on to his third point.

The third barrier to the Bible is the false notion that the Scripture is inerrant. "Conceding that finding errors in the Bible was disconcerting, Briggs nevertheless insisted that 'the Higher Criticism finds them, and we must meet the issue whether it destroys the authority of the Bible or not. . . . I shall venture to affirm that there are errors in the Scriptures that no one has been able to explain away; and even the idea and theory that they were not in the original texts is sheer assumption! If such errors destroy the authority of the Bible, it is already destroyed for historians. Men cannot shut their eyes to truth and fact. The Bible itself nowhere makes the claim that it is inerrant. Nor do the creeds of the Church sanction such a theory. Indeed, the theory that the Bible is inerrant is the ghost of modern evangelicalism to frighten children'."[14]

Briggs went on to his fourth point in which he struck out against the belief that "the authenticity of the Bible was founded upon the belief that holy men of old had written the various books of Holy Writ." Briggs spoke these words:

> But what do we know of the authors apart from the Bible itself? Apart from the sacred writings — Moses and David were not more inspired than Confucius or Sakya Muni. They were leaders of men, but how do we know that they were called of God to speak divine words to us? The only way in which we can prove their authority is from their writings, and yet we are asked to accept the authority of these writings on the authority of these authors.
>
> When such fallacies are thrust in the face of men seeking divine authority in the Bible, is it strange that so many turn away in disgust? It is just here that the Higher Criticism has proved such a terror in our times. Traditionalists are crying out that it is destroying the Bible, because it is exposing their fallacies and follies. . . . It may be regarded as the certain result of the science of Higher Criticism that Moses did not write the Pentateuch or Job; Ezra did not write Chronicles, Ezra or Nehemiah; Jeremiah did not write the Kings or Lamentations; David did not write the Psalter, but only a few of the Psalms; Solomon did not write the Song of Songs or Ecclesiastes, and only a portion of the Proverbs; Isaiah did not write half of the book that bears his name. The great mass of the Old Testament was written by authors whose names or connection with their writings are lost in oblivion.[15]

"From this point on, the inaugural address was a manifesto urging all liberals to join in the higher-criticism war against the conservatives. Casting himself in the role of a would-be-conqueror, Briggs finished his lecture with a spirited exhortation:

> We have undermined the breastworks of Traditionalism; let us blow

them to atoms. We have forged our way through obstructions; let us remove them now from the face of the earth. . . . Criticism is at work everywhere with knife and fire! Let us cut down everything that is dead and harmful, every kind of dead orthodoxy, every species of effete ecclesiasticism, all mere ,formal morality, all those dry and brittle fences that constitute denominationalism, and are barriers to church unity.

Let us burn up every form of false doctrine, false religion, and false practice. Let us remove every encumbrance out of the way for a new life; the life of God is moving throughout Christendom, and the spring time of a new age is about to come upon us.

Charles Augustus Briggs had crossed his Rubicon. The traditionalists would not pass up the challenge."[16] Surely one aspect of Briggs' character manifested itself in this challenge delivered at the end of his inaugural address. In 1889, just two years prior to this, in *Whither* he had said he had no objection to those who believed in inerrancy so long as they held them as private opinions and did not seek to impose them on others. Now he comes along with his opinions, labels them truth, and begins a campaign to impose them on everyone. Why should his opinions not also be privately held and not imposed on others either? His inaugural address and the positive response he got from the students indicated that he and others like him had been successful in imposing their views on the students. It also is notable that Briggs stated he was glad "the war had begun." This is no speech of a pacific personality. The war phrase did not come from orthodox believers. It came from this brash personality who was determined to change the direction of the seminary and the denomination to which he was attached.

THE REACTIONS TO BRIGGS' BOMB

One of the leading lights of the Union faculty took issue with Briggs. William G. T. Shedd was Professor of Systematic Theology and an evangelical. He cited reasons of conscience that made it necessary for him to "disarm this infidel in Traditionalist's armor."[17] He alleged that higher criticism was conjectural, a wholly modern theory and, in severing the traditional writers from books of the Bible, Briggs had made inspiration of no effect. It had become an inspiration of air.[18] Hatch, whose work shows considerable bias in favor of the liberals, concludes that "Shedd showed that the plainer the inconsistencies of the traditionalists were shown to be, the more reckless their arguments would become. In short, the old-guard theologians in time would resort to polemics rather than reason. This drift was eventually to drive many middle-of-the-roaders into the liberal camp."[19]

Briggs had stirred up a hornet's nest. It brought about two efforts to get rid of him. One effort centered around Union Seminary. His opponents wanted the board of the institution to remove him from the faculty. The other centered around the Presbyterian Church. Earlier, Union Seminary had entered into an agreement with that denomination by which the appointment of faculty members required the approval of the church. What was not clear, and this entered into the Briggs' case, was whether the denomination also had to approve a professorial change of status. It might have applied to Briggs because he had just been appointed to head up the new "Department of Biblical Theology," and conceivably this could be regarded as similar to a new appointment. On the other hand, he had been a member of the faculty since 1874. Had he been coming up for approval as a newcomer, the issue would have been clear. Thus his status was beclouded by the fact that it was an appointment to a new chair, of a man who had been on the faculty for some years in a different capacity. The Presbyterian Church, however, was finally to rule on the Briggs' case as though the change of status required its approval.

Philip Schaff, Professor of Church History at Union, was a close friend of Briggs. He was also a theological liberal. In his appraisal of the response to Briggs' inaugural he said that it was "the defiant and exasperating tone" in which Briggs delivered the address that made it sound "like a manifesto of war."[20] That probably was true. There is scant reason to believe that proceedings would have commenced against Briggs if he had conducted himself as he had during the previous seventeen years. His higher-critical views were being propagated during this period of his life, and nothing had come up by way of a challenge to unseat him. Union Seminary was already deeply infiltrated by liberalism and it probably would have gone along that way had Briggs been more discreet. But Briggs was the catalyst who forced the issue and brought the trend in the seminary to the light of day.

The directorate of Union Seminary was forced to take some kind of action with regard to Briggs. The board asked Briggs eight categorical questions to which Briggs gave his response. The questions were so phrased that Briggs did not need to comment on his basic convictions. It created the impression that the heretical teacher was not heretical after all.[21] Union Seminary then published an amplified version of Briggs' beliefs on the Bible. This was done to hamper the effort not to approve Briggs' appointment by the Presbyterian Church.

While this was in progress Briggs further damaged his own case by making comments to the press about his views on the Book of Daniel. He said that the book had not been written by Daniel as the book itself claimed. It had been penned by some unknown redactor who lived long after Daniel's time. Briggs went further than that. In an interview with a newspaper reporter he lost his cool and stated categorically, "The Bible is not inerrant," and he extolled the German-trained higher critics in Europe "for their imaginative and progressive discoveries in the field of biblical scholarship."[22]

BRIGGS AND THE PRESBYTERIAN CHURCH

The Briggs case went to the General Assembly of the Presbyterian Church. During the course of the proceedings many speeches were made, and many of the liberals in the denomination spoke in defense of Briggs. The liberals alleged that men like Hodge and Warfield had themselves used higher criticism in connection with their own work and writings. And they argued that if Briggs was guilty, so were they. Leading lights in the denomination such as Arthur C. McGiffert of Lane Seminary in Cincinnati said that Briggs was "one of the most helpful and inspiring teachers in our Church."[23] Dr. Herrick Johnson of McCormick Seminary in Chicago "demonstrated unusual courage when he contended there was no question that Briggs was 'evangelical.' "[24] It was all in vain, however.

The opponents of Briggs were successful in getting the church to refuse his appointment at the seminary, but this did not mean the seminary would agree to the decision of the General Assembly. After the Detroit verdict, which went against Briggs, Dr. Schaff, Union's church historian, said that he felt certain that Union would stand behind Briggs and defend him to the end. Francis Brown, another faculty member, said, "Now we will become more militant in our efforts to promote Higher Criticism and stand by Briggs."[25] He spoke prophetically, for Union indeed stood behind Briggs.

The board of directors of Union voted to defy the General Assembly's veto of Briggs' professorship at Union, an action that "struck many of the orthodox as a defense not only of the heretic's academic position but also of his teachings."[26] Two directors voted against Briggs at Union, but they were a small minority. "Union's defiance was taken to mean that the seminary was determined to propagate the German theology."[27] The reaction of New York newspapers to the Briggs trial and the sequel makes for interesting reading. The New York *World* "saw Union's decision to defy the General Assembly as a triumph for both Briggs and higher criticism. To the *World* it seemed that this crisis of conflicting wills had turned the New York seminary, almost overnight, into the chief citadel of the new theology in the United Sates."[28]

The New York *Times* agreed, and added some thoughts of its own. "Taking note of how the intellectual world was in the midst of a revolution that was overturning absolute standards, the *Times* urged Union, which it deemed the leading liberal seminary in America, to apply the pragmatic principles of this revolution to fields other than higher criticism. It recommended that Union expand its national emphasis to comprehend such subjects as sociology. In short, Union should not stop at establishing a department of higher criticism, but go on to found a department of 'Applied Christian Sociology.' New York City," concluded the *Times*, "would make an ideal laboratory for such a venture because of its teeming slums."[29]

THE NEW YORK PRESBYTERY TRIES AND ACQUITS BRIGGS

The Briggs battle was not over yet, however. A new phase began when the New York Presbytery tried him for heresy. On April 13, 1891, the Presbytery appointed a committee to consider the inaugural address Briggs had given at Union a few months before this. By the first week of May, 1891, the committee brought in its report. Briggs curtly refused to appear before the committee although he was invited to do so. Hatch indicates that a chief reason for Briggs' unwillingness to appear before the committee stemmed from another consideration. "He was in the midst of completing a pamphlet designed to neutralize the research of Birch [chairman of the committee] and his associates. In this publication he aimed at making his position on orthodoxy so clear that the prosecution's case would appear ridiculous. Here, as in previous moves, his intention was not to prove his orthodoxy but rather to prolong the theological debate. Each added day, he reasoned, meant that much more publicity for the liberal point of view."[30] Influenza caught up with Briggs, and he was unable to carry through on his plan. But he did give an interview to the press and again made some unguarded statements. "Waxing eloquent, he made a number of impolitic statements which played into the hands of the *reactionaries*. 'I do not know of one European teacher of the Old Testament,' he exclaimed, 'who believes in the inerrancy of the Bible. And the scholars of this country are with us as well' " (my italics). He was even less discreet when he followed these remarks with a call to arms. Showing that even illness could not dull his single passion, he said, 'We have not urged this fight, although we have been ready for it for some time. It was not considered advisable to force the fighting, but now that it is here against our will, we shall take up our arms and fight with all our energy and power'."[31] This interview convinced the committee of a need for a trial by the Presbytery.

The committee found Briggs' inaugural address to be theologically unsound on a number of crucial points. They noted "that whereas the Confession clearly proclaimed that 'the Old Testament in the Hebrew and the New Testament in the Greek were immediately inspired by God,' Briggs' peroration flatly denied this assumption."[32] One man dissented from the committee's report to the Presbytery. The majority report, once accepted, resulted in the appointment of a committee to draw up charges against Briggs.

Interestingly, "immediately after Briggs' inaugural address, liberal ministers and professors organized a secret fraternity called Chi Alpha. The sole purpose of this intellectual club was to 'convert young, orthodox ministers' newly arrived in the area to liberal theology. The Chi Alpha fraternity, in short, seemed an organization to entice fledgling ministers from their orthodox moorings. Its notable success was observed by the New York *Sun*, which said that 'an ever increasing number of young orthodox ministers are becoming infected' with higher criticism."[33]

On November 4, 1891, Briggs was called to present himself, and to offer his defense against the charge of heresy. The church where the Presbytery met to consider the case was packed. In making his defense, Briggs expressed "deep regret and sorrow if he had in any way over the past few months disturbed the peace of the church or given pain and anxiety to his brethren in the ministry."[34] This was effective, even though palpably false. "Briggs' new approach won over some of the moderates; his brilliant defense wooed the rest. Although his remarks were shrouded in ecclesiastical legalisms, he brilliantly laced his speech at strategic intervals with subtle pleas for higher criticism. This technique baffled and angered the Prosecution Committee, for they were expecting a militant and forthright justification of Wellhausen's ideas. Briggs' clever ability to becloud the major issue was especially astute when he insisted that the two leading charges against him did not comply with the procedural rules of the church's *Book of Discipline*."[35]

Briggs handled the charges against him cleverly, but what he said in the final twenty minutes of his discourse "was tantamount to an admission of heresy."[36] Dr. Shedd made the assertion, "Briggs' address could no more be squared with the Westminster Confession than you could square a circle."[37] But when the vote came, a vote that was based plainly on the question of German higher criticism, the New York Presbytery exonerated Briggs by a 94 to 39 majority.

The decision of the New York Presbytery was appealed to the General Assembly in 1892. It remanded the case to the New York Presbytery for a retrial. The New York liberals again returned a verdict to acquit. The case was appealed to the General Assembly again. In its meeting in 1893 in Washington, D.C., the General Assembly excommunicated Briggs from the church. There was no appeal from this decision. Six years later Briggs was ordained a priest in the Protestant Episcopal Church.

As a result of the General Assembly's action Union Seminary was faced with its own decision, but it did not wait until the 1893 General Assembly meeting. It already knew which way the wind was blowing. In 1892 Union Seminary separated from the Presbyterian Church, retaining Briggs on its faculty. He labored there until his death in 1913, a persistent and unyielding advocate of biblical errancy. The conclusions drawn by Hatch as a result of his doctoral study on the Briggs' case are very important. He states that higher criticism "made its initial impact upon intellectuals, particularly in the East" and the new German theology "was long confined to the rarified cloisters of theological seminaries." Higher criticism that started in the East moved westward "capturing all but a few bastions of fundamentalist resistance, some of which still defiantly [*sic*] fly their banners."[38]

THE LESSONS UNION SEMINARY AND BRIGGS TEACH

What lessons can be learned from the case of Briggs and Union Seminary? The first and most obvious is that the institution went on from the days of Briggs to become and remain one of the most liberal seminaries in the United States. At no time since Briggs' day has the institution reversed its position. Instead, it has moved farther and farther away from historic orthodoxy. Briggs, compared to Union Seminary today, would be considered relatively orthodox. This shows that once an institution moves away from biblical infallibility, it continues its course until its aberrations include denials of biblical essentials beyond inerrancy. Nor is there any evidence whatever that Union Seminary might conceivably return to orthodoxy. At this present writing the institution, which at one time was the most highly endowed seminary in the world, is in a precarious condition. Since the retirement of John Bennett as president, it has floundered, and its last president was dismissed from the institution with a generous financial settlement. Its student body has declined, and it has cut back its program.

Through the years, Union Seminary has had a profound influence on the churches. Of that there can be no doubt. But so far as one of Briggs' observations is concerned, it has failed miserably. It was Briggs who lamented that the masses in the great cities had not been evangelized. At least Briggs professed to believe in evangelization. Union no longer believes this, nor has the institution done anything of a significant nature through the years to evangelize New York City, where it is located. It has no gospel that faintly resembles the gospel revealed in the New Testament, and its orientation has been more and more leftward. But it has influenced generations of students in its graduate school, and many of them are firmly entrenched in colleges and seminaries around the world. Tillich, Niebuhr, and Bennett left behind them multitudes who embraced their viewpoints and now propagate them to others. It was Harry Emerson Fosdick, whom I have already quoted as disbelieving almost every fundamental doctrine of the Christian faith, who taught a generation of prospective clergymen how to preach at Union.

William Sloane Coffin, Jr. of Yale University fame, who was prominent in the disorders that struck that campus in the 60s, attended Union. Robert McAfee Brown of Stanford University, whose radical views are so widely known they need no documentation, is a graduate and former faculty member of Union. John Tietjen, the former president of Concordia Seminary at St. Louis, who is at the center of the struggle in the Lutheran Church – Missouri Synod over Scripture, is a graduate of Union with a doctorate. The question can be asked, "Does a poisoned well bring forth sweet water?"

The Briggs case teaches us still another lesson. In almost every case, unorthodoxy has its beginnings in the theological seminaries. They are the fountainhead of the churches. As the seminaries go, so go the churches. Almost inevitably, graduates of a theological institution reflect the viewpoints of their teachers. More than that, they usually go beyond their teachers, and carry their aberrant viewpoints to the farthest extreme. Once the theological seminaries go liberal, it does not take long for the denominations they represent to follow them. In the Presbyterian Church of which Dr. Briggs was a member (now the United Presbyterian Church), there is not a single theological seminary in the denomination today that is committed in principle and practice to historic orthodoxy. There are a few members of the faculties of these institutions who are truly evangelical, but their number is small and their ultimate influence minuscule. Before his death several years ago, J. Howard Pew, a staunch Presbyterian, sought to create a new United Presbyterian theological seminary that would operate within the framework of the denomination and stand forthrightly for the teachings of the Westminster Confession of Faith. He was willing to give millions of dollars for the effort. But the denomination politely refused permission. For years, Princeton Theological Seminary was the center of theological orthodoxy in the Presbyterian Church. Among its giants were men like Green, Hodge, and Warfield. They are gone, and the institution that once stood for historic evangelical Christianity is an inclusivistic school that has room for a variety of viewpoints that contradict each other. It has no integrated theology that can stand up in the face of the law of internal contradiction.

The Union Seminary illustration teaches us also that deviation from doctrinal commitments occur, but they are muted and do not come to the surface until someone or something brings them to the fore and requires a decision. Obviously, Union was infected with aberrant views before Briggs joined the faculty. Moreover, the majority of the faculty and the board of the institution were already committed to a liberal theology before the Briggs' case came to the forefront. Briggs was a catalyst who made apparent what was partially hidden. He brought the deviation out into the open for all to see.

Moreover, Union has a lesson to teach about the ethics of liberal theology. Briggs himself was devious. The board of the seminary was devious. Honesty and integrity were in short supply. Both Briggs and the board knew that Briggs was teaching contrary to the Westminster Confession of Faith. The board was fully aware that the institution's relationship to the Presbyterian Church committed the seminary to the standards of the Westminster Confession.

No one can fault the person who wishes to believe as he chooses. Freedom of religion includes the freedom to be an atheist, an agnostic, or a theist. But ethics requires that when a man no longer believes what he has sworn he believes, he must make that change of belief clear. He has two courses open to him. Either the institution or the church can then change its commitment to those doctrines he no longer believes, or he can demit the institution or the church. But for anyone to remain mute and to stay in a school or denomination when he disbelieves the standards the institution or church teaches is unethical. Yet both Briggs and Union Seminary were ethically and morally delinquent in this affair. And any church or school that has a commitment to a confession of faith but does not live up to it is hypocritical. What is stranger still is the mentality that passes adverse judgment upon fidelity to a doctrinal commitment. The literature of Briggs' controversy is full of loaded words that display contempt, if not hatred, for those who sought to remain faithful to the Westminster Confession of Faith. They were called "traditionalists" as though that was something evil; they were "reactionaries," a term that in anyone's book is slander; they were "die-hards," which suggests they were anti-intellectual and hidebound; the trial of Briggs by the New York Presbytery was termed an "anachronistic inquest."

Briggs' victory at Union and the later conquest of the Presbyterian Church by the liberals did not mean the end of evangelical faith. It was to survive this onslaught. Optimistic liberalism was dealt a death blow by 1930. Neo-orthodoxy rose in its place. But by the 1940s evangelicalism, which rose out of the earlier fundamentalism, experienced a resurgence of vitality. In 1947 Fuller Theological Seminary came into being. It was created for the express purpose of developing an apologetic for biblical inerrancy. Along with it came other tides of a literate, scholarly mentality comparable to that of the old Princeton school of Hodge, Warfield, Green, and Machen. It is among this new group of evangelicals that an incursion of disbelief in inerrancy has come just as in Briggs' day. And for them, the history of Union Seminary and the Briggs' trial has special reference. All they are doing is repeating history, and they can be sure that they will repeat what happened at Union subsequent to Briggs' day. Those who do not learn from history are bound to repeat its mistakes.

[1] Charles Augustus Briggs, *Whither? A Theological Question for the Times* (New York: Scribner's, 1889), p. 1.

[2] Ibid., p. 3.

[3] Ibid., p. 68.

[4] Ibid., p. 71.

[5] Ibid., p. 90.

[6] Ibid., p. 279.

[7] Ibid., p. 297.

[8] Carl E. Hatch, *The Charles A. Briggs Heresy Trial* (New York: Exposition Press, 1969), p. 23.

[9] Ibid., p. 25.

[10] Ibid., p. 26.

[11] Ibid., p. 27.

[12] Ibid., p. 29.

[13] Ibid., p. 32.

[14] Ibid., p. 33.

[15] Ibid., pp. 34, 35.

[16] Ibid., p. 35.

[17] Ibid., p. 39.

[18] Ibid., p. 40.

[19] Ibid.

[20] Ibid., p. 46.

[21] Ibid., p. 47.

[22] Ibid., p. 51.

[23] Ibid., p. 49.

[24] Ibid., p. 72.

[25] Ibid., p. 75.

[26] Ibid., p. 76.

[27] Ibid., p. 77.

[28] Ibid., pp. 77, 78.

[29] Ibid., p. 78.

[30] Ibid., p. 98.

[31] Ibid., pp. 98, 99.

[32] Ibid., pp. 100, 101.

[33] Ibid., p. 112.

[34] Ibid., p. 124.

[35] Ibid., pp. 124, 125.

[36] Ibid., p. 126.

[37] Ibid.

[38] Ibid., p. 132.

11

The Conclusion of the Matter

A journey of a thousand miles must come to an end. Even the rain water returns to the ocean from which it came. So the hour has come to draw some conclusions and let the reader make his own decision. I have presented an apologetic for biblical inerrancy. It is based on a legitimate concern. Simply stated, the concern is that evangelical Christianity is engaged in the greatest battle of its history. The central issue at stake in this battle is epistemological: it has to do with the basis of our religious knowledge. Does that knowledge come from reason, the church, or from the Bible?

THE ISSUE DEFINED

Ten years ago John Warwick Montgomery, in an article dealing with inerrancy, alluded to a statement made by James Orr in his book *The Progress of Dogma*. In that book Orr said that in each great epoch of church history, the Christian church has been forced to grapple with one facet of the Christian faith that has had a real bearing on the future direction of the church. In the early church the key issue had to do with the persons of the Godhead, and particularly the Christological problem involving the deity and the humanity of Jesus. The ecumenical creeds of Christendom express the orthodox, trinitarian views that prevailed as a result of that battle. Medieval Christianity dealt with the atonement of Jesus Christ. Anselm's

"Latin doctrine," which may have had some weaknesses, "gave solid expression to biblical salvation-history as represented by the Epistle to the Hebrews." In the Reformation era, justification by faith alone *(sola gratia, sola fide)* established the biblical teaching against an anthropocentric trend that nullified genuine Christianity. In bygone ages, the Christological crisis, the soteriological crisis, and the Reformation crisis arose, were faced, and solved. Today the great watershed is the issue of Scripture. This struggle over Scripture is unique in the history of the church. How the issue is settled remains to be seen. But if it is finally settled that Scripture can err, then the church and its theologians will learn that no source and no standard remains to solve further doctrinal problems that may arise.[1]

Years ago Charles Haddon Spurgeon understood the seriousness of the issue when he wrote:

> Believers in Christ's atonement are now in declared union with those who make light of it; believers in holy Scripture are in confederacy with those who deny plenary inspiration; those who hold evangelical doctrine are in open alliance with those who call the Fall a fable, who deny the personality of the holy Ghost, who call justification by faith immoral, and hold there is another probation after death; to be very plain, we are unable to call these things Christian Unions, they begin to look like confederacies in evil.[2]

So Clark Pinnock quoted Spurgeon as he went on to observe that James Stalker rightly said:

> Excessive aversion to controversy may be an indication that a Church has no keen sense of possessing truth which is of any great worth, and that it has lost appreciation for the infinite difference in value between truth and error.[3]

Pinnock, in his appeal to the Southern Baptists, then quotes Martin Luther:

> If I profess with loudest voice and clearest exposition every portion of the truth of God except precisely that little point which the world and the devil are at the moment attacking, I am not confessing Christ, however boldly I may be professing Christ. Where the battle rages, there the loyalty of the soldier is proved, and to be steady on all the battlefield besides, is merely flight and disgrace if he flinches at THAT point.[4]

WHERE THE BATTLE RAGES

Today that little point of conflict is the inerrancy of the Word of God written. The battle rages, not among those in the liberal tradition where the issue is already settled, but among those who profess to be evangelicals. It is among them that infiltration has come, and it is among them that the decision will determine the direction of evangelicalism for the future. Inerrancy right now is the crucial issue among evangelicals.

Richard J. Coleman (B.D. and Th.M. from Princeton Seminary) expressed this fact plainly when he said:

> Surprisingly enough the discussion of Biblical inerrancy swirls around us with almost the same ferocity as in the 1880s and the 1930s. The stance was taken then, namely by B. B. Warfield and J. Gresham Machen, that the traditional view of Biblical inerrancy should not be compromised by the promulgation of a limited view of inspiration. Well fought issues do not die easily and such is the case with the interrelationship between Scriptural inerrancy and its inspiration. The difficulties faced by Warfield and Machen in defending a strict view of inerrancy are still with us, if not more intensely, and thus the proponents of some kind of limited inspiration are still with us. The debate, however, has often been clouded by imprecisions and generalities. Thus, my purpose is to unpack some of the commonly used terms in this controversy leading to a more careful definition of alternatives.[5]

Coleman's conclusion, however, is a verdict against biblical inerrancy. "Scripture," he says, "is inerrant in whatever it intends to teach as essential for our salvation. . . plenary inspiration and inerrancy are not synonymous or inseparable. Unequivocally the doctrinal verses teach the inspiration of Scripture as a whole. But to impose on all Christians the deduction that plenary inspiration automatically guarantees total inerrancy is unwarranted. The gift of inspiration was granted not to insure the infallibility of every word and thought, though it did accomplish this in particular instances, but to secure a written Word that would forever be the singular instrument by which man learns and is confronted by God's will. . . . Evangelicals have the choice either to continue to react defensively or to advance positively a modified yet firm concept of inerrancy."[6]

We need only to return to the Briggs' case to note again that Briggs swore fidelity to the statement that the Bible is the only infallible rule of faith and practice. And this is neither more nor less than Coleman is doing. The issue is surely the same issue that was at stake in the Warfield-Briggs confrontation, in the Machen situation, and in the present-day struggle. Inerrancy is important, but what is equally important is what happens once inerrancy is scrapped. And this is where Coleman, for example, throws no light on the matter. Coleman is advocating "limited inerrancy." This term is meaningless; it is nonsense. The sooner we realize this, the sooner we will see the issue of inerrancy in its proper perspective. And, at last, every deviation away from inerrancy ends up by casting a vote in favor of limited inerrancy. Once limited inerrancy is accepted, it places the Bible in the same category with every other book that has ever been written. Every book contains in it some things that are true. And what is true is inerrant. Only two things remain to be determined once this position is acknowledged. The first is what proportion of the book is true and what proportion false. It may be 90 percent false and 10 percent true; or it may be 90 percent true and 10 percent false. The second thing that needs to be determined is what parts of the book are true. Since the book contains both error and falsehood, of necessity, other criteria outside of the book must be brought to bear upon it to determine what is false and what is true. Whatever the source of the other criteria, that becomes the judge of the book in question. Thus the book becomes subordinated to the standard against which its truth is determined and measured.

If inspiration means anything, and if inspiration pertains to the totality of the Bible, then we must see what limited inerrancy means. First, it means that something outside of and above the Bible becomes its judge. There is something that is truer and more sure than Scripture and whatever it is it has not been inspired by God. So a noninspired source takes precedence over an inspired Bible. Second, it leaves us in a vacuum without any basis for determining what parts of the Bible tell the truth and what parts do not. For the evangelical, the genius of inspiration lies in the fact that it disposes of these problems and provides for us a book that we can trust so that when we come to it, we do not need to do so with suspicion nor do we need to ask the question: "Is this part to be trusted?" This does not deliver us from the need to examine Scripture and to determine what it teaches. But it does give us a word we can trust, and leaves us with the assurance that once we have gotten its true meaning, we can test every other book against the Bible and not let other books determine the truth of Scripture.

ERRANCY LEADS TO FURTHER CONCESSIONS

I have already demonstrated that once inerrancy goes, it leads, however slowly, to a further denial of other biblical truths. In fairness, it should be said that there are evangelicals who, at this moment, have not yet gone beyond a modest denial of inerrancy. They are sound on the other major doctrines of the Christian faith, but they have made concessions rising out of their denial of inerrancy nonetheless. These concessions do not bear on essential doctrines other than biblical infallibility, which is a biblical doctrine. Among evangelicals there are those who accept the concept of two Isaiahs despite the clearest teaching of the New Testament that Isaiah 40-66 was written by the prophet Isaiah. There are evangelicals who believe that Daniel was written around 168 B.C., after the events described in the book, rather than before. They do this despite the claim of the book itself to have been written by Daniel and before the events took place. There are evangelicals who do not believe in a historical Adam and Eve and who regard the first eleven chapters of Genesis as nonhistorical. There are evangelicals who doubt that the apostle Peter penned 2 Peter, even though the text of the letter claims that he did. There are those who do not think Paul wrote the Book of Ephesians even though the inscription claims that he did. There are evangelicals who regard the Book of Jonah as a novella rather than history.

THE HISTORICAL-CRITICAL METHODOLOGY

There are evangelicals like George Ladd who take exception to the historical-critical methodology, but there are also those who call themselves evangelicals who have embraced this methodology. The presuppositions of this methodology, as we have already seen, go far beyond a mere denial of biblical infallibility. They tear at the heart of Scripture, and include a denial of the supernatural. Once we discard miracles, we automatically open the door that leads to a denial of the virgin birth and the bodily resurrection of Jesus Christ from the dead.

At the center of the controversey in the Lutheran Church–Missouri Synod and the Southern Baptist Convention lies the issue of the historical-critical methodology. The battle involves more than the view that inconsequential parts of Scripture are inaccurate. It involves the fact that once the historical-critical methodology is accepted, it takes one farther down the road, far beyond inerrancy in its simple stage. It has in it all of the seeds that lead toward apostasy. This point cannot be emphasized too strongly. It is hardly possible for those who embrace the historical-critical approach not to know in their hearts what this does to the interpretation of Scripture.

It should be obvious by now that one of the major confrontations that attends the battle over inerrancy centers about the interpretation of Scripture. No one is arguing that Scripture should not be studied to find out what the writer is saying. The problem is different from that. It is related to inerrancy, however. And it is also related to the historical-critical methodology. One of the important questions in this discussion is what the writers of Scripture intended to do. Rudolph Bultmann illustrates the case beautifully. He has adopted the principle of demythologization. He is saying that the biblical accounts are not true history. One must go beyond the accounts in Scripture to find out what lies behind them. The Jesus of the Gospels is not the Jesus of history. What the Gospel writers say cannot be trusted as true history. Accretions, nonhistorical incidents and viewpoints, and unfounded opinions are all there. Scholars must find the core or bedrock truths that lie behind this facade.

Evangelicals have always agreed that the writers of Scripture penned straight history, and that what they wrote was true. Now some may argue that they wrote what they *thought* was true, but that we know better today. For example, the two Gospel writers who gave us the account of the virgin birth believed what they wrote. But theirs was a prescientific age, and we know better now. Cancel out the virgin birth, since it is merely an effort to explain how the Incarnation took place. Two of the Gospel writers and the writer of the Chronicles give us genealogical tables. In two of these the authors trace the origins of man back to the first man, Adam. But today we say that man is millions of years old, and the notion that the first man was Adam is nonsense. Paul speaks of Adam as the first Adam and of Jesus as a second Adam. But Paul is not speaking historically. He is using this idea of the first Adam as a model, so it is not straightline history. And so it goes.

THE NEW HERMENEUTICS

Today there are evangelicals who, consciously or unconsciously, have drunk deep from the fountains of the new hermeneutic. They no longer regard Scripture as true history. They place the findings of science above Scripture and make science the judge of the Word of God. They also have drunk the wine of German rationalism that has found its way into their bloodstream so as to influence and affect their thinking. They are earnest and sincere men. They think they are serving the kingdom of God wisely and well in this their generation. They want men to be delivered from their ignorance and to enter into the new haven of advanced scholarship led by men with impeccable academic pedigrees rather than by men who are led of the Spirit of God and who have a spiritual discernment that comes from the Holy Spirit and not from doctorates — although the possession of a doctorate does not mean that those who have them, of necessity, have been corrupted. But it does mean that whatever it is that men drink from has a decisive influence upon them and generally conditions them forever.

When inerrancy is lost, it is palpably easy to drift into a mood in which the historicity of Scripture along with inerrancy is lost. And this drift is accompanied by the kind of thinking I encountered on the lecture circuit some years ago. One member of the Council of Churches in Indianapolis, Indiana, was expounding his beliefs about basic Christian doctrine. He readily admitted that Paul taught substitutionary atonement, the bodily resurrection of Christ from the dead, and the second coming of the Lord. Then he quickly and honestly said that he did not believe any of it. At least he knew what the apostle taught, but he wouldn't believe it. Evangelicals today need to return to a view of Scripture that regards it as historical and they need to be willing to believe what it says. The implications are clear. If this is done, then the questions about the authorship of Isaiah, Daniel, and Ephesians are resolved. Adam as the first man no longer becomes a problem. The Bible is taken at its face value and the claims of Scripture as to its own inspiration and inerrancy are the basis on which this approach is made.

ERRANCY AND OTHER DEVIATIONS: ETHICAL AND MORAL

I have said that history shows us where a belief in an errant Scripture takes us in the long run. I have shown *how* errancy leads to further declines and how institutions and denominations fall away. As men retreat from inerrancy, they lose any vital interest in evangelism and missions. Their zeal for finishing the job of world evangelization is replaced by socio-political-economic concerns. Their churches do not reach out even to the members of their own communities. How many first-rate evangelists and leading missionary lights have liberal theological seminaries turned out in the past twenty-five years? How many scholars have they nurtured who have arisen to defend the full trustworthiness of Scripture? How many of their graduates reflect the kind of life that demonstrates to a waiting world that they have been filled with the Holy Spirit? How was it possible for Union Theological Seminary and later the University of Chicago Divinity School to harbor on their faculties a "leading scholar" whose life was an uninterrupted series of adulteries known to them?

How is it that when errancy begins to creep in among evangelicals it always is accompanied by ethical deceit and moral failure? Does not the case of Briggs at Union make only too clear how this operates? How is it possible for evangelical schools that are controlled by orthodox doctrinal statements knowingly to permit members of their faculties to teach what is contrary to their confessional commitments? How is it possible for faculty members of seminaries to sign doctrinal statements as though they believed what they signed, but to do it tongue-in-cheek? How is it possible for evangelical schools to keep on telling their constituencies that they really are evangelical with regard to Scripture when they know they are not? Why don't institutions that have abandoned inerrancy in principle say so in such a way that people everywhere know this to be true? Why soft-pedal the change in position and pussyfoot around the issue?

Among denominations, why do men who dissent from their confessions of faith remain within those denominations with the intention of subverting others? Would not honesty and integrity lead them to dissociate themselves from these denominations and go where they could honestly agree with the doctrinal commitments or at least to places where there are no doctrinal commitments?

THE LUTHERAN CHURCH–MISSOURI SYNOD ETHICAL DILEMMA

Still another question begs for an answer. If liberal advocates are willing to fight against historic orthodoxy, why should not evangelicals in turn fight against the incursions of liberalism? Why is it not correct, indeed essential, for men like J. A. O. Preus to fight with all his might against those who do not believe the commitment of the Lutheran Church–Missouri Synod in favor of an inerrant Scripture? I am not unmindful of the fact that wherever liberalism has fought, it has won. But right now the issue is by no means decided in the Missouri Synod battle. Right now the evangelicals have the edge in the battle. Will this be the first instance of a large denomination that was able to maintain its theological purity against doctrinal subversion? And how can its doctrinal purity be maintained if those who fight against it are not willing to confess their error, repent, and believe and teach what the denomination believes and teaches, or unless they are removed from the denomination so that the infection can be stopped? The latter is a hard and difficult decision. But the history of the denominations who have turned away from inerrancy shows that the failure to stop infection leads to further disruptions and ultimately to the control of those denominations by liberals who have never been known for their affection for believers in inerrancy.

THE SOUTHERN BAPTIST INFECTION

The Southern Baptist Convention is another case in point. Probably 90 percent of the people in the pews believe in biblical infallibility. But the infection of which I speak has been spreading steadily in the convention and especially in its educational institutions. Among faculty members of Southern Baptist colleges and seminaries where do you find articulate spokesmen who come out in favor of inerrancy? The silence is deafening! Southern Baptists have not yet dealt with the matter decisively. Yet it is true that when it has surfaced and the messengers to the annual conventions have had a chance to express their viewpoints, they have voted in favor of inerrancy. So far the people have said that they favor doctrinal integrity, but they have not yet said whether they favor this over denominational peace.

Southern Baptists have stated repeatedly that Baptists are not a creedal people. Their cliché "no creed but the Bible" is well known. They always have favored freedom of interpretation. But when that freedom results in a denial of what Baptists have always believed, why then should the prostitution of that principle be allowed? The Sunday School Board some years ago defended Professor Elliot for whom they had published a deviant book on the Old Testament. The Board said, "The Broadman Press ministers to the denomination in keeping with the historic Baptist principle of the freedom of the individual to interpret the Bible for himself, to hold a particular theory of inspiration of the Bible which seems most reasonable to him [sic], and to develop his beliefs in accordance with his theory." But the Convention overruled this view and by this served notice that "the people are not yet committed to apostasy."[7]

Sooner or later, Southern Baptists will have to decide whether a person can really be a Southern Baptist and "develop his beliefs in accordance with his theory [of inspiration]." Does this mean anyone can continue to be a Southern Baptist and deny the virgin birth? Or the deity of Christ? Or the vicarious atonement? Or the bodily resurrection of Jesus from the dead? Or the doctrine of the Trinity? Or baptism by immersion? Or the symbolic presence of Christ in the bread and wine of the communion table? Or congregational polity? If and when that happens, then Southern Baptists have ceased to be Baptists; they have ceased to be a people of the Bible; they have become inclusivists and are on the road to apostasy.

ADVOCATES OF AN INERRANT SCRIPTURE

Not all Baptist denominations have been silent in the face of the inroads errancy has made in evangelical ranks. President Carl H. Lundquist of Bethel College and Seminary during the denomination's centennial year said this about the resolution passed by the Bethel Board of Regents: "Bethel faculty has affirmed continuously its belief that the Bible is without error in the original manuscripts. Beyond the question of inerrancy our faculty is committed to the plenary inspiration and final authority of the Bible as the basis of all we teach on the campus. In the current religious climate in America people are concerned about the position of the Bible taken by evangelical schools. The history of higher education generally has revealed a drift away from orthodoxy, Lundquist observed, and noted that theological liberalism 'originated with a faulty view of the Scriptures,' he said. 'Cleavages within evangelicalism have tended to foster suspicions in our day that oftentimes have been without basis in fact.' "[8]

The Conservative Baptist Theological Seminary of Denver, Colorado, has consistently stated its position that "Scripture is God-breathed and therefore infallible, indefectible, and inerrant; it gives us divine truth without admixture of error; it gives us truth which is fixed, objective, and propositional."[9]

But other evangelical seminaries have not been so clear. At its founding, Fuller Seminary had for one of its express purposes the task of creating an apologetic literature in favor of biblical inerrancy. But it has officially abandoned that commitment and stands today for a limited inerrancy having to do with matters of faith and practice but not extending to other areas of biblical revelation.

The North Park Seminary of Chicago takes a position similar to that of Fuller. We already have seen that its faculty is overloaded with those who have abandoned inerrancy and is represented by only one biblical faculty member who opts for inerrancy. How long will it be before this denomination is pulled forever into the camp of liberalism if it follows the pattern that always has accompanied this struggle in past generations? Or will the people of this denomination who hold to infallibility exert their influence in such a way as to change the situation in order to retain their historical evangelical position?

THE FINAL APPEAL

It is my conviction that a host of those evangelicals who no longer hold to inerrancy are still relatively evangelical. I do not for one moment concede, however, that in a technical sense anyone can claim the evangelical badge once he has abandoned inerrancy. The label "evangelical" has traditionally stood for a series of doctrinal convictions of which one has been biblical infallibility. Surely if the assertion that Christ is not God, or that the atonement was not vicarious, or that the virgin birth did not happen, or that Jesus is not coming again, or that Jesus did not rise bodily from the dead, is reason to deny the badge "evangelical," then he who denies the doctrine of infallibility — the only sure guarantee that these other doctrines are true — cannot truly be an evangelical.

My appeal to evangelicals who at this moment have moved or are moving away from biblical inerrancy is for you to rethink the situation in light of the historical data, and move back to a full commitment to this basic truth. It is highly unlikely that anyone can stop at a simple surrender of inerrancy without making more deadly concessions of a soteriological nature. It is true that a man can be a Christian without believing in inerrancy. But it is also true that down the road lie serious pitfalls into which such a denial leads. And even if this generation can forego inerrancy and remain more or less evangelical, history tells us that those who come after this generation will not do so. We have a responsibility for those who follow after us as well as for generations unborn.

My appeal is also to those evangelicals who still hold to biblical inerrancy. I urge you to contend earnestly for the faith once delivered to the saints. I urge you to dialogue with evangelicals who sit on the fence or have capitulated. I urge you to take whatever action is needed to secure a redress of this situation. I urge you to remember that godly men through the ages have come to the Scriptures without advanced theological training and have been better interpreters and more spiritual leaders than many who have undergone the most rigorous theological training. I urge evangelicals in the pews to remember that a good word spoken in love to college and seminary professors may serve as a catalyst to call them back to fidelity to Scripture. I urge you to remember that the so-called contradictions in Scripture do not stem from modern scholarship. These have been made known by critics ages ago, and have been dealt with in a variety of effective ways. The case for biblical inerrancy is a strong one, and answers to objectors have been made effectively for the past hundred years.

I do not doubt that if evangelicals in concert with each other would stand firm and tall for biblical inerrancy and the cardinal doctrines of the Christian faith, a new day would dawn and the blessing of God would follow. I can foresee, in that event, a new surge of spiritual power, a new advance in the task of evangelizing the world, and the establishment of churches around the world where Christ is honored, the true gospel preached, and the kingdom of God manifested in holy power before the eyes of unconverted men. May the Lord speed that day!

I do not look for or expect a time in history as we know it when the whole professing church will believe either in inerrancy or the major doctrines of the Christian faith. There will always be wheat and tares growing together until the angels begin their task of reaping the harvest at the end of the age. Truth shall forever be on the scaffold, and wrong forever on the throne as long as time shall last. But whatever the cost, whatever the sacrifice, God calls His people to faithful service based upon an unsullied adherence to His Word with the firm conviction that not one jot or tittle shall pass away until all has been fulfilled. When Jesus Christ comes, faith shall turn into sight and what we do not know now we shall know then. And when all of the mysteries of Scripture have been unlocked, we shall see what we have always believed — that the written Word of God is free from all error, and all parts of it in some fashion or another bear witness to the incarnate Word of God, Jesus Christ the righteous Branch, who is King of Kings and Lord of Lords.

[1] John Montgomery, "Inspiration and Inerrancy: A New Departure" in the *Bulletin of the Evangelical Theological Society* (Vol. 8, No. 2, Spring, 1965).

[2] Clark Pinnock, *A New Reformation: A Challenge to Southern Baptists* (Tigerville, S.C.: Jewel Books, 1968), p. 2.

[3] Ibid., p. 3.

[4] Ibid., p. 5.

[5] Richard Coleman, "Reconsidering 'Limited Inerrancy' " in the *Journal of the Evangelical Theological Society* (Vol. 17, No. 4, Fall, 1974), p. 207.

[6] Ibid., p. 214.
[7] Pinnock, *A New Reformation*, p. 17.
[8] *Bethel Focus*, November, 1970.
[9] *The Seminarian*, Vol. 13, No. 2, 1964.

Subject Index

Subject Index